GW00392331

OLD FORGE

OURS TO HOLD

RAF ALDERGROVE AT WAR
1939 – 1945

BY
TG DOCHERTY

First Edition 2008

Designed
by
Jupper Peep
www.jupperpeep.com

Published
by
Old Forge Publishing
39 Backgate
Cowbit
Lincolnshire
PE12 6AP
oldforgepub@aol.com
www.oldforgepublishing.org
01406 381313

ISBN 978-1-906183-03-5

Printed for Old Forge Publishing
By

LPPS Ltd
Wellingborough
Northants
NN8 3PJ

01553 764728

Contents

OURS TO HOLD

RAF ALDERGROVE AT WAR

1939 – 1945

Preface

In the 1990's I spent nine-and-a-half years at Aldergrove and I was fascinated by the number of wartime buildings and remnants of the Second World War remaining on the station, including the war graves in the churchyard. Whilst carrying out some research I came across the Form 540, the Operations Record Book, for RAF Aldergrove during WW2 and received permission to study it from the Station Adjutant. Until this point I had little idea of the major involvement of Aldergrove in the Battle of the Atlantic, the defence of Belfast and the training of crews for Coastal Command. I resolved to dig more deeply into the station history and the result is this book. The title 'Ours To Hold' is the motto from the station crest and with recent developments at Aldergrove it would appear that the RAF will hold the station for many years to come.

This book could not have been written without the unstinting assistance of many ex-Aldergrove air and ground crews and the officers in charge of the archives of those ex-Coastal squadrons still extant. My thanks go to them all (See acknowledgements). I hope the reader will enjoy this book as much as I did researching and writing it. RAF Aldergrove is deserving of its place in history. I hope this book goes a small way to achieving that.

Tom Docherty

INTRODUCTION

The airfield at Aldergrove, situated two and a half miles east of Lough Neagh, the largest lake in Great Britain, opened in early 1918. The site had been selected in 1917 and was intended for use as a testing airfield for Handley Page V1500 bombers which were to be constructed by the Belfast based company Harland & Wolff. The first of the V1500 bombers produced by Harland & Wolff, E4304 made a test flight of just over an hour at Aldergrove on 20 December 1918 and was flown to Bircham Newton the following day. The station was still under construction at this point and only a few of these large bombers were ever flown from the airfield. Just over a year after the Armistice the station closed in December 1919.

The airfield was retained by the newly formed Royal Air Force, however, and was re-opened on an annual basis for exercises in the Province. With the Nationalist struggle for independence from English rule gaining momentum No 2 Sqn brought its Bristol FE2b's to Aldergrove in June 1922. The squadron remained until September and left behind a detachment to counter any trouble until February 1923.

During the 1920's the RAF saw a small but steady expansion in its strength including the formation of Auxiliary and Reserve Squadrons. One of these, No 502 Sqn was formed at Aldergrove on 15 May 1925. The unit was initially equipped with Vickers Vimys and replaced these with Handley Page Hyderabads and later Vickers Virginias. The role of the squadron during this period was night bombing.

A view of Aldergrove in November 1925. The hangar, centre right, is still in use. The U shaped accommodation block, centre, was demolished in 2000. *(PHT Green via Geoff Gardiner)*

Officers of No 502 Sqn at Aldergrove in 1927. The Vickers Vimy Mk IV in the background sports the squadron's 'Red hand of Ulster' badge. *(PHT Green via Geoff Gardiner).*

An oblique view of the hangars at Aldergrove in April 1928. The buildings to the rear are now demolished and the Station Headquarters building would not be built on the site until 1932. *(PHT Green via Geoff Gardiner)*

Vickers Vimy of No 502 Sqn at Aldergrove in 1929. *(R Martin via Geoff Gardiner).*

After a decade in the night bomber role, No 502 Sqn became a day bomber unit equipped with Westland Wallaces, which were little better than the bomber types operated during the Great War. The unit next re-equipped with Hawker Hinds and by the time war broke out No 502 Sqn were flying Avro Ansons.

In January 1936, another bomber unit, No 9 Sqn, arrived at Aldergrove from Andover with Vickers Virginias. Whilst at Aldergrove, No 9 Sqn re-equipped with Handley Page Heyfords before returning to England in October 1936.

Handley Page Hyderabad J7742:2 of No 502 Sqn in formation with Avro 504N's at Summer Camp in July 1929. *(PHT Green via Geoff Gardiner)*

Handley Page Hyderabad J8811:3 of No 502 Sqn in July 1929. *(PHT Green via Geoff Gardiner).*

fast Telegraph
28-8-29

Handley Page Hyderabad J8814 of No 502 Sqn hit trees in a forced landing at Groomsport, near Bangor, County Down on 27 August 1929. *(PHT Green via Geoff Gardiner).*

Hawker Hind L7178 of No 211 Sqn during an Armament Practice camp at No 2 ATS in 1938. *(PHT Green via Geoff Gardiner).*

Westland Wallace Mk II, K6043 of No 502 Sqn at Aldergrove. This Wallace would be passed to No 4 AOS before being struck off charge on 27 Sep 1940. *(L Malcolmson via Geoff Gardiner).*

A major change to the station establishment occurred in March 1936 when No 2 Armament Training Station (ATS) was formed. The function of this unit was to provide armament training facilities for front line and other training units and soon the operational squadrons and Flying Training Schools (FTS) were sending regular detachments to Aldergrove. The size of Aldergrove's flying strength was to increase again in October 1936 with the establishment of a Met Flight equipped with Bristol Bulldogs and tasked with providing daily meteorological sorties.

F/O Corry crashed Hawker Hind K6763 after hitting a radio mast at Aldergrove on 14 Nov 1937. *(I Reynolds via Geoff Gardiner).*

Hawker Hind K 6762 served with No 502 Sqn at Aldergrove in 1938. This Hind was later passed on to the RAF College and then No 1 FTS where it undershot on landing at Stormy Down on 8 Dec 1940. *(L Malcolmson via Geoff Gardiner).*

On 17 April 1939, No 2 ATS was amalgamated with No 1 ATS and the unit was re-designated No 3 Air Observer School (AOS).

When war broke out on 3 September 1939, Aldergrove held No 502 Sqn with Ansons, No 3 AOS with a motley collection of Heyford, Swordfish, Sharks and Battles and the Met Flight with its Bulldogs. Over the next six years the striking power of the station would change out of all recognition and Aldergrove would play a significant part in the Battle of the Atlantic and the defeat of the U-boat menace.

A Handley Page Heyford at Aldergrove in July 1938. *(F McLintock via J Slater).*

Chapter 1

SEPTEMBER 1939 – DECEMBER 1939

On 3 September 1939, No 502 Sqn was based at Aldergrove with Avro Ansons under the control of No 15 (Reconnaissance) Group. The squadron carried out it's first operation on the day war broke out when Anson Mk I N5049 took off to patrol between the Mull of Kintyre and the Mull of Galloway. That same day, just ten hours after the declaration of war, the liner 'Athenia' was sunk by U30, 250 miles north west of Ireland. The Royal Navy would become stretched to the limit with the immediate introduction of the convoy system and the need for escorts meaning it would fall to Coastal Command to combat the U-boat threat, a threat with which Aldergrove was to become deeply involved. Just over a week earlier, the operations room at Aldergrove had been manned by a skeleton crew and after the outbreak of war sent No 502 Sqn out on its first patrols of the war both searching for submarines and on convoy duty.

For No 3 AOS, it was business as usual with courses being run for observers and air gunners using a variety of obsolescent types including Heyfords and Henleys. On the

The calm before the storm. An Anson of No 502 Sqn overflies the crowd at the last Empire Air Day to be held at Aldergrove in May 1939. *(Crown Copyright/RAF Aldergrove via Geoff Gardiner).*

evening of 8 September a trawler reported sighting a submarine in Dundrum Bay and the following morning No 502 Sqn sent an Anson to investigate the sighting. The first attack on a submarine carried out by No 502 Sqn was on 24 September when S/L Briggs took off in Anson N5104 with F/O Barclay, F/O Kirkpatrick and AC Davis for an air test. During the air test, Briggs sighted a U-boat off the Scottish coast and attacked it with anti-submarine bombs. The U-boat submerged immediately and the attack was made from 100 yards ahead of the swirl. Two bombs were dropped but the results were not observed. The sorties flown thereafter were generally unspectacular and the squadron continued convoy escorts and anti-submarine patrols at a rate of about thirty to forty sorties a month. On the afternoon of 22 October, however, F/O

Avro Anson N5104 of No 502 Sqn over Antrim. This Anson was flown by S/L Briggs during the Squadron's first attack on a U-boat on 24 September 1939. *(WH McGiffin via Geoff Gardiner)*

Bell in Anson N5234 with a crew comprising Sgt Butterworth, AC Jones and LAC Kerr sighted a possible periscope in the vicinity of a trawler and attacked it with two bombs. The trawler signalled that the suspicious object was, in fact, a minesweeping paravane!

By the end of October 1939, the Royal Navy was on the defensive and losing ships to the U-boats. HMS *Courageous* had been sunk in the Bristol Channel by U29 and U47 had sunk HMS *Royal Oak* in a daring raid on Scapa Flow. Coastal Command were also struggling to combat the U-boat menace and the Ansons of No 502 Sqn, equipped with primitive navigation aids, unreliable bombs and only the crew's eyesight to spot the

No 502 Sqn aircrew follow two ground crew manhandling a 100lb bomb out to one of the Squadron's Ansons. *(R Parsons via Geoff Gardiner)*.

U-boats were having little success. By the end of 1939, the Allies would have lost 114 ships to the U-boats.

No 3 AOS was redesignated No 3 B&GS on 1 November 1939 and continued its role of observer and air gunner training. The Province was sadly lacking in aerial defences and it was decided that No 3 B&GS would provide an emergency force of one fighter squadron and two light bomber squadrons equipped with Fairey Battles. The unit would also have a reconnaissance squadron comprising Sharks and Swordfish.

Westland Wallace Mk I, K3562 was operated at Aldergrove by No 2 ATS and No 3 B&GS. It was transferred to No 5 B&GS then No 1 GDGS before being struck off charge in June 1942. *(Westland Group).*

Another unit formed at Aldergrove in November 1939 was No 23 Maintenance Unit (MU). This unit would have a long association with Aldergrove and during its first months on the station it became responsible for the storage and preparation for issue to units of various aircraft types including Blenheims, Hampdens, Wellingtons and Bristol Bombays manufactured by Short Brothers in Belfast.

At this early stage of the war the threat of invasion was taken extremely seriously and several Coastal Patrol Flights (CPF) were formed around the country. No 4 CPF was formed at Aldergrove on 1 December with Tiger Moths. The unit was controlled by No 502 Sqn but remained only briefly at Aldergrove transferring to Hooton Park five days later.

On 2 December, No 3 Naval Air Observers Course commenced and the B&GS lost one of its Swordfish, L2799 in a taxiing accident when it collided with a tractor. The unit's aircraft strength was further depleted the same day with the departure of three Henleys to Sutton Bridge.

Lt Cdr WGC Stokes RN arrived at Aldergrove on 5 December and his unit, in the shape of No 774 Sqn of the Fleet Air Arm (FAA), followed him to Aldergrove on Christmas day. This squadron was a training unit for observers and telegraphist air gunners. No 774 Sqn arrived from Worthy Down with a mixed complement of Skuas, Rocs, Sharks and Swordfish. No 774 Sqn was parented by No 3 B&GS. The arrival of this unit ended the station's unit moves for the year and Aldergrove settled into a routine of convoy escort and anti-submarine patrol for No 502 Sqn and observer, air gunner and telegraphist air gunner training for No 3 B&GS and 774 Sqn. The year ended badly for No 502 Sqn, however, when Anson Mk I N5063:YG-N force landed in bad weather. The Anson had landed at West Freugh just after lunchtime due to bad weather and took off again during a temporary improvement in the weather coming down at Elliotts Farm, two miles east of Aldergrove on 29 December. Tom Pickering arrived at Aldergrove in

December 1939 to commence gunnery training. On his arrival he was treated to typical Irish hospitality and brought close to the tragedies of war:

"It was really wintry that night and there was freezing fog as we weighed anchor. I was leaning over the rail at the stern of the ship and, watching the sea being churned up by our propellers, I got that curious feeling of wanting to throw myself in! It was then that I moved my position. The ferry made a zig-zag course to avoid enemy submarines. I don't remember our having anything to eat or drink during the journey, but I remember we were mighty hungry by the time we entered Belfast Lough and finally docked. A clock in the harbour was just striking 9 o'clock as we left the ship. Eight hours we'd been on board. At school we were told that Ireland had a great deal of rain, and it was raining then! There were four of us. I remember Neville Kemp, a particular friend of mine, but I cannot recall the names of the other two. The first person we set eyes on was a policeman, complete with revolver in holster.

'Have yer had any breakfast yet, lads?' he asked, and continued, 'If you go across the road to Mrs Rafferty's, sure an' she'll fix you up with a foine meal an' all she will, an' she won't charge yer very much oither.'

We took his advice as no one had come to meet us and, sure enough, we did

---

STAFF PILOTS

Neville Cooper had joined the RAFVR pre-war as a sergeant pilot and, after training with several reserve units in England, was sent home to await developments. On the outbreak of war, Neville was called up along with thousands of others and soon found himself in a somewhat chaotic situation as the RAF tried to assimilate the huge number of men requiring training and accommodation.

"On the outbreak of war I was called up to full time service and posted to No 3 AOS at Aldergrove as a Staff Pilot. Aldergrove had so little accommodation that we all slept in a hangar. About three hundred, all in neat rows of beds, until it rained, then you moved to catch the least drips. After a week or two we were moved into new huts.

Most of the Staff Pilots were VR like myself and had not qualified for 'Wings' as we had done part time ground training but not taken the exams. We had also not completed the normal flying training; I had done 125 hours, well short of the normal 200. So we did a bit of conversion onto the unit's aircraft, Battles and Westland Wallaces, but then came to a halt as we could not take passengers, while the CO and OC Flying got stroppy with No 25 Group. For a time I was put in charge of a section amending Air Publications.

The name of the unit changed to No 3 BGS in February 1940 and in early April our 'Wings' were Gazetted. I do not recall taking any exams but I think the CO was instructed to make his own assessment and recommendation. I always felt I had missed out on part of the training. I was posted to No 8 BGS at Evanton in July 1940."

have a 'foine' meal – double bacon, double sausage and two fried eggs each, with as much fried bread as we could manage – and all for 1/7d apiece (about 8p in present currency)!

Replete and full to bursting we at last took our leave of dear old Mrs Rafferty and went outside. An RAF tender was waiting for us with four officers already on board – don't know where they came from, but I'll bet they didn't have a breakfast as good as ours!

'Where the hell have you been to? We've been looking all over the bloody place for you'. The corporal driver scowled at us. 'Next time, wait until you are bloody well told what to do. Don't bugger off on your own. You're in the air force now and you don't do as you bloody well like, understand?'

'Yes, corporal', we said in unison, 'there was no one to meet us when we docked, so we went for breakfast'.

'Of all the bloody cheek! Get aboard before I put you on a charge'.

We had arrived at Aldergrove and I was interested to see what kind of aircraft they had there. I saw a Westland Wallace, two-seater biplane; a Handley Page Heyford, also a biplane – a little more up to date than the old WW1 HP 0400, but not much. It used to cruise around the sky at a steady 90-mph and would even reach 115 mph in a steep dive! However, it was a lovely aeroplane in which to fly – but not operationally! There were a couple of Fairey Battles, three-seat monoplanes. I was very impressed with the Battle - –until we actually flew in them – then I pitied the poor blighters who had to crew them on operations. They were absolutely sitting ducks – and the Jerries shot them down on piece! A Hawker Henley and Blackburn Skua   used for drogue towing – completed the line-up.

Everything was very quiet and we were shown into a barrack block, which was to be our home for the next three months. No one was there, but kit-bags were beside some of the beds, so we asked the corporal who showed us in where the others were.

'Oh, they are at the funeral', was the cheerful reply. Our hearts sank. After seeing the antiquated aircraft in which we supposed we would have to fly, we wondered how often it occurred.

'What happened?' Neville asked.

'The chap was in the guardroom when someone pointed a rifle at him and pulled the trigger. The usual plea: 'I didn't know the gun was loaded'. So the boyo who pulled the trigger has to face a court martial'.

We were sorry for the poor chap who was killed, and for the one who had been careless, but we were somewhat relieved to find it had not been due to an accident in the air.

It was still pouring down when the other people whom we were to join on the course returned from the funeral. They had come from other ITWs and altogether, I believe there were twenty-six of us. The Heyfords could accommodate three gunners and the Wallaces one. Later, we flew in Battles, which took two gunners for air-firing practice. As it was New Year's Day, 1940, we were allowed the time to settle in, but work would start tomorrow. The nearest village, Crumlin, was three miles away, and the next nearest was Antrim, five miles away – rather bigger than Crumlin, but that is not saying much. A number of us trooped down to Crumlin for a try-out of the local beer. We were not allowed to go into the bar, but were put in the lounge, where we were more or less segregated from the locals. At that time I had never been in a pub before and I stuck to soft drinks at this point in my career.

Next day it was still pouring down but after breakfast, we had lectures to attend. For breakfast, I had my very first taste of baked beans on fried bread, but by no means my last!"

Before the prospective air gunners at No 3 B&GS were allowed into the air, and given live ammunition to fire at drogues towed behind aircraft, they had to undergo a period of ground training in several aviation and gunnery related subjects. Tom Pickering recalls this training:

"The lectures were to be a large part of the curriculum and comprised: pyrotechnics, stripping and assembly of the Vickers Gas Operated (VGO) machine gun, ditto for the Lewis gun, Browning machine gun and 20mm Hispano cannon. We also had to fire the machine guns, first of all on the ground, at silhouettes of German aircraft (the noise was terrific – in those far off days there were no earmuffs supplied). Lectures were given to us on how to use a parachute (when you jump, say to yourself 'Oh hell, oh hell, oh hell!' and pull the ripcord)!

Each evening at 1800 hrs a bus left for Belfast, returning to camp at 2130hrs, for the benefit of those who wanted a night out on the town. I went on it a couple of times, but it frequently ended up in a free-for-all with the locals and I found something else to do with most evenings. Another chap became a friend of mine. His name was Horace Kenworthy and he just couldn't get the hang of stripping the Browning gun and naming the parts. He asked me if I would come to the lecture room each evening to demonstrate. I agreed. I can still remember some of the awful names which were given to bits and pieces of the Browning gun; this is the rear sear, the rear sear spring retainer, the rear sear spring retainer keeper, and so on. We had to be able to do this blindfold, and in a very, very short time.

Day succeeded day and each morning we asked our instructors: 'When are we going to fly?'

'Don't worry, you'll be flying soon enough and we suggest you don't eat any chocolate before you go up, or you are likely to throw it all up, especially in those Heyfords – almost everyone is sick in those things!' Thus cheered, we had to concentrate on our lectures.

I found pyrotechnics a most boring subject, though I had to take it in to get through the course and I suppose if I ever we were adrift at sea, a knowledge of the various types of flares etc would be very useful.

Theory of sighting I found interesting – little bit of applied geometry here. Those neat patterns of holes you see appearing on the screen when an aircraft is fired on are just so much eyewash. The very first bullet goes almost true, but the rest are scattered in what is called a cone of fire, and the point of the cone is at the end of the gun. The further the bullets travel, the more scattered they become, so that the four Brownings at the rear end of the Lancaster bomber scatter the bullets at 400yards in a circle approximately 80 feet in diameter!"

Chapter 2

JANUARY 1940 – JUNE 1940

Avro Anson YG-Q of No 502 Sqn over County Antrim in 1940. *(R Parsons via Geoff Gardiner)*.

The New Year began badly for Aldergrove with an accident involving Heyford K6885 on 3 January. The aircraft was subsequently repaired and eventually struck off charge in August 1940. On the same day, a court of inquiry was convened to investigate a fire on Motor Boat PO 800 of the Marine Section, Crumlin. This unit operated boats on Lough Neagh in support of the ranges and the flying boat moorings. The Lough had been the scene of much aerial activity throughout the 1930s when bombing and gunnery ranges had been established and it would continue to be used until the 1950s. The bulk of the ranges were used by Aldergrove based aircraft, although aircraft from many of the other Ulster airfields also used the facilities. Henry McGarry, a professional net fisherman, who had moved to Ardmore on the shores of the Lough in 1929, was asked to lay the first targets and service them as required. His son, Jim, recalls the early days and the fun to be had as a young boy living close to the airfield and ranges:

"During the early 1930s bombing and gunnery practice was slow and leisurely, a kind of gentleman's pastime. A large proportion of the range time was taken up by the local No 502 Sqn. Between 1929 and 1936 the memory conjures up pictures of great lumbering bombers such as the Vickers Vimy, Vickers Virginia, Handley Page Heyford (which we christened 'The Flying Hayshed', Avro Ansons and Oxfords and, of course, the famous Gloster Gladiators of Malta fame. On the fighter front, the outstanding performers were the Hawker Fury and Hind biplanes; the latter had their forward firing machine-guns synchronised to fire through the propeller. How we watched them each day to catch the moment when the system might fail and give us the glory of racing to rescue the pilot from the Lough in the flat-bottomed cot which we used for schoolboy eel fishing, and whereby become famous heroes! (What did you expect from 10 and 12 year-olds living in wonderland?)

The Vimys and Heyfords seemed so slow that my brother and I tried to race them on our bicycles along the shore road parallel to their route, whilst the stand-up gunner in his open cockpit complete with leather helmet and goggles waved us on. It was not unusual in those halcyon days to have pilots and gunners visit us in their open sports cars at weekends to meet their young bicycle-mounted rivals, and to discuss with our father the design and positioning of targets.

Biplanes such as the Fury and Hind were still widely used as trainers up until 1939. Early In this period the air gunnery targets were used by a squadron of Short Stranraer flying boats. The floating targets were fitted with hessian screens and, after each gunnery mission, the flying boat would land, taxi up to the target, tie up and count it's own gunnery score! The whole thing seemed so natural."

No 502 Sqn also lost an aircraft when F/L Corry crashed Anson N5234 into a field adjoining the aerodrome. Corry was taking off at night for a patrol and the crash was thought to have been caused by frost on the wings. Luckily, though the Anson was written off, there were no injuries among the crew.

For Tom Pickering and the other members of the air gunners course at No 3 B&GS, the ground training was complete and on 6 January they were to commence flying training. Tom Pickering recalls this day and those that followed:

"On 6th January it had actually stopped raining for the first time since we arrived! There were loud cries of 'Hurray, we are going to fly at last!' We all trooped down to the flights and two Wallaces were standing there with their engines ticking over. The object of the first flight was to use camera guns, with 100-mph sights, and to try deflection shots on the aircraft which approached you. Two aircraft were going up together and the gunner in each had to take deflection 'shots' of the other machine which came up slowly alongside and then dropped back to come up on the other side.

A word about the camera guns. These were to be fitted on to the Scarff ring (the gunners cockpit was circular at the top, bearing the Scarff mounting for the camera-gun or machine gun The mounting was able to be swung manually through 180 degrees and bore a brake to stop it in the required position). The camera-gun would take a film having 16 exposures. For this first exercise we were issued with two rolls of film and we thus had to 'fire' 32 'shots' at the other aircraft as it was approaching alongside, but about two hundred yards away. This gave us various deflection shots.

The cloudbase was at a height of about two thousand feet and the sky was completely overcast – not very promising at all! I was lucky to be drawn third out of the hat along with Horace Kenworthy, which meant that we would be second to fly. The first two machines took off and we were left to await their return – hoping against hope that the weather wouldn't worsen in the meantime.

They were back within twenty minutes and then it was our turn. Horace climbed into his machine and I into mine. To a hook on the floor of my cockpit was attached a strap, just like a dog lead. The other end was hooked onto a ring at the base of my parachute harness and my parachute had to be put in a rack on the side of the cockpit. I pulled down a seat – reminiscent of the cinema but held in the up position by elastic cord – and sat after fixing the camera gun onto the mounting and inserting the first film. I was wearing a green Sidcot suit, flying helmet and goggles and parachute harness. The strap attached to the latter was all that prevented my parting from the aircraft by a sudden drop due to a downdraught.

The engine roared, the pilot turned and looked at me making a thumbs-up sign. (This was our only method of communication at Gunnery School)! I nodded and we were off. This was great – just what I'd looked forward to since I was about eleven years old, when I was first bitten by the flying 'bug'. We climbed steadily to about eighteen hundred feet, just below the cloudbase. Then I was once again given the thumbs-up sign, urging me to get cracking. So I stood up and that was when my troubles began!

I was not expecting the sudden blast of the 100mph slipstream – there was no windshield or anything to shield me from the rush of air! First of all, as I stood up, the cinema-type seat also rose and tucked itself under my parachute harness; my goggles flew over my head – fortunately still attached to a strap at the back of my flying helmet. I opened my mouth and let out an involuntary yell ––and I was unable to close it again! My camera-gun was almost torn out of my hands by the slipstream and, altogether, I was in a heck of a mess!

It seemed to take ages before I withdrew my harness from off the seat. That gave me an opportunity to duck down into the cockpit, close my mouth, pull my goggles over my eyes and tighten the straps, then pull my scarf over my mouth. All this while hanging on to the camera-gun like grim death with my other hand! Meanwhile, the other Wallace had flown by and then come up on the other side of us at least once. So I started taking pot-shots at it as it kept manoeuvring. When I had 'shot' the first film, the pilot turned around and gave his questioning thumbs up, to which I gave a thumbs-down! Then I had to change films in a 100mph gale! It is not to be recommended but I finally succeeded in getting off all my films and was eventually able to give a thumbs up.

We returned to earth once more and I climbed out after removing my parachute and the camera-gun. "What's it like?" was the cry from those still waiting. "Wizard!" and I walked around to the other machine to ask old Horace what was his impression. When I saw him I didn't have to ask. The poor lad was hanging over the side of his cockpit with his face as green as his Sidcot! Obviously he hadn't had an enjoyable first flight!

As luck would have it we were the last ones to fly because, as soon as we left the machines, the weather clamped down and flying was called off. So only four of us had flown that day. Back to the lecture rooms!

A couple of days later the sun came out briefly, so those remaining finally survived their first flights, but poor old Charlie Brown ended up like Horace Kenworthy – terribly airsick!

Then we had to take up a VGO and do some air-to-ground firing into Lough Neagh. We were allowed to fire into Lough Neagh only if the black cones were not hoisted. If they were, it meant that fishermen were out on the lough and we had to steer clear. This day there were no cones hoisted and I had my first taste of firing a machine-gun in the air. I got five rounds off before the gun jammed! I don't think anyone on the course ever succeeded in firing more than about fifteen rounds during any one exercise without having at least one stoppage! Can you imagine what it was like in a 100mph slipstream, to strip and remove the cause of the stoppage, and then reassemble the gun? During the stripping, the gunner had his Sidcot pockets stuffed with bits and pieces of the machine gun – fortunately they were large pockets – and the gun then had to be reassembled and remounted before any more air firing could take place.

The day came when we had to do some air-to-air firing. Two others and I were taken up in a Heyford. I had rounds of plain ball ammunition; the others had the noses of their bullets painted (with non-drying paint) red and blue respectively. We were to fire at a drogue target. The drogue was attached to a Henley by about 100 feet of towrope. The Henley was to come up on us about 150 yards away and we were to fire at the drogue. There was a red band painted around the drogue in the mid-position. Any bullet entering the forward section was counted as a score of 3, while bullets entering aft scored 1.

Sometimes we managed to nick the towrope with our bullets and the drogue dropped into the lough! One would-be gunner almost hit the towing aircraft. His bullets were so close that the pilot dropped the drogue and dived for the safety of the airfield!"

Jim McGarry and his young playmates would often observe the activities of the trainee gunners and observers as they daily flew over the Lough Neagh ranges:

"A late evening pastime for us youngsters was collecting the day's spent cartridges from along the shoreline. Bombing targets formed a solid basis for concentrated use both from a low level and also high level aspect. These were harmless practice bombs, which emitted a muffled sound and whitish smoke only. Special high rise observation towers were constructed at several locations from Langford Lodge point to Ballyginniff to observe and record hits and misses. A short period of bombing, using live 1,000lb bombs on a target in the centre of the Lough had to be scrapped due to broken windows and shattered nerves on shore! Night bombing onto the Lough targets also developed and for this purpose the targets had to be fitted with dim lighting.

Due to the introduction of air-to-air gunnery from fighters firing on a drogue target towed by another aircraft, it was found necessary to lay out a rectangular area of approximately 15 miles by 5 miles bounded by 52 danger area marker buoys. This was a drastic measure which inconvenienced the professional fishermen who were producing much needed food during the war and no doubt there was friction at times between the fast RAF patrol boats and themselves, but it seemed to resolve itself in that both sides learnt that sensible reading of the rules allowed both activities to survive side by side.

The towed silk drogues were often jettisoned by the towing aircraft well outside the aerodrome boundaries. These were worth five shillings (25p) each when returned to the operations hangar; good eyesight and a super bicycle were the tools of success and riches in this field.

Whilst servicing the above ring of danger area buoys I, and six other crew members aboard the usual mooring barge/towboat rig, were shelled by an artillery practice unit, who possibly had no proper lookout on shore. Even ten minutes crouched behind a steel winch on the open deck of a slow moving wooden barge is memorable!

No 502 Sqn was to suffer its first casualties of the war on 19 January when F/O Garrett and his crew, Sgt Moorby, AC Beattie and LAC McClure crashed on the foreshore four miles east of Rhyl in Anson N5050/B. Garrett lost control of the Anson in a snowstorm

Bombing up Anson YG-Q of No 502 Sqn at Aldergrove in 1940. *(A Stamper via Geoff Gardiner).*

and spun in. Moorby was killed and the rest of the crew was seriously injured. McCluro and Beattie later died of their injuries No 502 Sqn were flying thirty to forty sorties per month at this time and losing an average of one aircraft per month to accidents. By spring No 502 Sqn would be flying ninety sorties per month.

February was a relatively quiet month for the station with only a visit by the AOC 26 Group, AVM Champion de Crespigny MC DFC on the 21st and a collision involving Shark L2377 and a contractors lorry to break the routine. The Air Gunners Course at No 3 B&GS which had run from 10 to 24 February saw all twenty pupils pass out successfully with four of their number being granted commissions and a further four posted to instructors courses. Trainee air gunner, Tom Pickering, had his first flight in a Fairey Battle during February:

"I remember a trip in a Fairey Battle. This machine was obsolete when the war began but was extensively used in France and, during the attack on some bridges, forty of them were shot down. On this particular day, it was snowing and Charlie Brown was in the aircraft with me. We flew into some freezing fog but soon came out of it. All we did was joyride for about an hour. I enjoyed it but poor old Charlie was sick again!

The rear gun on the Battle was mounted under the rear cockpit fairing. This could be swivelled to reveal the gun. The mounting was then pulled up towards the gunner and the gun could be moved around. It also had the facility of firing under the tail of the aircraft but being so short, I had to unfasten my safety harness and then hoist myself up onto the cockpit rim in order to do this! If I lost contact with the gun I would be over the side without a 'chute in double quick time!

There was a glasshouse covering the wireless operator and gunner, which was equipped with hinges toward the forward end, where we entered and left the aircraft. This section could be tilted upwards for entry and exit and also to enable the gunner to operate his machine-gun and protect him from the slipstream. One day, when flying the Battle, we had just completed our air-firing task and I closed the cockpit cover. I still hadn't had time to strap myself in when, without any warning, the pilot indulged himself in doing a slow roll. Immediately, gravity exerted itself on me and, as I left my seat, my head hit the cover, which I had just closed! Had it still been open I would not now be relating this since my parachute was in the rack, as usual!

Once I had the task of firing from the 'dustbin' of a Heyford. The 'dustbin' was a 'belly turret', open to the elements and manually operated. In normal flight this was retracted, but for air firing it was lowered by the simple expedient of winding it down. There was a cat-ladder down which the gunner climbed to enter the turret. Once there, the turret could be rotated through about 120 degrees by means of a handle, which had to be pushed to engage a clutch and then wound in the direction desired.

It was a slow and tiring task and I wouldn't have liked to face enemy fighters in such an aircraft. The turret was intended to be wound up before the aircraft landed but on this particular day I stayed in the turret in its down position. That was the first and last time I did that! The base of the turret and my feet were sweeping the grass of the airfield as we landed and I made haste to climb the cat-ladder and wind up the turret."

No 3 B&GS lost Wallace Mk I K3672 in a crash near Langford Lodge on 4 March. Three days later on the 15th, Wallace K3562 collided with a steamroller and was damaged. The aircraft was subsequently repaired and went on to serve with a number of other units until 1942 when it became an instructional airframe. Ground taxiing accidents with vehicles were fairly common at this time due to the amount of contractors vehicles involved in the expansion of the station. The month closed with the departure of the Station Commander, G/C CS Richardson MBE, to No 1 Air Armament School (AAS) at Manby for a Station Commanders course and conference. W/C JP Barnett MC took temporary command of the station. During the month, the B&GS/774 Sqn had run two Air Gunners Courses and four Naval Observers Courses passing out a total of 44 RAF air gunners and 25 Naval Observers.

Tom Pickering was among the gunners who passed out from the B&GS during March and recalls his final days on the course:

"In the end the written and oral exams were the proof of the instructors teaching. Afterwards we awaited the results with impatience. I believe only one chap failed. I was quite pleased with my result – I came second on the course – yet I was niggled that the loss of one mark prevented my being first equal.

The next day we were issued with our air gunner brevets and it was a proud moment when we stitched them on to our tunics. Originally, a brass 'flying bullet' was worn on the sleeve but that changed shortly before we finished the course to a cloth half-wing worn on the left breast of our tunics. Then it was time to join our first squadron. I went to Manston in Kent to join No 235(F) Squadron."

No 502 Sqn continued to increase its sortie rate throughout the spring and several oil slicks were attacked in the hope of sinking a U-boat. A periscope was sighted on one of the sorties and an attack was made with no result. With a lack of U-boat targets, the squadron continued its routine of convoy patrols to deter submarine attacks. With the fall of France in May 1940, the threat of invasion from the Continent was feared and on 10 May all leave from the station was cancelled until further notice. The following day Henley K3308 was involved in an accident (The serial K3308 was allocated to a Avro Tutor so the real identity of the Henley is not known.) On the same day P/O Gilmore, flying Anson N5216/S, was escorting the armed merchant cruiser 'Asturias'. On taking over the escort duty, he fired the correct signal cartridges and received six rounds from the ship in return, luckily no hits were scored.

On the 12th, there was an accident involving Wellington L4231 and Magister P2402 of No 3 B&GS when the Wellington, from No 15 OTU, had overshot on landing after the flaps jammed and collided with the Magister. No 6 (War) Observers Course commenced on 20 May and with the threat of invasion still high, a conference was held on the station on 8 June at which all of the station's officers were present. The Station Commander gave an appraisal of the situation and the defence of the station was discussed. Three days later, on the 11th yet another taxiing accident occurred when Battles L5011 and N2228 collided. On the 15th, Battle L5386 overshot the airfield and crashed in a ditch. Observers courses continued apace and No 7 (War) Air Observers Course commenced on the 17th. A week later, No 5 Course passed out and on 28 May the station received a signal giving warning instructions for No 3 B&GS to prepare to move at short notice. Whilst the B&GS was preparing to move out another unit, No 416 Flight arrived from Cosford on 25 June, under the command of S/L Humphries for

Anson YG-E of No 502 Sqn on convoy escort duty in 1940. *(R Parsons via Geoff Gardiner).*

army co-operation duties. The unit comprised eight aircraft; seven Lysander Mk II and an Oxford, 15 officers, 23 other ranks and 32 vehicles and was initially accommodated in tents. The signal of the previous day was followed by another on the 29th ordering the B&GS to move immediately to its dispersal station and the month ended with preparations in full swing.

Since the outbreak of war, Aldergrove had been under the control of No 15 Group, which had its HQ at Plymouth. No 15 group was responsible for convoy escort and anti-submarine patrols in the Western Approaches and, until the fall of France, the Aldergrove based units concentrated on this area. After the French collapse, No 15 Group transferred its headquarters to Liverpool, co-located with the Royal navy's C-in-C Western Approaches. The role of the group was greatly expanded and now included the Western and North-Western Approaches. The threat of invasion forced the Government and the service chiefs to review the position of Northern Ireland and they decided to bolster its fighter defence and also boost the number of Coastal Command assets operating from the Province. The following months would see a marked increase in the use of Aldergrove.

The south-east corner of Aldergrove airfield in early 1940 showing the original runway layout. The runways would be realigned in September 1941. *(Crown copyright/RAF Aldergrove via Geoff Gardiner)*.

Chapter 3

JULY 1940 – DECEMBER 1940

The first day of July saw No 416 Flight being upgraded to squadron status and being numbered No 231 Sqn and carried out its first patrol when P/O Joel made a dawn coastal patrol the following day. With the departure of No 3 B&GS, No 774 Sqn was also on the move. On 2 July, the unit was informed that it was to move to Evanton in the north of Scotland and commenced to move out the following day. Eight Swordfish and five Sharks of the squadron left Aldergrove for Evanton but unfortunately one of the Sharks, piloted by Sub Lt Miller, crashed on landing and the pilot was killed. The aircraft of the B&GS were dispersed to several stations. The Battles were spread among West Freugh, Evanton, Penrhos, Manby and Warmwell. Ronaldsway and Cranwell received Wallaces. The Henleys were flown to Manby and a single Magister was allocated to Reading. Eight unserviceable aircraft were left behind.

On the 4th, the remainder of No 774 Sqn, 5 Rocs, 1 Skua and a Shark departed for Evanton with the final aircraft, a Skua, leaving on the 5th. The station was not to remain quiet for long though as personnel of No 61 Group began to arrive the same day followed by another batch on the 6th. No 231 Sqn received a Mentor on the 6th and a Tiger Moth on the 9th for communications duties and were able to move its Lysanders into Bellman hangars with the departure of the B&GS and the next few days were busy with the re-shuffle of sections and units on the station. On the 8th, four more Battles departed for Manby and the influx of new personnel and units continued with the arrival of No 64(F) Wing Servicing Party under the command of W/C Brake. Another unit arrived the same day in the guise of No 11 Repair & Salvage Unit (RSU).

The staff of the Operations Room pose for a photograph in 1940. *(I Reynolds via Geoff Gardiner).*

Lysanders, similar to this preserved example, were operated at Aldergrove by No 1 APC, No 9 OTU, No 231 Sqn and No 416 Flt. *(Westland Group).*

No 231 Sqn began carrying out dawn recce sorties on the 9th but almost immediately were warned of a possible move of the squadron to Newtownards. Over the following days, the squadron awaited further news and began packing. On 11 July, No 231 Sqn lost Lysander P9097, when P/O Baldwin crashed at Castlewellan. Baldwin escaped without injury after his engine cut and he hit a wall in the forced landing. Then, on the 15th, No 231 Sqn moved out to Newtownards. The following day, a further group of No 11 RSU personnel arrived with the unit's transport.

Over the next week, the last remnants of the B&GS departed the station and, on the 20th, Aldergrove had an influx of operational aircraft in the shape of No 254 Sqn and No 245 Sqn and a four aircraft detachment of Ansons from No 48 Sqn which joined two others already on the station. No 254 Sqn were transferred from No 18 group and brought six Blenheim Mk IV aircraft from Sumburgh in the Shetlands. No 245 Sqn commanded by S/L EW Whitley DFC, brought its Hurricane Mk Is from Turnhouse to take up the fighter defence of Belfast. No 245's ground party arrived the following day and the Sqn carried out a sector recce with nine aircraft to familiarise themselves with the area. No 245 Sqn had their first operational scramble from Aldergrove on 23 July but returned with nothing to report. On 28 July, Sgt P Killick, of No 245 Sqn, crashed his Hurricane on landing sustaining severe head injuries and a broken arm. The Hurricane was wrecked in the crash. On the 30th, No 254 Sqn were suddenly detached to St Eval for operations.

Aldergrove was not to be devoid of a Coastal Command presence for long as four Hudsons of No 233 Sqn arrived on 2 August, followed by a further six on the afternoon of the following day. No 233 Sqn was another 18 Group unit and had been based at Leuchars in Fife prior to being transferred, under the command of W/C HA Purvis

Station Headquarters, pictured in 1953. Constructed in 1932 and still in use today. *(RAF Aldergrove)*

DFC AFC, to Aldergrove and No 15 Group. The Hudsons were a mix of Mks II and III. By 2 August all of the Ansons of the No 48 Sqn detachment had been fitted with self sealing fuel tanks, adding greatly to the mental comfort of the crews. Other Coastal Command units also used Aldergrove from time to time and No 206 Sqn lost Hudson Mk I T9272 which was damaged beyond repair in a heavy landing returning from an anti-submarine patrol. No 245 Sqn almost lost another aircraft on 5 August when P/O ER Edmunds made a forced landing in the squadron hack, Magister N3861, near West Freugh due to lack of fuel. Edmunds was uninjured but the Magister was slightly damaged. On 7 August, No 502 Sqn received three of the much-maligned Blackburn Botha general reconnaissance aircraft from No 33 MU. The Botha was not to remain on the squadron strength for long though, as on 23 August F/L Corry, F/O McGiffen and Sgt Paterson were detached, along with seven groundcrew to Abingdon for instruction on the Whitley.

On the evening of 25 August, Sgt Barnfather, in Anson J/502, sighted a long trail of oil with patches forming ahead of it at 30-foot intervals. Barnfather went to find surface vessels to assist and returned to the area at 2050 hrs. The trail had disappeared but oil patches were still forming. Barnfather dropped a smoke float and checked the course of the patches. Movement was confirmed and Barnfather attacked from 300 feet. His first bomb was a direct hit on the last patch of oil to form on the surface. The second bomb dropped 60 feet dead ahead of the first on the course of the object. Oil continued to form but altered course from the position of the last bomb. No further results were observed.

With the Coastal Command presence now comprising Nos 233 and 502 Sqns and 254 Sqn detached to St Eval and No 245 Sqn representing Fighter Command, Aldergrove was becoming a potent operational unit. With No 64(F) Wing Servicing Party and No 11 RSU also sharing the station the unit was extremely busy.

During August, night flying trials with Martin Maryland Mk I bombers were being carried out at Aldergrove and these were marred by the loss of one of the aircraft on the night of 28/29 August when AR704 (recorded as having hit trees on the approach to Aldergrove) crashed, killing the crew, Sgt TF Meathrell (pilot), Sgt WJ Davies and Sgt DFG Sanders. Sanders was a member of No 22 Sqn and was buried on 3 September with full military honours in Glenavy, not far from Aldergrove. The Maryland had flown in from North Coates for the trials. John Wightman, who had joined the RAFVR pre-war, was a member of a fitting party detached to Northern Ireland in July and August 1940 and he recalls this incident:

"The number of personnel at Aldergrove had probably quadrupled since the start of the war and temporary huts for sleeping accommodation were dotted all over the place. The one assigned to us was just one hundred yards from the end of the main runway – fortunately the downwind end, so that aircraft took off away from us into the prevailing wind. Coming in over the top of us as they landed, they made much less noise as engines were not on full boost and did not disturb our sleep too much.

Another two hundred yards behind our hut was one of a type of prefabricated hangar, shaped like a giant Nissen hut (half a cylinder lying on its side). The in-line set up of hangar, hut and runway was a disaster waiting to happen, and happen it did.

One evening, about 10.30pm, three Martin Maryland light bombers flew in from England, the crews never having been to Aldergrove before. The runway lights were switched on, but for some reason the red obstruction lights on top of the hangar were not turned on. The three aircraft lined up for their landing, not knowing that they had to be high enough to clear the hangar. The flight leader clipped the top of the rounded roof with his wheels and bounced, causing the aircraft to stall. The pilot reacted perfectly, ramming his throttles into the emergency boost position and undoubtedly saved the lives of himself and his crew, not to mention mine and those of the other guys in the hut with me. At this moment, I was sitting in pyjamas on the edge of my bed and heard the thump of the undercarriage on the hangar, without realising what it was. Thus I was completely unprepared for what happened next – the shattering roar of two Pratt & Whitney radials over the top of us, windows and blackouts blown into the hut and being plunged into total darkness. What made us go weak at the knees later was the realisation of by how little he had missed us by. On the gable end of our hut was an eight-foot pole which carried the overhead wiring for our 230-volt supply. Some part of the aircraft, probably the undercarriage, had carried away both the pole and the wiring, hence our loss of lighting. In spite of this, the pilot made a safe touchdown on the runway.

That was not the end of it – worse was to come. In the darkness, the pilot of the second machine would have been unaware that anything was wrong, because he would have seen the lights of No 1 as it rolled down the runway. He proceeded with his approach but sadly he must have been a few feet lower, as he hit the roof much harder and crashed about fifty yards behind our hut. We rushed outside but there was nothing we could do; the intensity of the fire drove us back and the crash tenders had difficulty in reaching the site. Fortunately, no bombs were being carried but the heat caused the turret ammunition to explode and bullets were whining in all directions. We retired even further and lay on the ground until the barrage had finished. The poor devils in the third aircraft aborted their landing and circled for half an hour. The obstruction lights had belatedly been turned on, so they got down safely. Next day, we were given the job of recovering the IFF gear from the wreck, though I don't know why they bothered as it was unrecognisable. It took me a long time to forget the stench of burnt human flesh which hung around the site."

August saw No 502 Sqn continue its convoy escorts and anti-submarine patrols in the obsolete Ansons, but new equipment was on the way in the shape of Armstrong Whitworth Whitleys. Crews began to be detached to Kinloss for conversion to the Whitley and initially a flight of five Whitleys equipped with ASV were allocated to the squadron and named the 'No 502 Sqn Special Flight'. The squadron used these aircraft to test ASV under operational conditions.

While the Battle of Britain was reaching its height in the south east of England, Aldergrove saw more unit movement when No 7 Mobile Oxygen Plant (MOP) moved out to Dromore on the 6th and the following day No 22 Wing Servicing Unit departed for the same location. No 8 MOP also moved out on the 7th. On 13 September, the first four aircraft of No 224 Sqn arrived. The remainder of No 224 Sqn brought their Hudson Mks I and III to Aldergrove the following day to relieve No 233 Sqn which departed for Leuchars. No 224 Sqn was commanded by S/L CFC Wright DFC and comprised 24 officers and 126 other ranks. The No 48 Sqn detachment managed to fly over 400 hours on patrols during September. A further detachment had arrived at the beginning of September in the shape of No 102 Sqn from Bomber Command. Coastal Command was hard pressed to cover the convoys at this time and had asked for help from Bomber Command. No 102 Sqn sent a three aircraft detachment to Aldergrove on 3 September. Two of the Whitleys carried out the squadron's first convoy escort on 6 September by which time there were six aircraft detached.

At this stage of the Battle of the Atlantic, the Focke Wulf Condor, a four engined long-range reconnaissance bomber, was causing great problems to the Atlantic convoys. To counter this threat, Coastal Command transferred a detachment of long range Blenheims of 'A' Flt, No 236 Sqn to Aldergrove from St Eval on 17 September. No 236 Sqn brought eight Blenheims, 9 officers, 18 NCOs and 28 other ranks to the station. The groundcrew were transferred by air and quickly found the refuelling arrangements at Aldergrove unsatisfactory. There was no bulk storage for fuel and the petrol bowsers had to be filled by hand from four-gallon tins.

It was hoped that the squadron would be able to counter the Condors harassing shipping and shifting the area of enemy shipping attacks further west into the Atlantic. The squadron launched its first sorties on the 18th when three Blenheims, 2798/G, 5739/H and 5737/A flown by F/L Dennison, P/O Van Wayenberghe and Sgt Dennison searched the Irish Sea for an enemy aircraft reported to be regularly patrolling the area. Nothing was sighted.

No 502 Sqn saw some action on 24 September when the CO, S/L Briggs, flying an

Anson, sighted a submarine off Fair Head and attacked it, dropping two bombs one hundred yards ahead of it. His hopes of sinking it were not realised, however. On the same day, F/L Dennison left Aldergrove in Blenheim 1954/V with Rear Admiral King as a passenger to deal with an enemy aircraft reported to be attacking a convoy four miles north north west of Larne. Sgt Barrow and P/O Van Wayenberghe flew the other two aircraft in the formation, 2798/G and 1811/W. On arrival over the convoy there were no enemy aircraft to be seen and they escorted the convoy into the North Channel before returning to base. The next day P/O Herrick, 5740/J, P/O Dejace, 3600/R and Sgt Haylock, 1942/U were scrambled on an enemy aircraft patrol and sent to Islay where a convoy was being attacked. By the time they arrived, the enemy were gone and they returned to Aldergrove.

Just over two weeks after their arrival, No 224 Sqn suffered its first loss at Aldergrove when Hudson Mk I T9326:V crashed after take off on 30 September. The Hudson was tasked to escort an inbound convoy, HX74, arriving from Halifax, Nova Scotia. The pilot, Sgt AJ Gibbs and his crew, Sgt K Postgate, Sgt RC Cox, Sgt S Swann and Sgt JP O'Connor were all killed.

On 7 October, Whitley Mk V P4995:DY-P of 102 Sqn, piloted by F/O HR Young, force landed in the sea owing to engine trouble and sank in less than five minutes. The crew, F/O HR Young, Sgt R Collier and P/O DK Fosdyke were picked up by the destroyer HMS *St Mary* after being in the dinghy for 22 hours. The next day, the No 102 Sqn detachment left Aldergrove for Prestwick. Also on 2 October, Sgt Hughes of No 245 Sqn lost his bearings and made a forced landing at Rothesay, on the Isle of Bute. Hughes was uninjured but the Hurricane was slightly damaged. Five days later, No 245 Sqn suffered its first loss at Aldergrove. P/O Beedham crashed Hurricane N2707 on the edge of the aerodrome when, after an engine failure, he turned back and stalled. Beedham was killed in the crash.

October 1940 saw plenty of activity for No 502 Sqn with its Ansons and newer Whitleys. One of its crews found the liner 'Empress of Britain' on fire in the Atlantic and three days later, another aircraft made an attack on a U-boat. On 16 October, Hudson Mk I T9328, captained by F/L FC Scott of No 224 Sqn, took off from Aldergrove for a patrol and tragically flew into Slievenanee Mountain. Scott and his crew, P/O RJ Davies, F/O AB Tisdall, Sgt AB Nayler and Sgt AF Thomas were all killed.

Aldergrove was honoured by a visit to the station by Group Captain HRH the Duke of Kent KG KT GCMG GCVO on 21 October. The Duke arrived in a Hudson piloted by W/C EH Fielden AFC, the Captain of the King's Flight for a welfare inspection of the station. The Duke was met by the Station Commander, G/C Richardson and Air Cdre Carr. The Duke met all of the squadron commanders and senior officers on the station and lunched in the Officers' Mess before departing to Sydenham in the afternoon in a Proctor piloted by Air Cdre Carr. The day did not go well for everyone however. No 245 Sqn lost Sgt Greenwood, who had taken off to carry out a battle climb practice. Police at Toomebridge reported that the aircraft was observed to dive into Lough Neagh at high speed and explode on impact.

'A' Flt of No 236 Sqn departed Aldergrove for Sutton Bridge and night fighter duties on

26 October. Sgt Wilkinson in Whitley KI/502 sighted a conning tower on the morning of 26 October at a range of five miles. The U-boat dived as the Whitley reached the spot and no bombs were dropped and on 29 October, the squadron made its first successful ASV location of a U-boat. ASV was still very secret and in the words of one squadron member "When you receive instructions you destroy them before reading!" F/L Corry in KI/502 was on escort duty to convoy SC8 when a strong ASV contact was picked up at a range of three miles on the starboard beam. Corry turned onto course and sighted a U-boat on the surface 400 yards away. The U-boat proceeded to submerge and Corry went into attack. On the approach, the port wing dropped making aiming difficult and no bombs were dropped. Corry made a tight turn and released a salvo of four 250lb anti-submarine bombs from 700 feet. The bombs appeared to burst either on or within five yards of the stern of the U-boat, which was just awash with its periscope retracted just above the surface. Unfortunately, contact was lost due to the poor visibility immediately after the bombs exploded.

On 5 November, there was a change of command for No 48 Sqn when W/C Findlay was posted and S/L RH Harris became the new CO. The same day, No 502 Sqn received bad news from Kinloss. Whitley Mk V P5064 crashed on operational training killing the WOp/AG Sgt Nicholas. No 245 Sqn continued its run of bad luck at Aldergrove on 7 November when Sgt Dykes damaged Hurricane N2486 on landing, Dykes had been forced to make a flapless landing and hit a spraying machine. The Hurricane was so badly damaged it was not repaired. Two days later, P3099 was totally destroyed by fire. The pilot, Sgt Killick, escaped with slight injuries and shock.

11 November 1940 was a historic day for the station when the first transatlantic delivery flight of seven Hudsons led by DCT Bennett, who later found fame leading No 8 (Pathfinder) Group, arrived from Botwood in Newfoundland. On 13 November, another No 245 Sqn Hurricane, P2906, was damaged when F/L Sczcesniewski hit a lorry on the runway on landing with his starboard wing. Luckily, only two of the workers in the lorry were injured. The Hurricane wing was replaced. Twenty five minutes after this incident Sgt Koscik damaged P3385 on landing. Again the Hurricane was repairable. The losses continued to mount at Aldergrove and the winter weather was to take a hand when icing caused Hudson Mk I T9338 of No 224 Sqn to crash on take off on the 15th. The ice caused the Hudson to hit a hut on take off and the aircraft was destroyed in the resulting fire. The pilot, Sgt Castle and one other crewmember, Sgt Norman, survived but Sgt E Mill, Sgt FL Ingersent and Sgt EE Owen were killed. Whilst Aldergrove was coping with the Hudson crash, F/L Corry brought his No 502 Sqn Whitley, P5054, back to base with some damage, but no injuries to the crew, after being fired on by an unknown vessel. No 502 Sqn was to lose another aircraft when Whitley Mk V, P5054 crashed into the sea near Downhill, Co Londonderry in the early hours of 18 November killing Sub Lt LEH Scholefield, a naval officer flying with the squadron.

On 19 November, a new unit, No 272 Sqn, was formed at Aldergrove from a flight each of No 235 and 236 Sqns. The new squadron was equipped with Blenheim Mk IVf. S/L AW Fletcher DFC from No 235 Sqn was the first CO, 'A' Flt was made up of personnel from No 236 Sqn and commanded by F/O AS Moore while 'B' Flt came from

No 235 Sqn and was under the command of F/L RJ Peacock DFC. The following day, S/L Fletcher arrived from Bircham Newton with eight Blenheim Mk IVs. The squadron began training and the first operation was carried out by P/O Snow the same day. During the period, the squadron was busy carrying out 'armed rover' sorties. No 48 Sqn, which had held a detachment of Ansons at Aldergrove during the summer months,

Whitley YG-O of No 502 Sqn. *(G Gray)*

left the same day. No 224 Sqn lost another Hudson on 20 November when N7272 crashed near Luss in Dumbartonshire. The Hudson, piloted by P/O Atkinson, had departed Aldergrove at 1115 hrs to carry out a convoy escort for Convoy OB245 and, while returning to Aldergrove, was abandoned by the crew when they ran out of fuel three miles north west of Luss. The Hudson crashed into Loch Lomond but all of the crew escaped.

On the night of 21 November, Aldergrove was hit by an 82 mph gale which luckily did not damage any aircraft but did make it unsafe to taxy over the boggy grass the following day. On 24 November, No 272 Sqn suffered its first loss in unfortunate circumstances. P/O Herrick, with his crew, Sgts Smith and Hair, had taken off to escort convoy SC11 and never returned. It transpired that, on leaving Aldergrove, they spotted a small convoy, which was not the correct one, and flew towards it.

Eyewitnesses on the destroyer HMS *Vesper* reported that a dogfight took place between the Blenheim and a Fulmar during which the Blenheim stalled and fell into the sea, disappearing immediately. A search was made, but despite rescue craft being on the scene in three minutes, only the rubber dinghy and a fuel tank were found. There was no sign of the crew. No 502 Sqn lost one of its most experienced crew on this day. Sgt Barnfather crashed Whitley Mk V, P5090:YG-L into a mountain one mile west of Balquidder in Perthshire. Barnfather, Sgt Westoby, P/O Whitsed, Sgt Curtis and Sgt Perfect were all killed. The only survivor was Sgt Hamilton, an air gunner, who was badly injured.

No 245 Sqn lost another Hurricane on 30 November. During dogfighting practice with another pilot at 12,000 feet, Sgt Pretkiewicz disappeared and was later reported to have crashed at Crockeneel, west of Cushendall. The Hurricane was wrecked and Pretkiewicz was killed. Once again, No 502 Sqn was to suffer a loss in the continuing war against the U-boat. Whitley Mk V, T4219 left Aldergrove at 1255 hrs for a patrol and never returned. F/O DEM Thompson and his crew, Sgt Hutchings, Sgt Wain, F/S Scragg and Sgt Kerr were posted missing. The squadron also had a change of command on this day when W/C TB Cooper replaced W/C LR Briggs as CO.

No 233 Sqn returned to Aldergrove from Leuchars on 7 December. The first two Hudsons of No 224 Sqn returned to Leuchars the same day. Three Harrow transports were utilised to move the squadron's personnel back to Leuchars. The following day

AIR GUNNER – 272 SQUADRON

Peter Mullen OBE was a WOp/AG with No 272 Sqn at Aldergrove from December 1940 to April 1941 before serving briefly on No 1405 Met Flt, also at Aldergrove. Here he recounts some of his experiences:

'I was at Aldergrove for about six months, until the squadron was posted elsewhere to convert to Beaufighters, which, of course, do not have WOp/AGs. I then went on to form a new Canadian squadron, again on Blenheims. My work with 272 Sqn was solely as long range fighter escort to North Atlantic Convoys, so I was often frustrated because of the difficulty in finding the convoy in bad weather. The North Atlantic is rather a vast area in which to find a fairly small target.

My experience with 1405 Met Flt was limited to two sorties, for which I was pleased, because as you can imagine, it was a dreadful bore for the man in the mid-turret, whilst the pilot and navigator were collating met information as a very uncomfortable height – without oxygen if my memory serves me correctly.

I remember little about our accommodation at Aldergrove, but do recall the incredible hospitality so freely given by the locals, who revelled in feeding us up with the most incredible Irish breakfasts whenever they could get hold of us. We did go by bus to Belfast occasionally, but I was teetotal in those days. I was only 19! Whilst I was there, I do remember a fairly violent German air raid on Belfast, after which anyone in an RAF uniform was held to blame because there were no fighter squadrons available in the area. The public could not see why we should not have taken off and done something about it.

Coming back to Ireland was always made simpler by reason of the lights in the Republic towns, whereas the towns in the North were completely blacked out. One of our aircraft had spent too long looking for his target convoy and was running dangerously low on fuel. He knew he could not reach an airfield in the Northern Ireland and found an airstrip in the South who surreptitiously put sufficient fuel in his tank to get him home! All is fair in love and war!

When escorting convoys our main object was to seek the huge German bomber, the Focke Wulf Condor. They rarely came out into the open except to attack a convoy, spending most of the time in and around cloud cover.

I do remember being most surprised to come across a gaggle of He 111s and determining from our debriefing that there was no doubt they had come from Norway in a concerted effort to bomb the convoy which we were escorting. I do know that the ones which we met did not even attempt a pass on our convoy and must have gone straight back to Norway. The biggest menace in that respect was the Focke Wulf Condor, a huge machine with a fair bomb load. The Heinkels would not have been able to stay around for very long, having only an average fuel capacity.

the remainder of No 224 Sqn ground party departed again using the Harrows. The final Hudsons departed on the 9th and 10th. On the 7th, No 502 Sqn lost Whitley Mk V T4277 which crashed near Ballykelly. No 272 Sqn had an aircraft damaged on 9 December when Sgt Demoulin taxied his Blenheim into a stationary Whitley and

Time carried forward :— 63·25 | 2·00

Date	Hour	Aircraft Type and No.	Pilot	Duty	Remarks (Including results of bombing, gunnery, exercises, etc.)	Day	Night
		BLENHEIM				·30	
6·1·41	1455	T 1950	SGT. SMITH	TO LIMAVADY.	EXPLAIN,	1·55	
7·1·41	1500	T 1950	"	A.S. SWEEP.		3·00	
13·1·41	1425	Z 5752	"	ESCORT.		·30	
14·1·41	1455	Z 5756	F/LT. MOORE	M/c TEST.		2·00	
16·1·41	1035	T 1954	SGT. SMITH	ESCORT.		1·10	
31·1·41	1410	Z 5733	"	-		·30	
9·1·41	1510	Z5750	P/O SALTER	FROM LIMAVADY		5·45	
12·1·41	1100	N 3526	SGT. SMITH.	FIGHTER ESCORT.	INTERCEPTED 5 He. 111's.		
						78·45	2·00

SUMMARY FOR JAN 1941.

	DAY	NIGHT
HOURS FLOWN DURING JAN	15·20	—
HOURS FLOWN ON UNIT	43·20	-
GRAND TOTAL	78·45	2·00

O.C. "A" FLIGHT .. W Moore P/O.

O. C 272 SQDN. . . . - - - - . .

TOTAL TIME ....

Extract from Peter Mullen's logbook for January 1941, whilst serving with No 272 Sqn, showing an entry for the interception of five He 111s on 12 January. *(Peter Mullen OBE).*

the next day another Blenheim was damaged when Sgt Smith failed to put his Blenheim's undercarriage lever into the down position and the undercarriage collapsed on landing.

On 11 December, a party from Farnborough arrived to carry out flare dropping trials. The aircraft used for the trial were a Boston, flown by S/L Clouston and a Whitley flown by S/L Bickford. The party was unable to carry out the trials on the night of arrival due to the lateness of their arrival and the fact that both aircraft had been damaged by hail on the flight to Aldergrove. The weather on the next two days held up the trials until the 14th and the party left for Farnborough on the 15th. On 16 December, No 245 Sqn had a change of command when S/L JWC Simpson replaced S/L EW Whitely. S/L Simpson had previously been serving with No 43 Sqn at Drem.

The Station Commander, G/C Richardson was replaced by G/C GW Bentley DFC on 18 December on posting to Sydenham. The previous day, seven more Hudsons departed Botwood for Aldergrove. Led by Captain Storr, they arrived just before lunchtime having crossed the Atlantic in 10 ½ hours. Among the passengers carried was Sir Walter Latham, Economic Adviser for the government. Six of the seven Hudsons arrived at Aldergrove, the seventh putting down at Prestwick. The 17th also saw the departure of another of Aldergrove's smaller units when No 12 WIS left for Glengormley, near Belfast. The six Hudsons left Aldergrove on the 18th and all arrived safely at Speke.

Date	Hour	Aircraft Type and No.	Pilot	Duty	REMARKS (including results of bombing, gunnery, exercises, etc.)	Time carried forward :— 176·15 2·00	
						Flying Times	
						Day	Night
5·4·41.	1915.	B. ENHEIM IV M 5736	Sgt. SMITH.	W.OP/A.G.	ESCORT. NOT MET.	2 05	
6·4·41.	1520.	BLENHEIM IF Z 3638(114).	"	PASSR.	To NEWCASTLE. Co DOWN.	1 40.	
6·4·41.	18 30	ANSON N1338	F/o LUNN	"	To ALDERGROVE.	·30	
7·4·41.	10 10	BLENHEIM II M 5736	Sgt. SMITH	W.OP/A.G.	ESCORT CONVOY.	5·15	
10 4 41.	12 30	N 5736	Sgt SMITH	"	ESORT CONVOY.	4 50	
13·4·41.	08 05	G 3542.	"	"	FIGHTER PATROL.	5·15	
13·4·41	1330	M 5736	"	"	ESCORT CONVOY	5·10	
				1405 MET. FLT.	ALDERGROVE.		
19·5·41	10·30	BLENHEIM IF V 5692	F/LT. RICHIE.	W OP/A·G.	MET. FLIGHT.	3·30	
24·5·41	10 30	V 5691	"	"	"	3·00	
29·5·41	16·10	...4291	F/Sgt KELLY	PASSR.	To HATLON.	2·00	
						194·15.	
					TOTAL TIME ...		

An extract from Peter Mullen's logbook showing his last flights with No 272 Sqn and the two sorties flown on meteorological reconnaissance with No 1405 Met Flt. *(Peter Mullen OBE).*

G/C Bentley officially took command of the station on the 21st. The same day, No 272 Sqn sent four aircraft out on convoy escort duties. Sgt Hobbs in T/272 failed to return. The Blenheim was later reported to have crashed ten miles south of the Eire border. Hobbs, Sgt Ricketts and Sgt Newport had all escaped by parachute. On Boxing Day 1940, P/O Longhurst was on escort duty in Whitley YG:F when a suspicious object was sighted thirty miles astern of the convoy. Longhurst proceeded to the position and a dark patch with bubbles breaking the surface, trailed by a long streak was sighted. One bomb was dropped which scored a direct hit on the bubbles. A faint trace of oil appeared but nothing further was seen.

On 29 December, a special flight arrived from Botwood. This flight of seven Hudsons contained a special Hudson, which had been gifted to the RAF by the people of Burbank, California. This particular aircraft was planned to be built and delivered within a week of leaving the factory. The first aircraft of the flight arrived at 1245 and thirty minutes later two others followed. The fourth aircraft landed at Speke and it was learned that the sixth aircraft had crashed on take off at Botwood, obstructing the runway and preventing the departure of the seventh Hudson. A few hours later, the Hudsons departed for Speke and all arrived safely. Also on the 29th, one flight of No 272 Sqn moved temporarily to Limavady complete with groundcrews. The last day of 1940 saw

Aldergrove with a total strength of 3,308 personnel comprising station personnel and those of the squadrons and lodger units.

The end of 1940 saw the threat of invasion diminish to almost nothing but between June and November most of the Royal navy's assets were deployed against this threat. The U-boat crews called this period the 'happy time' and the ill-equipped units of Coastal Command could do little about the havoc being wreaked on the convoys. The best a convoy escort commander could hope for was an obsolete patrol aircraft, circling overhead, which would hopefully keep the U-boat submerged and lessen the chances of a successful sinking.

Chapter 4

JANUARY 1941 – JUNE 1941

On 7 January, No 502 Sqn sent the ground party for a four aircraft detachment to Wick by boat and train. The four aircraft left the following day led by F/L Foster. The same day, tragedy struck the station when Hudson Mk II T9379 of No 233 Sqn crashed, a few minutes after taking off, in a field about three miles north of the airfield. P/O Stone and his crew P/O Quemby, Sgt Haddon and Sgt Joseph were all killed. Stone and Joseph were buried on the 11th.

The detachment that had carried out flare dropping experiments in December returned on 9 January. S/L Clouston flew in a Boston, S/L Fulton brought a Blenheim and P/O Johnson arrived with a Whitley. The aircraft flew throughout the night carrying out the experiments and the following afternoon they were joined by a Defiant piloted by F/O Knocker. The trials continued into the night of 10/11 January and the detachment departed for Farnborough again on the 11th.

Mid-January saw, heavy fall of snow and, on the 19th, the station became unusable with drifts of snow on the runways and roads. The next day, the roads were still blocked and the road to Antrim was finally re-opened on the 25th. Station personnel spent the intervening days digging out the aircraft and clearing roads and runways of snow. The constant battle against the U-boats and the elements was taking its toll on No 502 Sqn and on 23 January they lost yet another Whitley. Whitley P5041 crashed near Campbeltown on the Mull of Kintyre, killing the crew, F/L Billing, F/O Holmes, Sgt Hooker, Sgt Pilling and Sgt Bradley. On the 24th, No 502 Sqn suffered again when the crew abandoned Whitley Mk V T4168 which was short of fuel. F/O Johnson was killed, F/O Ward and Sgt Jefferson were interned in Eire and Sgts Hogg and Greenwood were posted missing. The Whitley crashed near Lough Foyle. On the same day, one of No 233 Squadron's Hudsons, P5123, force landed in Eire and the crew. P/O Welply and P/O Cowper, were interned. The Hudson was repaired and taken into use by the Irish Air Corps. While the survivors from these crashes were contemplating waiting out the war in an internment camp in Eire, No 502 Sqn was sending an advance party to Limavady, the squadrons new base. Three days later, the Sqn HQ moved to Limavady and No 502 Sqn bade farewell to Aldergrove, its pre-war base.

In February 1941, an Area Combined Headquarters was established in Liverpool to co-ordinate naval operations with those of No 15 Group. The area covered by Western Approaches Command and that of No 15 group were adjusted so that all of the reconnaissance, fighter, flying boat and long range fighter assets, including those based at Aldergrove, could be utilised efficiently.

The Farnborough detachment returned to Aldergrove again on 1 February led by S/L Fulton, with a Whitley and two Blenheims to carry out night fighting experiments. Major Roper of No 257 Searchlight Unit and Mr Jones of the Air Defence Experimental Establishment (ADEE) also arrived with a searchlight to take part in the experiments. Over the next week there was much 'to-ing and fro-ing' by the detachment with Whitleys, Defiants and Blenheims arriving from and departing for various airfields.

STATION ENTERTAINMENT

Like all RAF Stations, Aldergrove had a number of former professional entertainers as well as a host of gifted amateurs. The Station often put on shows to entertain the personnel and the RAF had troupes of travelling entertainers who would visit. On 3 February 1941, BBC radio broadcast a live show from Aldergrove, one of a series entitled "Airman Smith Entertains." George Martin was serving at Aldergrove as a ground gunner, awaiting posting in his own trade of electrician. He was a musician and vocalist and performed at various functions. George decided to do a comedy routine, as there were other singers on the bill. This was a success and his act from then on concentrated on comedy. After being demobbed he was resident comedian at the famous Windmill Theatre for two years following this by doing radio and television work including script writing for acts such a magician David Nixon and the puppet Basil Brush.

On 3 February, No 272 Sqn moved from the far side of the airfield into a hangar vacated by No 502 Sqn and their accommodation situation was much improved. On 4 February, No 245 Sqn sighted its first enemy aircraft since the move to Aldergrove. The Poles of Yellow Section were ordered to scramble at 1315 hrs and fifteen minutes later sighted a He 111 near Rathlin Island. The Heinkel was at 30,000 feet with Yellow Section below at 20,000 feet. The Poles gave chase but were unable to make contact.

On 7 February, the Station Operations Record Book notes that 'A' and 'B' Flts of No 245 Sqn left for Limavady on a 'special mission' returning the following day when the mission was cancelled. While No 245 Sqn were at Limavady on the 9th, a flight of Hurricane Mk Is from No 607 Sqn based at Macmerry, south of Edinburgh, arrived to provide air defence cover. That night F/L Mowat of No 245 Sqn sighted an enemy aircraft, possibly a Heinkel, passing close to him in the opposite direction. By the time he turned to pursue it, the enemy aircraft had disappeared.

Hudson N7372 of 233 Sqn was damaged beyond repair in a crash at Aldergrove on 13 February when the pilot overshot his landing and the undercarriage collapsed. Night flying experiments continued at Aldergrove on 15 February when P/O Hanley brought a De Havilland DH89 in from Hendon and on the 24th S/L McArthur flew in a Boston from Farnborough. No 233 Sqn sent off two aircraft to search for the missing 'SS Anchises' on 28 February. One of the two was successful in finding six boatloads of survivors who were subsequently picked up by a ship.

The first day of March was particularly busy for Aldergrove as detachments of No 206 Sqn, 224 Sqn and 236 Sqn arrived from Leuchars, Bircham Newton and St Eval respectively. No 206 and 224 Sqns brought Hudsons and No 236 Sqn flew in with their Blenheims. No 233 Sqn were involved in another search when two Hudsons were tasked with the escort of the 'SS Simaloer' on 2 March. The ship had been bombed and had launched some lifeboats. When the ship was found she had a slight list to port and P/O Russell in T9372 began a search for the lifeboats. Having successfully found one, Russell directed the 'SS Clan Cameron' to the spot to take on the survivors.

Sgt Carruthers in N7223 was also on the scene but, despite continuing the search and finding a second upturned lifeboat, none of the 40 passengers it had contained were found. Four days later, No 233 Sqn launched four aircraft to search for survivors of the 'Nichalau Zografia'. One of the Hudsons guided a destroyer to the boatloads of survivors. While the Coastal squadrons were being kept busy on convoy escort, No 245 Sqn were busy shooting down balloons. On 3 March, F/L Kitson and F/L Mowat were scrambled to search for a drifting balloon. After some time they found it over Lough Erne and shot it down.

No 23 MU maintained its busy schedule of receiving aircraft for storage, flight-testing and dispersal and delivery of aircraft to other operational units throughout the period. Reginald Carter, one of the unit test pilots, recalls life at the MU during this period:

"I was posted from the Continental Ferry Pool to No 23 MU at Aldergrove on 5 March 1941 and was engaged in flight testing, delivering and dispersing of various types of aircraft. Frequent deliveries were made to training and operational stations in England, Scotland and Wales, often having to return to Aldergrove by train and ferry from Stranraer to Larne. Dispersals were made to a number of landing strips in Northern Ireland, some of which had been hastily laid down and were in poor condition. One I remember was laid out on one field and extended to another via a gap made in a large hedge. A couple of these strips were very rough indeed and most unsuitable to aircraft such as Bostons and Havocs with their tricycle undercarriages.

Accommodation and food were very good at Aldergrove and I was involved in plenty of interesting flying on the different types of aircraft. I even managed three days leave in Dublin, in 'civvies' of course!

The pilots at the MU were mostly older than the squadron pilots and the MU consisted of both civilian and service people. They carried out repairs and major inspections on the aircraft, maintained them in airworthy condition and controlled dispersals. We carried out regular air tests on the various aircraft sometimes combining this with delivery. We had several pilots and the CO was Wing Commander Gainer.

Aircraft that I flew included the Wellington, Whitley, Blenheim, Bombay, Botha, Hereford, Havoc, Short Scion, Fairey Battle and Lysander. Taxi aircraft which we used for transporting pilots included the Anson, Rapide, Oxford and even a Tiger Moth.

Typical deliveries would have been Wellingtons to Stradishall, Wyton, Syerston and Marham; Whitleys to Dishforth; Blenheims to Leuchars. There were few problems encountered, mostly minor. On one occasion on a delivery I had to turn back with engine trouble in a Whitley. There was an occasion when control cables on a Wellington were reassembled incorrectly, causing the pilot to sweat a bit. Another I remember was when we delivered two Herefords to Langford Lodge. I put mine down safely but the other one struck a wooden barricade at the approach end of the unfinished landing strip. The undercarriage collapsed on touchdown resulting in a ground loop in a cloud of dust. As the aircraft burst into flames, the pilot did an exit and a sprint clear in a time that an Olympic athlete would not have equalled. Not quite the recommended way to deliver aircraft.

The test pilots of No 23 MU in 1941. L to R: P/O Farrow, F/L Parker, P/O Statham, Sgt Cheetham, P/O Kelly, P/O Carter, Sgt Bone. *(RWH Carter)*

The dispersal airfields and airstrips which we used in Northern Ireland were Maydown, Langford Lodge, Murlough, Limavady, Newtownards, Ballywalter and Blaris. We often carried passengers on delivery flights, generally people going on leave. On one such flight in a Wellington, I dropped off nine people at Sealand on my way to Stradishall. There could well have been a few bottles of Irish whiskey among them! I left Aldergrove on posting to the RAE at Farnborough on 20 July 1941."

On 10 March, tragedy struck No 272 Sqn when two aircraft failed to return from operations. P/O Van Waeyenberghe in L/272 and Sgt Chanler, a Canadian, in E/272 took off on escort duty and are thought to have collided in bad weather. Van Waeyenberghe, a Belgian, had escaped from France and joined No 236 Sqn in July 1940. He was posted to No 272 Sqn in November 1940. He was a very experienced and popular member of the squadron. Sgt Chanler had recently joined the squadron from the OTU at Catfoss. Sgts Thompson, McWatt, Pass and Newton were also lost in the tragic accident. The squadron sent out aircraft to search for survivors the following day with no success. Two other No 272 Sqn aircraft on escort duty had a lucky escape on the 11th when they were fired on by the convoy they were escorting. Three shells burst near the aircraft but no damage was caused.

△ Hudson of No 206 Sqn being serviced in a hangar at Aldorgrovo. *(No 206 Sqn).*

Also on the 11th, the No 236 Sqn detachment departed again to St Eval and two days later a detachment from No 235 Sqn arrived from Penrhos with Blenheim Mk If long-range fighters. Another unit formed in March was No 1405 Met Flt under the command of F/L Ritchie. This unit was tasked with carrying out daily 'Bismuth' meteorological reconnaissance flights into the Atlantic with Blenheims. The unit's first sortie was flown by F/L Ritchie in Blenheim V5692. No 224 Sqn lost another Hudson to the weather on 16 March when Hudson N7369 overshot landing in bad visibility and the undercarriage collapsed. No 206 Sqn lost one of its Hudson Mk IVs when AE611 crashed at Aldergrove on 20 March. The aircraft dived into the ground after a night take off killing the crew; P/O Richard James Fuller, P/O Maurice Kingsley Warren, Sgt Frank Leslie Holyoake and W/Op AG Sgt Cecil Henry Funnell. On 23 March, No 272 Sqn was informed that it was to re-equip with Beaufighters and on 27 March, the CO and F/S Nelson went to Chivenor to fly the Beaufighter prior to instructing other squadron pilots on receipt of the new aircraft. The CO and F/S Nelson returned from Chivenor in a No 252 Sqn Beaufighter and caused a sensation on the station when they 'beat up' the aerodrome. The Beaufighter did not remain however, returning to Chivenor with a No 252 Sqn pilot.

The station became even busier when half of No 252 Sqn arrived from Chivenor with its Beaufighters on 3 April. Preparations had begun at Chivenor for the move of the Squadron's 22 Beaufighter Mk Is and the solitary Blenheim Mk IV on 2 April. 'A' Flt moved the following day bringing 11 Beaufighters and crews and a skeleton staff of maintenance personnel to operate as a detached flight. The remaining 'A' Flt personnel arrived the next day in two aircraft of No 271 Sqn. Preparations for the despatch of the second flight began on 5 April and the following day 10 Beaufighters set out for

Aldergrove. No 252 Sqn was now under the operational control of No 15 Group and carried out its first sorties the same day. The squadron was tasked with carrying out convoy patrols. The squadron work up had been slow due to aircraft unserviceability and, though declared operational at the end of March, 252 did not carry out their first patrol from Aldergrove until a convoy anti-aircraft patrol was flown on 6 April. The rear party left Chivenor by road and air on 7 April and the squadron quickly settled in to its allocated accommodation of one Bellman hangar with two adjacent offices and a further two offices on the opposite side of the aerodrome. The accommodation was hardly adequate but they had been promised an improvement on the departure of another squadron. The squadron had its first accident on 7 April when F/O McDonald failed to check the contents of his Beaufighter's port fuel tanks and the port engine cut out on approach to land. McDonald force landed T3241 on the airfield. On 10 April, the road party, which had left on the 7th, arrived. Two days later, No 252 Sqn moved into a new hangar and took over two married quarters, adjacent to the dispersal points, as the Sqn HQ and Flt accommodation.

No 245 Sqn continued to lose aircraft and pilots and on 4 April Sgt Gault, whilst flying on a convoy protection patrol in Hurricane V7678, crashed at Carrickfergus. The Hurricane dived through cloud into a hill and Gault died from his injuries.

The defence of the Province was not given great priority compared to other areas at this time and there was not one single searchlight in the whole of Northern Ireland. The anti-aircraft gun situation was little better with only twenty-four heavy and eight light guns allocated. Two of the heavy 3.7in guns were positioned at Aldergrove. On the night of 7/8 April, Belfast was raided by the Luftwaffe between 2330 and 0300 hours. No 245 Sqn carried out patrols with single aircraft. On one such patrol, S/L JWC Simpson DFC shot down an He 111 over Downpatrick. Simpson was airborne at 0125 hrs, patrolling east of Strangford Lough, when he sighted two enemy aircraft above him at 7,000 feet. He closed to investigate and drew fire from both aircraft. Simpson broke away and re-engaged the rearmost Heinkel 111, which blew up after his third burst of fire.

On 8 April, No 272 Sqn departed Aldergrove to convert to Beaufighters at Chivenor, the move being completed on the 9th. No 245 Sqn were to suffer further losses in April when, on the 13th, L6780, carrying S/L McEwen, F/L Kitson and W/O Johnson to Aldergrove crashed on take off at Squires Gate. An engine failed on take off and the Blenheim turned over crashing out of control, killing all three on board.

Beaufighters were a familiar sight at Aldergrove, being operated by No 9 OTU and Nos 143, 248 and 252 Squadrons. *(Authors collection)*

No 233 Sqn sent out eight aircraft on convoy escort duty on 15 April and unfortunately lost one when Hudson T9432, piloted by Sgt Green, became lost and crashed at night in Scotland. The Hudson flew into Ben Laoigh in Perthshire in bad visibility at night. April 15th also saw the arrival of the remainder of No 224 Sqn from Leuchars bring the squadron up to full strength and the No 206 Sqn detachment left for Bircham Newton the same day. The night of the 15th also saw the first serious raid on Belfast when the Luftwaffe bombed the city from 2245 until 0530. Hurricanes of No 245 Sqn took off to intercept the bombers but, due to difficulties in co-ordinating the defences the Sector Controller held the fighters off ordering them not to approach closer than five miles to Belfast.

On 16 April, Sgt Westcomb of No 233 Sqn was on escort duty in Hudson T9313 when he spotted and gave chase to a FW200 but he was unable to overtake it and the Condor escaped. No 252 Sqn, however, had more success this day when F/L Riley of 'A' Flt, flying Beaufighter K/252, encountered a FW200 and shot it down into the sea. Riley spotted the enemy aircraft at the end of his patrol and closed on the Condor making his attack from the port beam to the quarter finishing up astern. He opened fire at 300 yards and continued in short burst to point blank range when astern. The Condor returned fire with a midships gun. The Condor caught fire near the port wing root and both engines appeared completely unserviceable as the Condor swung to the left, straightened out then dived into the sea in flames. There were no survivors and very little wreckage seen. This was the squadron's first success since its formation and was scored after eleven days of operations from Aldergrove. The squadron's delight at this success was somewhat dampened due to the loss of F/O Lane and his Beaufighter the same day. The squadron also began to detach aircraft to Sumburgh for operations off the Norwegian coast. On 23 April, No 252 Sqn were warned of an impending move to Malta and all leave was cancelled. Two days later, the move was reduced to detachment strength of 15 aircraft for a period of one month. One aircraft which would not be going on the detachment was Beaufighter Mk I 2269, piloted by F/O Hirst, which was damaged by a Wellington taxiing into its starboard wingtip. Three days later, six Beaufighters left for St Eval under the command of S/L Yaxley MC. The following day, ten more departed under the command of F/L Riley, leaving seven aircraft and nine crews at Aldergrove. The ground echelon remained behind and was renumbered as No 143 Sqn on 15 June 1941. No 233 Sqn received a new CO when W/C Kidd DFC AFC arrived on 26 April.

On the last day of April, P/O Perrott and Sgt Pilfold of No 245 Sqn took off for a dogfighting exercise. Both aircraft failed to return. They had collided during the practice and crashed into Lough Neagh. Sgt Pilfold's body was recovered but P/O Perrott was not found. Also this day, No 252 Sqn was allocated an Anson, on loan from No 48 Sqn, to improve the efficiency of the squadron's observers. On the night of 4/5 May, the Luftwaffe carried out a heavy raid on Belfast and followed this up with a further raid on the night of 5/6 May when S/L Simpson of No 245 Sqn was again successful, shooting down a bomber for his 12th victory. S/L Simpson had no searchlights to assist him in locating the enemy bombers but just after 0130 hrs flying at 7,000 feet, above cloud, he saw three enemy aircraft flying in line astern. He made a head on attack on the nearest Heinkel, thinking he was attacking from astern. He closed on the bomber and opened fire. The bomber blew up in mid-air and the debris fell into the sea. The other enemy aircraft opened fire and Simpson broke away and returned to base.

5 May also saw the arrival of a flight of Blenheims of No 254 Sqn on detachment from Sumburgh under the command of F/L Illingworth DFC. Three Handley Page Harrows brought in the ground personnel. The following day, the remaining flight of No 236 Sqn returned to Bircham Newton. On 7 May, the first operations by No 254 Sqn were carried out from Aldergrove.

S/L Simpson was in action again on 13 May. He took off at 1105 hrs to fly to Ayr to collect spares and, crossing the Irish Sea on the outward trip, he spotted an aircraft flying northwards, very low over the sea. The aircraft was dark camouflaged and bore yellow roundels and was identified as a Do 17. S/L Simpson flew ahead of it and made a head on diving attack. The enemy aircraft attempted to gain height but a second attack forced it down again and after a third attack it hit the water and turned over. The Dornier remained on the surface for about three minutes before sinking. Simpson returned to base with his thirteenth victory. No 1402 Met Flt lost one of its Gladiators, Mk II N5620, when it crashed that night at Langford Lodge hitting a tree and overturning.

No 233 Sqn lost Hudson Mk I N7296 at Nutts Corner after a brake seizure caused it to crash on 21 May and on 22 May four of No 252 Sqn's Beaufighters were returning from the Malta detachment when F/O MacDonald's aircraft, T3249, crashed into the sea off Mounts Bay after running out of fuel. MacDonald, F/O Lemar and Sgt Booth were picked up by a small coastal vessel. A second Beaufighter, T3235, piloted by F/O Holgate, also went missing and was later reported to have crashed in Eire. Holgate, F/O Verity and Sgt Barnett were interned. Verity, who would later gain great fame as a pilot flying SOE agents into occupied Europe with the Lysanders of No 161 Sqn, managed to make an escape from internment in disguise and with the assistance of MI9. On 25 May, the squadron was warned of an impending overseas posting and the following day a Blenheim Mk IV, Z6245, was fitted for wireless telegraphy instruction for the observers.

No 233 Sqn had success on 28 May when W/C Kidd in Hudson N7218/I attacked and shot down a He 111. The Heinkel had been attacking a ship from high level and Kidd climbed to attack it opening fire from 500 yards at full deflection. No hits were observed and the Heinkel turned and dived taking evasive action. At 1000 yards the Heinkel rear gunner opened fire and the dogfight continued for a few minutes. Kidd closed to 400 yards and scored some hits before the Heinkel escaped into cloud cover. Kidd's crew then spotted a second Heinkel dead ahead at about 7000 feet and as his front gun ammunition was exhausted Kidd climbed to engage with the rear guns, closing to 200 yards. The Heinkel tried to evade the Hudson with short plunging dives but Kidd maintained formation and the gunner poured continuous fire into the Heinkel at 50 yards range. The He 111 burst into flames and crashed into the sea. Two of its crew were seen to bale out.

Also on 28 May, the rest of No 254 Sqn arrived from Carew Cheriton to bring the squadron up to full strength. These were followed by a flight of No 236 Sqn but they returned to Carew Cheriton the next day. While the remainder of the squadron was arriving, F/L Illingworth was airborne in Blenheim Mk IV Z6027/Q on escort to Force LY. At 0952 hrs the Force was being shadowed by a He 111 and Illingworth attacked the bomber. The Heinkel dropped four bombs from 4,000 feet, missing the ships, and Illingworth succeeded in driving it off although no hits were observed.

On 29 May, Blue Section of No 245 Sqn left Limavady at 0900 hrs en route to Aldergrove. They intercepted an enemy aircraft at 18,000 feet south west of Lough Neagh and Sgts Hill and Srom gave chase. They chased it all the way to Dublin, expending all of their ammunition and setting its port engine in fire. The bomber eventually escaped.

During May, experiments were carried out at Aldergrove with a view to concealing the flare path and obstruction lights as much as possible whilst still allowing aircraft to land using them. The experiments were to discover the most suitable cowling for this purpose. The work was being carried out under the control of OC No 233 Sqn. Construction work on the station gathered pace during the month and a decontamination centre and sick quarters were making satisfactory progress.

On 1 June, the remaining crews of No 272 Sqn along with the groundcrew joined No 252 Sqn and two days later the personnel of both squadrons were informed that they would be absorbed by No 143 Sqn on 15 June. No 254 Sqn had its first action and some unwanted attention from a convoy on 2 June. P/O Sise was escorting convoy CB329 in Blenheim J/254 when a 4,000-ton motor vessel was torpedoed. Sise dived the Blenheim to sea level in an attempt to find the U-boat and the ships in the convoy opened fire on the Blenheim, forcing Sise to move away. The aircraft was badly damaged but luckily, the crew was unhurt. Three days later, Blenheim Mk IVf N3524 failed to return from a Norwegian patrol.

More success came No 233 Squadron's way in June when aircraft of the squadron made two attacks on U-boats claiming them both as damaged. Sgt Simpson lifted Hudson N7226 off the runway at Aldergrove on 6 June and made his way out to sea. At 0634, his air gunner, Sgt McMillan, sighted a wash on the port beam, half a mile away. Simpson hauled the Hudson round to the north to investigate and quickly sighted a periscope 400 yards away. The periscope submerged as the Hudson passed over the spot dropping three depth charges thirty seconds later. Two of the depth charges exploded fifty feet to port of the wash, the third failed to explode. As Simpson turned after the attack, a periscope was seen to rise out of the water thirty yards to port of the explosions. Simpson continued to circle but when no further results were observed he informed the convoy escort of the U-boat position and left for base. Later the same day, Hudson N7209 was on submarine strike duty when, at 1257 hrs, HMS *Skate* signalled that there was a submarine two miles ahead of the convoy. The navigator, Sgt Scott, spotted a periscope breaking the surface 200 yards ahead, before submerging. The Hudson was turned hard to port and dropped three depth charges on a shallow dive at a height of 10 feet, 250 yards ahead of the swirl. The depth charges fell 60 feet apart, one falling directly on the aiming point. Unfortunately, only one exploded but a large number of bubbles appeared followed by a large mass of thick, brown, pearly looking mud

A No 233 Sqn Hudson patrols over a convoy 120 miles west of Benbecula in June 1941.
(J Griffith via J Meadows)

and a very thin streak of oily water continued to be disturbed for the next ten minutes. After this nothing further was seen. Shortly afterwards, HMS *Skate* arrive on the scene and marked the spot with a smoke candle.

No 254 Sqn suffered another loss at Aldergrove on 9 June when P/O CLH Werner crashed Blenheim Mk IV Z6025 near Garvagh. Werner, Sgt R Shaw, the observer and Sgt JJEM O'Donnell (WOp/AG) were all killed.

On 15 June, all of the personnel of No 252 Sqn were posted to No 143 Sqn which formed with Beaufighter Mk Ic aircraft. No 233 Sqn lost Hudson Mk III T9447 in a crash one mile south west of Coleraine on 18 June. An engine cut on take off and the Hudson crashed while attempting a forced landing. No 245 Sqn lost another pilot on 26 June when Sgt Hill, on an army co-operation sortie, crashed near Ballymena and was killed. On 28 June, the Fighter Sector HQ was transferred to Ballyhalbert on the Ards peninsula when this station opened under the control of No 13 Group. The experiments on the airfield lighting carried out in May continued at a reduced level when it was decided in June that the airfield would be equipped with Drem lighting. No 233 Sqn continued to investigate cowlings for the obstruction lights. Work on the decontamination centre and sick quarters continued and construction of a YMCA building began during the month.

BEAUFIGHTER OBSERVER

In June 1941, F/L T Armstrong DFC was serving with No 235 Sqn at Bircham Newton flying in Blenheim Mk IVf.

"On 9 June 1941, some of the squadron were moved to Aldergrove to form No 143 Sqn and convert to Beaufighter Mk Is. We had, I think, five Beaufighters, the first we had seen, and a couple of Blenheim Mk Ifs. According to my logbook, I managed to get eight practice trips in Beaufighters and three in the Blenheims. We then did two ops into the Atlantic, neither very successful. The CO was S/L Stockdale. On 4 July 1941, we moved to Thornaby prior to flying out to Malta and the Middle East. Such was my experience of Aldergrove. I don't think it was completed and I have vague recollections of it being rather primitive."

Chapter 5

JULY 1941 – DECEMBER 1941

July 1941 saw the departure of No 143 Sqn to Thornaby on the 5th on completion of its work up on Beaufighters. No 245 Sqn departed for Ballyhalbert on the 15th to continue in its role of air defence for the Province. With the departure of No 245 Sqn the station was transferred to Coastal Command under No 15 Group. Two days

Three ZS coded Hudsons of No 233 Sqn in formation. *(J Griffith via J Meadows)*.

later, AVM Robb visited the station to inspect it after the transfer.

F/S Larkins was on patrol in Blenheim S/254 on 8 July when the port engine began to vibrate and misfire. Larkins had been on patrol for several hours and made for Port Ellen, the nearest airfield. Now on one engine, he made an approach to land. Larkins was aware of the limitations of Port Ellen with its short runway and elected to land, but rain on the windshield obstructed his vision and he did not see the boundary markings of the unserviceable ground and ran into a soft patch and overturned. The following day, Sgt F Aspinall crashed his Blenheim whilst on convoy escort. The starboard engine cut out in flight and Aspinall was unable to maintain height, force landing in the sea. A destroyer picked up Aspinall and his observer, though the observer later died of his injuries. The WOp/AG, Sgt GM Carnall was not found. A week later on 16 July F/L Randall was taking off from Aldergrove in Blenheim L8841 when the port tyre burst just before the aircraft became airborne. Randall throttled back both engines and by use of the rudder and full brake kept the aircraft fairly straight until the end of the runway. At this point, the aircraft swung to port and travelled broadside until it came to a standstill. The port wing and undercarriage were damaged beyond repair. The port propeller blades were damaged and the centre section of the fuselage showed signs of severe strain. Randall and his crew had a very lucky escape.

On 17 July, F/L Winnicott of No 233 Sqn was escorting convoy OB346 when he sighted a Condor ten miles away. He gave chase but the Condor escaped into cloud. The Condor had been responsible for the shooting down of Q/502 who were picked up by an escort vessel.

On 18 July, a Whitley of No 502 Sqn, piloted by F/O Lindsay, overshot on landing at night, ran across the Crumlin to Antrim road and ended up in a line of trees, luckily no one was injured. On the same day, F/L GCB Bernard-Smith arrived to take over command of No 254 Sqn. The following day, a Blenheim of No 254 Sqn Mk IV T2120, piloted by F/O King was involved in a serious crash. The pilot had dived the aircraft to low level over the airfield but, unfortunately, hit a telegraph pole and lost control of the Blenheim. The aircraft crashed into the roof of the NAAFI building then the fuel tanks burst and set the building on fire. Some of the wreckage was thrown in the direction

BLENHEIM BOY

Ron Smith served with No 254 Sqn during 1941-42 and was at Aldergrove when the tragic NAAFI crash occurred:

"I was with 254 Sqn on the station on two separate occasions before 1942. My first visit was on a detachment and I returned in May 1941. On the first visit I recall the shock of seeing the lights still on in Belfast and I think around the station. By the time we arrived in '41 Belfast had been bombed – lights out! One of our Blenheim Mk IVs flew into the top floor of the NAAFI, killing several besides the crew, and I recall taking hurried cover one day when a Beaufighter of another squadron opened fire with most if not all of its four cannon and six machine guns – right in the hangar! What a racket!

I was a Fitter II, ex-Halton Apprentice and I later became an Engineer. On one detachment I remember working like stink when we hit a bad luck streak and had two out of three aircraft unserviceable. I think I was a corporal at the time. One job involved changing a fuel tank and the main cock had to be locked open, the snag being that the cock lever position varied according to its manufacture. Due to the panic situation this one got locked wrong – like closed! It should have been fo8und on the ground test, but incredibly it was not. As NCO in charge of detachment Maintenance it was my responsibility. By chance I went on the test flight and when we were over the lake there, the port engine cut out (you take off on both engines running on both tanks and separate them after being clear of the airfield). The CO, having established some mitigating circumstances, and the fact that I was suitably scared by the engine cut out called it quits.

In a local village pub in Crumlin we often saw a chap knocking back pints of stout with hardly a gulp and with little obvious effect. So, one night, some idiot in our group told him that we were buying and that we were going to see if we could keep pace with him. I have only a hazy idea how it ended but when he bid us "Goodnight Boys" he was in much better shape than we were! We met WAAF's for the first time at Aldergrove. It was pretty embarrassing at first, our language being pretty loud and coarse as in most 'all-male' societies. I was posted away from 254 in early 1942."

of one of the 23 MU hangars and caused thirteen casualties, some fatal, among a party of the ground defence force who were drilling there. Some of the girls employed by NAAFI were trapped in the burning building and were killed outright. Several others were injured. The station fire tender, assisted by another from Nutts Corner, managed to put the fire out. The three crew, six NAAFI girls and one airman were killed and a further ten airmen, four NAAFI girls and a civilian worker were injured.

After the tragedy of the previous week, the station had something to celebrate when a Hudson of No 233 Sqn shot down a Focke Wulf Condor which was attacking a convoy on 23 July. P/O Down and crew in Hudson AM536/J were about to leave convoy OG69 when a message was received from the escort of a suspicious aircraft to starboard. Down turned to investigate and spotted a Condor four miles ahead. The Hudson approached from the port quarter with Down forcing every ounce of speed out of it. He closed to 400 yards in a shallow dive and opened fire with the front guns. The Condor returned fire while Down closed to 20 to 30 feet beneath and to port of the Condor enabling the turret guns and the side fuselage guns to be brought to bear at point blank. Smoke and flames billowed out from the Condor's port engines and it made a steep turn to starboard. The Hudson gunners continued to pour fire into it and only ceased firing when the Condor had passed the starboard tailplane and flown out of range. The crippled Condor continued to lose height and crashed into the sea. P/O Down was relieved by Sgt Ballantine in Hudson AM582 and two minutes later the SNO of the convoy escort signalled that the Condor was ahead of the convoy. Ballantine flew ahead and spotted the Condor in the sea and a dinghy containing survivors. The corvette HMS *Begonia* picked up six survivors.

On 27 July, Sgt Donner and crew were escorting convoy SL80 in Hudson AM541. They had arrived over the convoy at 1820 hrs and, at 1910 hrs, were about to leave when the Hudson suddenly crashed into the sea. The crash was observed by P/O Down, in AM536/J, who was able to report that the destroyer HMS *Broke* had picked up the entire crew.

No 233 Sqn began to move out to St Eval in Cornwall on 9 August. They were replaced by No 206 Sqn, which brought its Hudsons in from St Eval. The squadron's first patrol from Aldergrove was carried out by Sgt Ireland in Hudson AM622/L.

The station lost another aircraft on 16 August when Hudson MK V AM588 of No 206 Sqn, piloted by P/O T Hayston, crashed into a hill four miles north east of Lady Hill near Antrim. The pilot, P/O Thomas Lunston Hayston and the WOp, Sgt Robert Elliott Ramsay, were killed. The navigator, Sgt Stait had both legs broken and was very seriously injured. The fourth member of the crew, Sgt Mann, who was in the turret at the time of the crash, escaped uninjured. On the same day P/O Howard left Aldergrove in Hudson AM604:J to escort the '*Imperial Star*'. The ship was not met but at 1108 hrs Howard spotted a FW200 and gave chase. The Condor disappeared into cloud and a few minutes later he spotted a He111, which he also gave chase to. Once again the enemy escaped into cloud.

On 26 August, eight Beaufighters of No 248 Sqn arrived from Detling. While the Beaufighters were arriving at Aldergrove, F/L Patrick was on patrol in Hudson T9453/Q of No 206 Sqn. While escorting convoy OS4, he sighted a U-boat but was unable to make an attack. The following day, two officers, F/O Moir and P/O Beckingham arrived at Aldergrove to prepare for the arrival of a Group Training Flight.

By the end of August, the work on the decontamination centre was almost complete and the new sick quarters were ready to be opened. The YMCA building involved in the crash was abandoned and the ORB noted that this did nothing for the tidiness of the station.

On 1 September, F/L Patrick took off from Aldergrove in Hudson T9444/A to escort convoy OG73. He met the convoy and established R/T contact only to be fired upon by the convoy! On 4 September, G/C Bentley, who had taken over the station some nine-months earlier left the unit to take up a new post at St Eval. W/C WK Le May took over the duties of Station Commander. No 1402 Met Flt was to lose yet another of its

Gladiator Mk II, N5592 of No 1402 Met Flt which crashed on 6 September 1941. *(E Cromie via N McGarry).*

aged Gladiators on 6 September when Mk II N5592 crashed at Lady Hill, Co Antrim. On 12 September, Sgt AA McIntosh of No 254 Sqn and his two army passengers had a lucky escape, though slightly injured, when an engine cowling came adrift and part of it struck the tailplane, jamming the elevators and causing McIntosh to make a forced landing. McIntosh landed the Blenheim, N3610, in a field at Ballymaguire near Stewartstown, Co Tyrone, with the undercarriage up.

During September, the 206 Sqn diarist recorded that after two years of war only five of the original September 1939 aircrew members of the squadron remained; F/O CN Crook, P/O EE Fitchew, F/S WD Caulfield DFM, F/S R Field DFM and Sgt GH Livingston. The rest of the squadron were casualties, missing or posted.

Air Cdre Kirby and Lord Londonderry visited the station on 18 September and inspected the sites of the new runways, construction of which had just commenced. The building of these runways necessitated the demolition of the officers sleeping quarters and two officers' married quarters, which had been in use as the WAAF Officers Mess. Two days later, the station lost another aircraft when a Blenheim of No 254 Sqn crashed into Lough Neagh. Two of the squadron's Blenheims had been carrying out a practice formation flight over Lough Neagh when the Blenheim struck the water and sank immediately. The three crew, Sgt KF Kuhle, Sgt R Steel and AC2 TW Vickers were posted missing. Two of the crew were recovered on the 25th and the third crewmember was recovered from the Lough two days later. Four days after the Blenheim crash, tragedy struck again when No 206 Sqn lost a Hudson in a crash just outside the airfield boundary. Sgt Dunn had taken off in Hudson AM664/B to escort the 'Australia Star' but had a problem with the ailerons and decided to return to base. The Hudson crashed near the aerodrome and burned out. The crew, Sgt Frederick Dunn, F/S Bernard Morgan (both pilots), WOp/AG Sgt Victor Charles Donald Hayward and WOp/AG Sgt Geoffrey Owen Linhart were all killed.

Sgt Joe Peet with his bride in September 1941. Peet joined 206 Sqn in October 1941 and was shot down over Bremen on 25/26 June 1942. *(206 Sqn)*

Sgt EH 'Ted' Nelson, WOp/AG No 206 Sqn. Ted joined the squadron in September 1941 and took part in the '1000 Bomber raid on Bremen the following June. *(EH Nelson)*

The strength of the station was increased once again with the arrival of a flight of No 48 Sqn, under the command of S/L Wherry, on attachment. The flight was not to remain long however, leaving for Skitten on the 15th. No 206 Sqn were thwarted in their attempts to sink a U-boat once more when P/O Wills sighted a wash and disturbance caused by a submarine in heavy seas on 16 October. Wills, piloting Hudson AM722/R, escorting convoy TC14, dived and dropped a sea marker to mark the U-boat's position, then, turning to attack at depth charge height, failed to spot any sign of the marker or the U-boat wash.

On 20 October, the station was informed that the Group Training Flight that was to be formed at Aldergrove would henceforth be known as No 15 Group Operational Practice Flight. In response to a request for search and rescue aircraft, No 206 Sqn launched Hudson's 206/C, 206/R and 206/W to search for a Whitley crew in a dinghy. S/L Holmes, piloting AM722/R, found the dinghy with the crew of six safe. A No 502 Sqn aircraft relieved Holmes and a destroyer picked up the crew of the Whitley. On 25 October, the author of the books "Battle of Britain" and "Bomber Command", Mr Hilary-Saunders, visited the station accompanied by G/C Willoughby de Broke to obtain 'local colour' for the book "Coastal Command".

Two views of a No 206 Sqn Hudson named 'Little Gel II'. These photos were not taken at Aldergrove but show the Hudson in some detail. As well as the name the coloured wheels are of note. *(No 206 Sqn).*

Hudsons of No 206 Sqn in November 1941. This scene depicts one of their fairly regular 'beat ups' of the station. *(EH Nelson)*

The beginning of November saw Aldergrove accommodating two squadrons, Nos 206 and 254, and three flights, 1402, 1405 and 15 Gp Operational Practice Flt, the latter becoming No 1 Armament Practice Camp on 5 November. No 1 APC would remain as a lodger unit until 1 September 1945, utilising Lysanders, Masters, Battles, Martinets and Dominies. The first day of the month saw an aircraft from the station in action when Hudson AM570/P of No 206 Sqn, captained by P/O Miller, which had been on convoy patrol, successfully fought off a Condor which escaped into cloud after having some damage inflicted upon it by the Hudson. Miller made quarter attacks with the front guns and several beam attacks to allow his gunners to attack with side guns after the turret jammed. Several hits were observed on the Condor. The Hudson returned to Aldergrove with engine trouble after the fight, which had lasted for seven minutes.

The following day saw more action for the station when 12 aircraft of No 254 Sqn carried out a patrol and reported sighting a submarine submerging. Following this report, No 206 Sqn sent out three Hudsons on an anti-submarine sweep. S/L Holmes in AM762/S sighted a submarine at position 5430N 1210W and depth charges and a sea marker was dropped. Later, a whale surfaced near the marker.

During November, Nos 206 and 254 Sqns carried out numerous convoy escorts and anti-submarine patrols and on 14 November, eight Blenheims from No 254 Sqn were detached to Carew Cheriton to operate under the control of No 19 Gp. These aircraft returned the next day. On 16 November, No 206 Sqn began sending detachments to Wick to operate with No 220 Sqn under No 18 Gp control.

No 206 Sqn at Aldergrove in 1941. *(No 206 Sqn).*

While the patrol aircraft of Nos 206 and 254 Squadrons carried out their patrols and escorts, the Blenheims and Gladiators of Nos 1405 and 1402 Met Flights continued to make their daily meteorological flights. In addition to its Blenheims, No 1405 Met Flt began to receive Hudson Mk IIIs in December to extend the range of the daily 'Bismuth' sorties. These flights, though often routine, were vital to both Coastal and Bomber Commands who relied on the meteorological information supplied by these Flights to plan the long range coastal patrols and bomber sorties to Germany and Occupied Europe.

No 206 Sqn continued to detach Hudsons to Wick throughout December and also

A group photo of No 206 Sqn aircrew at Aldergrove in 1941. *(No 206 Sqn)*

began detaching aircraft to Speke. On 5 December, seven of the squadron's Hudsons proceeded to St Eval on detachment. No 254 Sqn which had been at Aldergrove since May, departed for Dyce in December, the move taking place over the period 8-15 December. During the move, the squadron lost Blenheim Z/254 which force landed at Turnberry on the 8th. Two days later, another Blenheim was lost en route to Dyce when aircraft P/254 crashed at Glenisla in Scotland, killing the crew, W/C Bernard Smith, Sgt Harris and Sgt Strather and two passengers, Sgt Sinclair and LAC Lovell. On 11 December, No 206 Sqn were in action again when Hudson B/206 attacked a U-boat with its front guns south west of the Faroe Islands.

While No 254 Sqn were leaving the station, their place was being taken by No 143 Sqn which began arriving from Dyce on 14 December under the command of W/C GV Garey. Pilots of No 254 Sqn began ferrying in Blenheim Mk IVs for No 143 Sqn on 9 December. The first three to arrive were coded 'A', 'L' and 'M'. The following day, No 143 Sqn's unit equipment was transported to Aberdeen Docks from Dyce for shipping to Aldergrove. On 14 December, thirteen Blenheims took off from Dyce for Aldergrove but bad weather forced three to land at Prestwick. Another landed at Ayr and one Blenheim force landed at Perth due to engine trouble. The last of No 143 Squadron's Blenheims arrived from Dyce, piloted by F/L AB Parker and F/L JW Blennerhassett on 16 December. Two days later, the unit's equipment began to arrive and on the 19th the squadron was loaned two Magisters by the station for training.

On 17 December, No 206 Sqn began to detach Hudsons to Chivenor and on 21 December, No 206 Sqn sent a Hudson out to search for a reported U-boat but with no success. The No 206 Sqn detachment to Chivenor lost an aircraft on the 22nd when a Hudson, captained by F/L Terry, failed to return from a sortie to St Nazaire. This raid was carried out by Coastal crews to assist Bomber Command in an attack on the Donge oil refinery. Terry and his crew are thought to have come down in the sea as the Germans claimed no Allied aircraft shot down that night. The detachment returned from Chivenor on Christmas Eve.

On Christmas Eve, L9391:V, a Blenheim Mk IVf of 254 Sqn was ditched on patrol and a somewhat sombre Christmas evening was celebrated in darkness by the station when the camp lights failed. On Boxing Day, No 206 Sqn sent three aircraft on a patrol on which a large oil streak was sighted. The streak was thought to have been of recent origin and depth charges were dropped. The aircraft circled the streak for thirty-five minutes with no result and proceeded with their patrol. The last patrol of the year was carried out on 28 December, escorting the ship 'City of Edinburgh' throughout the day.

Despite the increase in attacks on U-boats by the Aldergrove-based aircraft and by Coastal Command as a whole, the battle of the Atlantic was at a stalemate. By the end of 1941, the Allies had lost over ten million tons of shipping, half of it to U-boats. Construction was not keeping up with losses and, though the Kriegsmarine had lost thirty-five U-boats, the number sunk never exceeded the number available for operations. Coastal Command desperately required new equipment and better methods of hunting and killing the U-boat.

Hudson VX-V of No 206 Sqn taking off. The aircraft serial number has been deleted by the censor for security reasons. It is possibly P5178, which used the code letter V. *(No 206 Sqn)*.

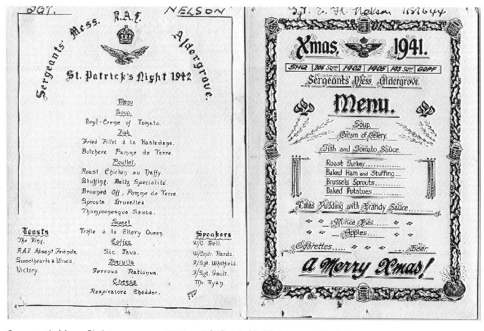

Sergeant's Mess Christmas menu, 1941 and St Patrick's Night menu 1942. *(EH Nelson)*

Chapter 6

JANUARY 1942 – JUNE 1942

The first sorties of 1942 were on 3 January but several were recalled due to adverse weather. On 5 January, No 206 Sqn sent a Hudson out to search for another Hudson of No 220 Sqn which had gone missing and a second Hudson carried out a search for a missing Spitfire. This aircraft was recalled when it was reported that the wreckage of the missing Spitfire had been found. The previous day, the unit was able to take its mind off the war for a few precious moments when the entertainer George Formby visited the station and gave two performances.

The Hudsons of No 206 Sqn carried out many sweeps over the next few days and the squadron lost a Hudson on 8 January when it crashed on landing. The crew escaped without injury. No 143 Sqn's Blenheims began to be ferried away by crews from No 489 Sqn the same day and the squadron was informed that others would be allocated to Nos 415 and 254 Sqns. On 25 January, an accident involving two of No 143 Sqn's Blenheims, Z5972 and Z5731, occurred on the tarmac. Whilst a fitter was running up the engines of one of them, the chocks slipped away from the wheels and it ran forward. Z5731 ran into Z5972, which was stationary, causing damage to the leading edge and nose. Z5972 had the Perspex of the observer's cabin in the nose badly damaged and both propellers written off.

Patrols and convoy escorts continued with little to report until 26 January, when No 206 Sqn sent ten of its Hudsons on sweeps. Hudson AM613/G, captained by F/O Nelson, sighted a U-boat on the surface at 1153 hrs. The U-boat appeared to submerge quite slowly and the Hudson was able to make an attack, dropping four depth charges. The Hudson remained in the area of the attack for over an hour but no results were observed from this attack. Two days later, Hudson G/206 was on patrol again when the crew sighted and unidentified aircraft 10 – 15 miles distant. Unfortunately it disappeared into cloud. The next day Hudson G/206 ran off the runway while taking off and its place was taken by AM604/J under the command of F/O Goddard. Whilst on patrol, J/206 located a U-boat on the surface using ASV. The U-boat quickly submerged as the Hudson made an immediate attack. Four depth charges were dropped; one of which was estimated to have hit the submarine. No results were observed and shortly afterwards the Hudson directed a destroyer to the scene of the attack. Both the Hudson and the destroyer continued to search the area to no avail. During the attack, the wireless operator found his Morse transmitter key to be broken and tapped out the attack message to base with his fingers in direct contact with the live wires.

While this attack and the subsequent search was going on, Hudson 'M' of No 1405 Met Flt sighted another U-boat on the surface and signalled this information to base. Hudson 'B' of No 206 Sqn was ordered to search the area. Later, Hudson 'K' of No 206 Sqn made a further search for the U-boat attacked by J/206 but again with no luck.

More of No 143 Sqn's Blenheims were ferried away by crews from Nos 415 and 254 Sqns on 28 January as the squadron awaited re-equipment with Beaufighters.

On 30 January, while No 206 Sqn were patrolling with three Hudsons, Aldergrove commenced an anti-invasion exercise at Alert No 2. The following day, the exercise continued with the Alert state being increased to Alert No 1 in the afternoon. During the continuation of the exercise on 1 February, two of No 206 Squadron's Hudsons crashed. The crew of Hudson G/206 (possibly AM613) escaped uninjured but unfortunately the crew of Hudson J/206 (possibly AM603), one officer and four SNCOs were all killed. The station was brought to 'action stations' on the morning of the 1st and the exercise ended that afternoon.

No 206 Sqn were shouldering a large share of the Coastal Command burden of patrolling during this period and a signal from Coastal Command on 2 February shows that 206 Sqn were the leaders in flying hours:

'At present 15 Group consists of six Squadrons at five different Stations. Between 30/12/41 and 2/2/42, the total number of flying hours (excluding Met Flights) amounted to 1719. Of this total Aldergrove, (206 Squadron) were responsible for 578, or roughly one third of the total flying hours of the Group. Their nearest rivals were 93 and 502 Squadrons at Limavady with a joint total of 378 hours. In the same period 206 Squadron made three attacks on U-boats.'

On 5 February, No 206 Sqn sent out four Hudsons on patrol and at 1443 hrs Hudson

Logbook entry for February 1942 showing details of Ted Nelson's crash in AM622:VX-L on St Valentine's Day. *(EH Nelson)*

HUDSON CRASH

Ted Nelson joined No 206 Sqn at Aldergrove on 24 September 1941 and remained at Aldergrove until 30 June 1942. During this period he completed thirty-five operations on Hudsons, a total of 210 operational flying hours, before being posted to Benbecula and Flying Fortresses. Among the sorties he flew were the longest Hudson flight of nine hours and ten minutes, a Met flight up to 18,000 feet, no mean achievement in those days and he also took part in the 'Thousand Bomber Raid' on Bremen. Ted was on board Hudson AM622:VX-L when it crashed on take off on St Valentine's Day 1942. "There are several points to bear in mind when considering our operations during those days. We had no radar in the early days and no binoculars were issued for searching. There were no modern comforts in wartime aircraft. We wore three pairs of gloves – silk, wool and leather. Long johns, fur-lined Irvine jackets and trousers and fur lined boots. Flying out of Aldergrove due west was not allowed as we would cross into Eire. Valuable time was lost over submarine infested waters due to the extra time taken in flying up to Coleraine before heading west. The Hudson's maximum flying time was 6-7 hours. I joined No 206 Sqn on 24 September 1941 and was assigned to 'A' Flt. I was a Sergeant WOp/AG paid 7s/9d (less than 40p) a day which increased over the ensuing 12 months to 10s/2d (50p) per day. My first flight from Aldergrove was on 4 October 1941 and my first operational flight was on 8 October."

8 October 1941 – Hudson AM622

"The very first one – returned after thirty minutes with a failed wireless set. Took off again when repaired but were back again within four hours as mountainous seas and a sea level cloud base precluded any hopes of sighting a U-boat."

2 November 1941 – Hudson AM587

"Seventh operational flight but the first one with Sergeant pilots Marriott and Goodson and Sergeant WOp/AG Peet and Nelson allowed out together since forming as a crew at OTU in September. Close escort to an aircraft carrier. Four young lads, average age just about 19, found it difficult to accept the enormity of being responsible for such a great aeroplane laden with deadly depth charges and guns galore. (In the ensuing months the novelty soon wore off as we aged really fast.)"

11 November 1941 – Hudson AM788

"Returning from an air search for a ditched Hudson crew in Lough Eyre and flying low down the Bann valley we collided with a large bird which wrecked the aerial system and smashed the astrodome and gun turret. Les Goodson kept us airborne – guess we were all too young to die just yet.
The 1941/42 winter was appalling, with so very many operational flights resulting in – 'Returned – bad weather'- being entered in the logbooks. Gale force winds, high seas and virtually nil visibility were not conducive to our locating convoys or sighting U-boats. (Imagine the conditions on the ships). The Battle of the Atlantic moved northwards and more and more operational flights were being made out of Stornoway and Tiree in the Hebrides after overnight stops by Aldergrove crews."

14 February 1942 – Hudson AM622

"St Valentine's Day. A 0645 take off for yet another anti-submarine sweep saw us fail to clear some power cables and we crash-landed in a field. We had a full load of fuel and depth charges. Twenty-seven seconds after take off she crashed in flames and disintegrated. The two pilots and WOp/AG Joe Peet escaped through the pilot's hatch, slid down the wing and somehow forced open the main door in the fuselage, which was tightly jammed, and dragged me, lying injured in the rear of the aircraft, out. In a mad scramble the four of us reached the nearest ditch before the fuel and depth charges exploded and left nothing but a hole in the ground. All within 27 seconds. In those early days we took two homing pigeons in a brown wicker basket to send back U-boat sighting/attack messages. There was probably more anguish about the loss of the bird than relief at our escape from almost certain death. The birds were tended by the WAAF in the Parachute Section. Sadly the crash meant the end of AM622, the very Hudson in which I had made my first operational flight, just four months earlier. At the time it seemed like four years."

May 1942

"An active month – Six operational flights and one meteorological flight of 7hrs 20 mins at 18,000 feet – I can still feel the cold! A single engine landing in T9431 on the 17th and a spell aboard the destroyer HMS Keppel escorting the Queen Mary on the first part of an Atlantic crossing in atrocious weather – seas actually breaking over the bows of the huge liner. (Part of a PR exercise to acquaint aircrew with the difficulties of life at sea in the Royal Navy. We failed to persuade any naval types to see the war from our vantage point in the air. They felt safer with a deck beneath their feet)."

18 June 1942 – Hudson T9458

"Longest Hudson flight to date. 9 hrs 40 mins. Anti-aircraft escort to convoy – guess we carried less depth charges and extra fuel tanks."

25 June 1942 – Hudson AM722

"Target Bremen. The second '1000 Bomber raid', code named 'Millennium Two'. Bomber Command had wasted us for the first 'Millennium' at the end of May (Target Cologne) but we had to withdraw as there was massive Atlantic activity – some aircraft had already been re-camouflaged only to be returned to bright colours the next day. Our crew split for this raid and flew with others. Three of us returned. My best mate, Joe Peet, was shot down and became a POW. Another casualty in another Hudson was our new CO – he had literally just been appointed on 12 June. The memory of that night will live forever particularly the outward flight when, in whichever direction you looked, there were aircraft, hundreds and hundreds of them. Even over Bremen you could see black shapes and marvelled at the way we all stayed apart from each other. On the ground, even from 12,000 feet, you could see all the different areas of the city afire, with the occasional spurt, much as if you had poked the embers of a very hot wood bonfire. In the air there was the most beautiful firework display of all time as the AA shells burst; hypnotic and impossible to believe they were all fatal if they hit your aircraft.

Originally, on the 23rd, we had flown from Aldergrove to North Coates and from there to a satellite airfield nearby called Donna Nook. After the raid we landed at North Coates for the debriefing and then went back to Donna Nook to sleep, returning to Aldergrove on the 27th.

The living conditions and social life at Aldergrove were as good as anyone could wish for bearing in mind largely wooden huts. An excellent Mess – slight snag when we 18/19 year olds arrived as sergeants when the NCOs we had to live with were mainly regulars who had taken years to reach NCO rank. At a welcoming party 'THEY' lined up on one side of some long tables put together end to end which we youngsters lined up opposite. Each man was served with a pint of beer, which remained untouched until his neighbour turned his empty glass upside down. The 'regulars' seemed to down theirs in one gulp and all their glasses were empty before we had hardly begun. One by one we were taken outside, debagged and had mustard smeared all over our testicles – then made to 'adjust our dress' and return to the Mess. DO NOT DO THIS AT HOME – the pain is excruciating. The 'regulars' seemed more kindly disposed towards us after this! Socially a lot of leisure time was spent drinking in the Mess, nibbling extra rations in the NAAFI, moderately flirting with the WAAF and enjoying the occasional visit to Belfast. The Grand Central Hotel was our main 'stamping ground'. Happily our two pilots learnt to dance and gradually the four of us were invited into the homes of the two young ladies they went dancing with. I can vividly remember the way we were escorted to these homes and advised about the streets we should avoid. I guess we had 'the Troubles' in 1941/42 – certainly there was a perceptible atmosphere away from the main roads.

There is no more beautiful sight to Coastal Command aircrew than that of a huge Atlantic convoy appearing out of the dawn light on the horizon. A most emotional moment enhanced with relief when a ship count proves no overnight losses. There is no deeper sadness than when at first sighting it becomes obvious that the convoy is in disarray after heavy losses – a feeling of total helplessness, of depression and of real youthful anger that nearby, just below the surface, lie the U-boats and the crews who cruelly did this to 'our' convoy.

AM875/U, piloted by F/S Gauntlett sighted a U-boat. The Hudson attacked with four depth charges and nothing further was seen of the U-boat. The same day, No 206 Sqn lost Hudson Mk V AM706 in a crash at Aldergrove, which caused the aircraft to be damaged beyond repair.

On 9 February, two Hudsons were detailed to search for a Spitfire which had gone missing the previous day but with no success. The pilot of the Spitfire was washed up near West Freugh in his dinghy, but sadly he was dead. The detachments from the station continued and No 206 Sqn sent six Hudsons to Stornoway. The Hudsons at Stornoway carried out a sweep on the 10th during which Hudson G/206 sighted a raft. The raft held two survivors and the Hudson remained with the raft until it reached its endurance limit and had to return to Stornoway. The next day five Hudsons left Stornoway for Aldergrove and Hudson U/206 sighted the raft again. A Catalina was circling it and a trawler appeared half a mile away. The Hudson signalled base that the raft had been found and that the trawler had rescued the two men alive.

On 14 February, only one Hudson managed to get airborne from Aldergrove, tasked with the escort of Convoy SL 99, comprising 39 merchant ships and five escort vessels. The rest of the day's patrols were delayed by the crash of Hudson AM622:VX-L of No 206 Sqn

No 206 Sqn aircrew 21 April 1942. Ted Nelson 3rd row, 11th from left. Note the blanking out of the ASV aerials on the nose by the censor. *(EH Nelson)*

immediately on taking off. Hudsons W/206 and V/206 eventually managed to get off and completed uneventful patrols. Hudson AM587/D of No 206 Sqn, however, sighted the periscope of a U-boat about seven miles distant and launched an attack. Four 250lb depth charges were dropped and one was estimated to have struck the U-boat. Immediately following the explosion of the depth charges, oil was seen to rise in a patch. D/206 assisted by G/206 remained in the area but nothing more was seen to confirm the sinking.

During February, the detachments to Stornoway continued and four Hudsons were sent there on 18 February to carry out operations. The following day A/206, which was one of the detachment, sighted a U-boat at 6040N 1450W and attached it with depth charges. No hits were observed and, following this attack, another U-boat was sighted but they could not attack having expended all of their depth charges

The 22nd saw three Hudsons airborne to search for a U-boat, which had been sighted near a convoy, but no trace of this submarine was seen. Changes of aircraft for the Stornoway detachment continued throughout the rest of February and though U-boat sightings had been frequent during January and February and several attacks had been made, results were inconclusive even when hits were observed. No U-boats were recorded as lost to aircraft in February and only two had been sunk by ships.

March began with a reorganisation of assets at Aldergrove when No 1405 Met Flt was absorbed into No 1402 Met Flt. This increased the strength of the Flt by three Blenheim Mk IVs, two Hudson Mk IIIs, nineteen aircrew and thirty groundcrew. From its formation in March 1941, under the command of F/L Ritchie, the Flight had carried out 291 Bismuth sorties in 330 days.

On 4 March, No 206 Sqn lost another Hudson when W/206 crashed on take off, luckily no one was injured. No 143 Sqn, which had lost its last Blenheim only two days previously, was informed on 10 March that, pending re-equipment with Beaufighters, it would operate as a temporary Blenheim OTU.

On 15 March, a Hudson of No 206 Sqn was detailed to escort a convoy and whilst carrying out a search of the area, observed an underwater explosion. The explosion was thought to be a mine and no wreckage was observed. (German navy records show that U133 was lost on 14 March and is recorded as having been sunk by a mine, possibly one of her own. Allowing for the proximity of the dates perhaps the No 206 Sqn crew had observed the sinking of this U-boat?). F/L Chave-Jones of No 1402 Met Flt had a lucky escape on 23 March when flying Blenheim Z7349. Returning from a Bismuth sortie, the Blenheim burst a tyre on landing and crashed. The crew escaped injury but the aircraft was written off in the crash. Two days later, Chave-Jones was promoted to acting S/L.

At the beginning of April, No 143 Sqn received a new CO when W/C Thornhill was posted in to take command of the squadron on 5 April. Two days later, the newly promoted S/L Chave-Jones of No 1402 Flt was killed along with Sgt Gihl of the flight. They had been taking part in a night flying practice in Hudson T9431 of No 206 Sqn and Chave-Jones was receiving night flying instruction from F/L Goddard of No 206 Sqn. F/L Goddard was seriously injured in the crash.

The Hudsons of No 206 Sqn were active again on the 13th and one of them AM734/O, piloted by F/O Wills, sighted a circular track of oil narrowing to a point with small circular blobs of oil coming to the surface at the point. Wills decided not to attack as he assessed the U-boat to be too deep for effective use of depth charges. A Hudson of No 1402 Met Flt, Mk III V9159, crashed on take off at Aldergrove on 13 April but luckily the crew, P/O Hill and Sgts Bergh, Cotter and Doak were unhurt. Another oil streak, 200 yards long, was sighted on the 17th but again nothing conclusive was seen. Another aircraft accident occurred on 19 April when one ran off the runway. The crew, P/O Camps and P/O Alford, were unhurt. The sightings of oil streaks continued on the 20th when two suspicious streaks were observed across the track of the vessel 'Canadian Star'. The Hudson, AM788/A, piloted by W/C Hards of No 206 Sqn, warned the ship and the convoy. An escort vessel signalled that contact had been made and carried out a depth charge attack raising bubbles and debris. The Hudson then made a further attack dropping four depth charges but no results were observed. The attack continued with further depth charges being dropped by the escort vessel following which a brown whirl was observed. The target later transpired to have been a wreck from some time before.

Squadron moves at Aldergrove were frequent and on 23 April, No 143 Sqn took its

GUINNESS GALORE

Joe Griffith joined the RCAF as an observer in 1940 and after training arrived in the UK in January 1942. Completing the Hudson OTU at Silloth he was posted to No 206 Sqn at Aldergrove joining Glaswegian Willis Roxburgh's crew.

"I joined 206 Sqn at Aldergrove. They were on Hudsons, just a four-man crew. One of the crew, Richard Thomas, was at Aldergrove long before I came in May 1942. 206 took part in the first 1,000 Bomber raid on Bremen where Roxburgh's plane got shot up so badly it was a write off. At that time Aldergrove had runways but they went up and down over small bumps, two or three in number. The ground had never been levelled so it was a difficult place to operate and was said to separate the men from the boys. Warrant officer Dinger Bell was in charge of all catering and messing affairs. In those days, beer was always in short supply in every RAF station in England. This was not so in Aldergrove. Guinness stout was available in unlimited quantities from Southern Ireland. It was a good product and most people, having cultivated the taste for it, didn't care if they ever saw beer again. So the allocation of beer accumulated and Dinger Bell traded it off to RAF stations on the mainland for spirits. It was said that the Officers' Mess in Aldergrove was the best supplied bar of any RAF station In the UK. Ah, well. Those were the days."

Joe Griffith moved with No 206 Sqn to Benbecula but returned to Aldergrove later with the Liberators of No 86 Sqn. Commissioned in late 1943, he went on to become the personal navigator to Air Chief Marshal Sir Sholto Douglas.

Joe Griffith navigated Hudson FK745 in 1944-45 for the C in C Coastal Command, ACM Sir Sholto Douglas. *(J Griffith via J Meadows).*

Beaufighters to Limavady. The following day, G/C Kubita, a Czechoslovakian serving with the RAF, arrived with W/C JM Southwell and F/L Fantl, the operations officer, to discuss the move of No 311 (Czechoslovakian) Sqn to Aldergrove. No 311 Sqn were based at East Wretham in Norfolk and were a Bomber Command unit equipped with Wellingtons. The squadron was about to be transferred to Coastal Command.

The advance party of No 311 Sqn arrived at Aldergrove on 26 April. Two days later, No 206 Sqn began detaching aircraft to Tiree for operations. The No 311 Sqn move continued with the arrival of a party moved by road and rail on the 29th and the last day of the month saw the air party arrive completing the move. Training commenced immediately with the first submarine bombing practice carried out at Lough Foyle with No 206 Sqn. Crews flew many anti submarine sweeps with No 206 Sqn and practised periscope bombing, cross country navigation and low level bombing. Training flights in co-operation with Royal navy submarines were also carried out. The squadron was commanded by W/C Josef Snajdr with S/L Josef Sejbl commanding 'A' Flt and S/L Josef Stransky in charge of 'B' Flt. There were seven crews on each flight. During the early

Ted Nelson's No 206 Sqn crew on 21 April 1942. Left to Right: Joe Peet, WOp/AG, Les Goodson, pilot, Ted Nelson, WOp/AG and Allan Marriott, pilot. *(EH Nelson)*

part of the month, ground training on 'Depth Charges and Submarine Destruction', 'Navigation in Coastal Command', 'WT/RT and Lorenz Facilities' and 'Ship Recognition' was carried out.

May was a busy month for No 206 Sqn with patrols, escorts and sweeps of up to six aircraft each day. A Blenheim of No 143 Sqn crashed on landing on 1 May but only one of the crew, Sgt GF Browne, was injured slightly. P/O RK Roberts and F/O CA Wales were uninjured and all of the crew were returned to Limavady. On 3 May, four Hudsons on patrol sighted an oil patch but after investigating it they were unable to verify its source. No 1402 Met Flt received a new commanding officer when F/L WD Heaphy was posted in to take command on 12 May. Heaphy was promoted to acting S/L on 5 June.

No 311 Sqn had been at Aldergrove less than a month when they lost their first aircraft when an 'A' Flt Wellington, DV716:KX-Z, flown by F/S Zezulka, was damaged during a low level bombing practice. The crew was unhurt and the Wellington was sent to No 23 MU for repair. The port wing, engine, engine cowling and landing gear were replaced before the aircraft was returned to the squadron in July 1942. This was followed by the loss of Wellington Z1150:KX-R, of 'B' Flt which crashed into Lough

Neagh, near Rams Island, on 20 May. The Wellington had been carrying out a low level bombing practice and turning back for base the pilot, Sgt Dostal, began to climb. At 100 feet, an engine failed and the aircraft crashed into the Lough and sank. The six crew on board, three of whom were from No 206 Sqn, were rescued and Sgt NH Wright (206 Sqn) suffered a fractured humerus. The rest of the crew, Sgt JG Edwards, Sgt D Harborne (206 Sqn), Sgt H Dostal, Sgt V Orlik and Sgt R Pancir received cuts and abrasions and all suffered from shock. On 21 May, F/S Clark in Hudson T9458/H of 206 Sqn was on a met recce sortie when he sighted a U-boat. Clark dropped sea markers to mark the position and continued with the sortie. Returning later, he sighted the U-boat a mile away but made no attack. Having settled in at Aldergrove and trained in the techniques necessary for

Wartime photograph of the No 311 Squadron badge. *(Karla Zuber).*

over water operations, No 311 Sqn sent five Wellingtons out on its first operations from the station on 22 May.

The following day, No 206 Sqn once again started to detach aircraft to Stornoway. No 143 Sqn suffered a further loss on 23 May when Blenheim Mk IV P4835 crashed at Limavady. Both squadrons continued patrols over the next few days and a Hudson of No 206 Sqn sighted and oil patch on the 28th, which it attacked with depth charges. F/O Wills in AE648/N sighted bubbles and fresh oil moving westward from an oval oil patch. After circling for one hour one depth charge was dropped 300 yards ahead of the streak. The streak altered course 45 degrees to starboard. Wills then released his remaining depth charges singly. The oil streak continued slowly on course and as was often the case with these attacks, once again, no results were observed.

The next day a Hudson of No 206 Sqn, AM605/K, piloted by F/S Biddell was sent on an air-sea rescue sweep for a training unit Whitley reported to be in difficulties and located two dinghies and dropped Thornaby Bags to them before contacting a nearby destroyer and giving the position of the dinghies. The destroyer rescued the survivors.

On 30 May, change was once again in the air for Aldergrove when Air Cdre HG Smart of No 17 Group visited to discuss the possibility of locating a Coastal Command OTU at Aldergrove and on 6 June, the station was informed that No 9 (Coastal) OTU was to form at Aldergrove. Another of the unit's Hudsons crashed on 9 June. F/S Weir and crew, Sgts Bunney, Brown and Powditch crashed on take off but were lucky to escape with only a small cut to Sgt Bunney's hand. With the training unit due to move in

A Wellington (possibly of No 311 Sqn) bombing a towed target on Lough Neagh, 13 May 1942. *(via 206 Sqn).*

L to R: Pierse, Roxburgh and Wills of 206 Sqn at Aldergrove *(206 Sqn)*

No 311 Sqn, which had barely settled in, moved out to Talbenny on 12 June. The squadron had carried out its last patrols on 26 May and they had had no successes whilst based at Aldergrove. On 14 June, three Hudsons of No 206 Sqn carried out a search for the crew of a Lancaster. An escort vessel picked up the crew and the Hudson's were recalled. On 18 June, six Hudsons of No 206 Sqn were ordered to carry out the escort of a convoy. Prior to the arrival of the aircraft, the convoy was engaged by a Focke Wulf Condor but the Condor slipped away before the Hudsons arrived.

On 23 June, twelve Hudsons of No 206 Sqn were detached to North Coates and then to Donna Nook. On the night of 25/26 June, these Hudsons took part in operations over Bremen as part of one of the famous 'Thousand Bomber Raids'. The target was the Deschimag U-boat yard but, unable to locate it due to heavy cloud, the Hudsons dropped their bombs in the vicinity of the large fires. There were no engagements with night fighters though several were seen. F/L Roxburgh

WOp/AG Sgt Joe Peet of No 206 Sqn was shot down and made a POW on the '1000 Bomber Raid' on Bremen in June 1942. *(EH Nelson)*

in A/206 returned with flak damage, landing at base with a broken main spar. Two of the Hudsons were reported missing. The missing aircraft were S/206, captained by W/C Cooke, OC No 206 Sqn with P/O Watson, F/S McGlynn and F/S Hubbard and M/206 captained by the 'B' Flt commander S/L Crook with Sgt Wright, P/O Phillips, Sgt Payze, Sgt Speed and Sgt Peet. W/C Cooke was on his first operation with the squadron. The Hudsons, which had been detached to North Coates for the sortie, returned to Aldergrove the next day. The bodies of S/L Crook and his gunner F/S Hubbard were recovered from the sea by the Germans on 3 July. W/C RJS Romanes was posted in from No 500 Sqn as the new commanding officer on 29 June.

No 206 Sqn was also forced to move out of Aldergrove to make room for No 9 OTU, which had formed on 7 June, and the squadron departed to Benbecula on 29 and 30 June having been at Aldergrove since August 1941. The departure of the operational squadrons left Aldergrove with only the operational training role with No 9 OTU and No 1 APC. The OTU was equipped with Beauforts and Beaufighters and a small number of Masters, Martinets, Tiger Moths, Oxfords, Magisters and Lysanders for communications and target towing duties.

Date JUNE	Hour	Aircraft Type and No.	Pilot	Duty
		JUNE. 206 SQUADRON.		ALDERGRO
		HUDSON		
13.6.42	0745	AM 58M.	F/SGT GOODSON 32	AG O
17.6.42	1115	AM 722	F/SGT MARRIOTT 33	WOP
19.6.42	1450	T 9458	F/SGT GOODSON 34	AG and WOP
23.6.42	1745	AM 822	F/SGT BIDDELL	PASSENGER
23.6.42	2125	AM 822	F/SGT BIDDELL	PASSENGER
25.6.42	2320	AM 722	F/O BLAND 36	AG
26.6.42	0815	AM 722	F/O WOOSLEY	PASSENGER
27.6.42	1200	AM 722	F/O WOOSLEY	PASSENGE
29.6.42	1325	AM 587	F/SGT MARRIOTT	WOP
29.6.42	1555	AM 587	F/SGT GOODSON	WO P
30.6.42	1350	AM 822	F/SGT MARRIOTT	WOP

A page from Ted Nelson's logbook showing the entry for the '1000 Bomber raid' on Bremen on 25 June 1942. *(EH Nelson)*

Time carried forward :—	333.40	44.0

REMARKS (including results of bombing, gunnery, exercises, etc.)	Flying Times	
	Day	Night
ANTI-SUB SWEEP. NOTHING SEEN	6.45	
ANTI-SUB SWEEP NOTHING SEEN	4.50	
	LONGEST HUDSON FLIGHT	
ANTI-AIRCRAFT ESCORT TO	9.00	0.40
CONVOY 200 OPS		
ALDERGROVE TO NORTH COATES	2.25	
400 i		
NORTH COATES TO DONNA NOOK	0.10	
MILLENIUM TWO		
MASS BOMBING RAID ON BREMEN		6.35
TARGET BOMBED. 2 1/2CLEST 1,000 %. INCLUDING ICE PORTS 1000		
NORTH COATES TO DONNA NOOK	0.10	
DONNA NOOK TO ALDERGROVE	2.15	
ALDERGROVE TO BENBECULA	1.25	
BENBECULA TO ALDERGROVE	1.10	
ALDERGROVE TO BENBECULA	1.45	
TOTAL TIME ...	363.35	51.15

Chapter 7
JULY 1942 – DECEMBER 1942

July 1942 saw Aldergrove settle in to the routine of training aircrews for Coastal Command. No 9 (Coastal) OTU was operating Beauforts and Beaufighters alongside the mixed types of No 1402 Met Flt and No 1 APC. In addition, the station administered No 2880 Sqn RAF Regiment and No 23 MU, which came under the control of No 41 Gp. The station had been transferred to No 17 Group on the first day of the month and two weeks later Air Cdre Smart, AOC No 17 Gp arrived to inspect his new charge. No 23 MU had remained active at Aldergrove throughout

An aerial view of Aldergrove in 1942. *(206 Sqn).*

Another 1942 view of Aldergrove. *(206 Sqn)*

this time and was now busily preparing and despatching Wellingtons and Hampdens to the operational squadrons.

During August, No 9 OTU continued to work up to its full training capacity but the unit was destined to leave Aldergrove without getting fully organised. In the short spell it was at Aldergrove that the OTU managed to lose Oxford ED177 in a crash at Lisnaw near Killyleigh. The crew, Aspirant Dugot and Adjutant Caillaux were admitted to Downpatrick Infirmary with injuries. W/C Woodruff and S/L Morris left for an inspection of Crosby on Eden on 3 September and the main party of the OTU moved to Crosby on Eden between 6 and 9 September. The advance party departed on 5 September and the move was completed by 14 September.

Aldergrove was once again transferred to No 15 Gp control on 15 September. The following day, Hudson 'J' of No 1402 Met Flt, captained by Sgt Horn, went missing on a

'Bismuth' met flight. Four days later, on 20 September, F/L Proctor of No 1402 Met Flt was on a 'Prata' sortie. During the flight he entered cloud at 30,000 feet. Descending to 20,000 feet, still in cloud, all of his gyro instruments froze. He baled out and landed in Eire from where he quickly returned in time to carry out the evening 'Thum' sortie! The perils of flying on Met sorties continued to show up at Aldergrove when Sgt Fox crashed on landing at base. He had been on a 'Bismuth' sortie when severe icing caused his engine control to be lost causing the forced landing. The excitement continued for the Met Flt when S/L Heaphy and his crew diverted from a 'Bismuth' sortie with engine failure and landed Blenheim Z7345 at St Angelo. With its major units departed for other stations, Aldergrove settled into the routine of meteorological flights for the remainder of the year. Though routine, this work was vital to the planners of Bomber Command. The information provided by the Met Flt allowed them to select the targets most likely to have suitable weather conditions and also to forecast the likely weather conditions for the bombers returning to their bases in the UK. On 3 October, yet another 1402 (Met) Flt aircraft was involved in an accident when Hudson FH404 swung on landing and crashed at Aldergrove.

Blenheim Z7345 was to feature in yet another incident on 29 November when P/O Alford had a tyre burst on take off for an air test and the Blenheim swung off the runway and turned over in the mud. The pilot and a passenger, P/O George, were uninjured. The last days of 1942 were sad ones for No 1402 Met Flt. Hudson FH407, piloted by F/S SR Millar, failed to return from a 'Bismuth' sortie. After departing Aldergrove at 0900 on 30 December, nothing more was seen of this aircraft.

Chapter 8

JANUARY 1943 – JUNE 1943

The New Year was to see a change of role once again for Aldergrove and on 21 January W/C NMS Russell of No 15 Gp visited the station to discuss the proposal to operate Liberators from Aldergrove. This proposal would bring Aldergrove back into the forefront of Coastal Command operations in the Atlantic. Two days earlier, S/L Heaphy of No 1402 Flt crashed Gladiator N5637 when he ground looped on landing at Langford Lodge. The aircraft was written off but S/L Heaphy was unhurt. On 10 February, W/C PA Gilchrist DFC, the CO of No 120 Sqn and W/C LHC Auys, the Chief Technical Officer at Ballykelly arrived at Aldergrove to discuss the move of two squadrons, No 120 and No 220 Sqns from Ballykelly to Aldergrove. Four days later, the main parties of both squadrons arrived from Ballykelly and a Fortress of No 220 Sqn carried out the first sortie from Aldergrove on the 15th landing at Nutts Corner on their return. No 120 Sqn were credited with the destruction of U529 in position 5545N 3109W on 15 February – an auspicious start to the squadron's sojourn at Aldergrove. The combat report and intelligence analysis of this sortie make interesting reading:

Combat Report	F/O Turner		
1204/15/2	S/120	Liberator III VLR	Camouflage white underneath.

On A/S sweep flying on track 001 degs at 3000ft., in weather 10/10 cloud, bearing 030 degs Green distant 7-8 miles, in position 55 degs 45 mins N 31 degs 09 mins W course 260 degs 6 knots. U/B appeared to be German 517 ton type with gun forward of conning tower, mottled brown and grey camouflage. Aircraft attacked from U/B's port bow at angle of 40 degs to track releasing from 70 ft 6 Mark XI Torpex depth charges, set to shallow depth, spaced 36 ft., while conning tower and stern were still visible above surface. Evidence states that depth charges straddled U/B just abaft of conning tower with centre of stick on port side. (4 to port, one to starb). After depth charge explosion oil and air bubbles were seen, the oil was heavy and formed a streaked patch 150-200 ft in diameter. Wreckage was also seen in the form of a dark cylindrical dome headed object of which about 2 feet was showing in the oil patch, a rectangular box like object, black and 6 x 4 feet together with numerous small pieces of dark coloured debris. Aircraft remained in area for 10 minutes and then sighted 1 M/V, "Shooting Star", in position 56 degs 56 mins N 30 degs 50 mins W course 270 degs 10 knots, details of attack being reported to this M/V by V/S. At 1348 aircraft sighted another M/V, "Sidney Star", in position 50 degs 17 mins N 30 degs 33 mins W course 215 degs 10 knots, again details of attack were reported to this M/V by V/S. The position of U/B was 210 degs 15 miles from "Shooting Star" and 235 degs 37 miles from "Sidney Star"

Analysis

The excellent photo confirms position of entry of DCs and shows in the air just above the U-boat's after deck an object which may be No 5 DC having bounced off the hull. No 4 and possibly No 3 should have been lethal if the 35 ft advance underwater and the 19 ft lethal radius are upheld.

Result

Excellent attack. The after results indicate severe damage or possible destruction. The good and very valuable photograph confirms the visual evidence of position of entry. This successful attack undoubtedly saved "Shooting Star" from later trouble.

U529, a Type IXC with a crew of 48, was launched on 15 July 1942 and was captained by Kapitanleutnant Georg Fraatz. She was lost with all hands.

The health of personnel on the station was a cause for concern in the two weeks following the arrival of the squadrons from Ballykelly. There was a fairly severe outbreak of Trench Mouth, which lasted for ten to twelve days with sixteen cases being reported. Luckily all cases were cleared up quickly.

DFC Citation – 10 October 1943 – Acting Flight Lieutenant Reginald Thomas Frederick Turner, RAFVR, No 120 Squadron

"This officer has completed three attacks on enemy submarines in recent months, one of which, in February 1943, was assessed as sunk. Since the beginning of 1943 he has been operating as Captain of an aircraft on operations over the North Atlantic. His keenness, enthusiasm and devotion to duty have been of a high order and he has frequently demonstrated his determination to complete his duties in the face of adverse weather. Flight Lieutenant Turner has, at all times, displayed a fine fighting spirit and great perseverance."

During this period, the crews of No 120 Sqn were living the lives of Gypsies, taking off from one base and landing at another. The Squadron was in the process of moving from Ballykelly to Aldergrove and maintaining a large detachment at Reykjavik in Iceland. Jack Colman was with the squadron during this period and recalls the turmoil caused by the move. As is often the case, those detached from the squadron knew little or nothing of the activities of other members of the unit. Colman would arrive at Aldergrove ferrying an unserviceable aircraft after a forced landing, diverted from Reykjavik to Benbecula:

"After lunch we went to have a look at P for Peggy, although the folks here would call her P for Peter, which was strictly correct but, she was always P for Peggy in Reykjavik. Poor old Peggy, she looked buggered. There was a jagged hole in the cowling on No 2 engine on the outboard side, which we could not see from the cockpit where something must have flown out, a mysterious hole in the port fin and rudder, up on jacks with the main wheels off and a floppy nosewheel door. Freddie linked up with the ground crews to supervise their activities as none of them had experience of Libs and the Fortresses

Boeing Fortresses similar to this one were operated from Aldergrove by No 220 Sqn and later by No 1674 HCU. *(Geoff Gardiner)*.

they worked on had Wright Cyclone engines not our Pratt & Whitney Twin Wasps. We met Norman and Les and before the day was over it had been arranged that the Engineering Officer, together with a sergeant and corporal, would fly up from Ballykelly the following day to see what was what. That night we found the Mess full of rumour – it's amazing how rumour gets around. They thought we had been shot up, been on fire, the navigator had lost his leg and our engines had cut through lack of fuel whilst landing. It seemed that someone on the tannoy had told them to remove the blackouts and put all lights on to make sure we did not crash on the camp. To start with this was worth quite a few drinks, but then we had to tell them the truth, especially when they saw Fred running around on two legs, and we took the Mickey out of them for getting in such a panic.

The Engineering officer and his team duly arrived and decided what spares were required. These along with a replacement engine were flown in, in a Dakota, and after seven days we were jolly thankful to be getting away – even though it was only to be to Ballykelly to get some jobs finished off. But, P for Peggy was not wanting to go. As we did our final pre-take off check, a pillar of smoke arose from the control pedestal as I exercised the prop switches and they all stuck in fine pitch – good job the electrics burned out then and not just after take off. So it was two more days before we boarded her again, together with the ground crew lads, for a gentle one hour forty minute cruise to Ballykelly, all but ten minutes being in cloud. For the next six days we seemed to be flying backwards and forwards between Ballykelly and Aldergrove as one of the new squadrons was moving in to Ballykelly and the rest of our squadron was getting ready to join us in Iceland. Some of our servicing was being done at Aldergrove and the new ASV was being fitted. We learned there were a couple of changes on our crew; Les and

Harry were to come off for a rest and two most colourful characters joined us. Two more Yorkshiremen so we were five out of seven. 'Ginger' a very colourful lad from Sheffield, a ruddy complexion like a rising sun, topped with a mass of curly ginger hair, medium height, stocky, a broad smile and 'down to earth'. He had been 'The Bulls' No 1 WOp/ASV Operator and led 'The Bull' on to many U-boats in the early days when they were not picking up the old ASV and they were operating far out where the U-boats did not expect to find aircraft. 'The Bull' had now completed his tour and was leaving the Squadron so his crew had been split up, or else gone on rest so we would be getting a new CO. The other lad 'Joe', from Hull, was a complete contrast. New to the Squadron, straight jet-black hair plastered down, a thin pencil-line Clark gable type 'tash, big round face but not very happy looking. Ginger took over from Les as No 1 and Joe became No 3.

We managed to get a couple of dropping exercises fitted in, as we had not been able to do any for a long time. This also enabled us to get to know Ginger and Joe. Ginger was a great bloke, full of fun and expert at his job, he thought the new Mk II was a piece of cake compared with the old stuff and was picking up the smallest of things with ease – even though we could not pick them out when he let us have a look. Joe was a bit quiet and although we tried our best to make him feel at home, he seemed very aloof. I met a Flight Lieutenant who was going to be our Flight Commander when we all got together in Iceland so I had a bash at him about getting a crew of my own. He looked at my file, my competence card from Ferry Command was not there, so the other Flight Commander must have chucked it out, but I assured him that he would be able to see from my logbook, which was in Iceland, that I had checked out on Libs and had done over twenty ops. I pointed out that if I went on doing nothing but second pilot work I would be losing my touch. He seemed reasonably sympathetic and, to my delight, the next day he asked me to fly over to Ballykelly with him. For the return flight he let me start off in the left hand seat and do the lot whilst he acted as second pilot – we did a bit of a detour to fit in a few climbs, descents, turns and a mock dropping run over Lough Neagh. The landing went OK and I began to think that I may be getting somewhere – he seemed a nice guy.

By 19 February P for Peggy is flying again, new engine and all patched up, so we take her for an Airframe and Engine Test, swing the compass and decide she is all ready to go again. We took a WAAF officer with us – she was one of the Air Traffic folk in the Watch office at Aldergrove, it was a novelty for us to speak to a girl on the R/T and she wanted to see for herself what it was like from aloft. She was a grand girl and we had a lot of fun with her, making her make our R/T calls for us to the bewilderment of those on the ground."

In February 1943, No 86 Sqn was operating from Thorney Island with Liberator Mk III. By 23 February, the squadron was detaching aircraft to Aldergrove for operations, the Liberators returning to Thorney Island for inspections. The first No 86 Sqn sortie from Aldergrove was an anti-submarine escort flown by S/L RB Fleming in Liberator Mk IIIA FL931:M. No 120 Sqn carried out its first sortie from Aldergrove on 6 February when F/O Goodfellow took Liberator Mk III FL933 on patrol. A U-boat was sighted but no attack was made. The squadron would not fully move into Aldergrove from Ballykelly until 14 February, whilst maintaining a detachment in Iceland. Five days later, the squadron received a new CO, W/C Gilchrist.

On 21 February, Jack Colman was airborne on a convoy escort sortie:

"Couple of days later we are sent off on a Close Escort to a slow outward bound convoy on the southern route – ONS166. We met her at 5010N 2800W. It seemed funny being so far south with the compass

Liberator Mk IIIa FK223:T of No 120 Sqn. *(120 Sqn)*

working properly and no radio interference. The weather was a bit mixed but never bad. Somehow or other, it was thought that U-boats were gathering but we did not see anything – the convoy was in good order – we kept searching in areas passed to us by the SNO by lamp – stayed till dusk and landed after 17 hours. Only pity was that we were in a Modified IIIA, so no hot food and cold drinks towards the end."

Later the same day, 120 Sqn made a U-boat attack from Aldergrove when S/L DJ Isted DFC, in Liberator Mk III FK223/T, escorting convoy ONS166, sighted two U-boats. Using cloud cover to approach, he broke cover and attacked the first submarine stem to stern with six depth charges. The conning tower was still visible 1 ½ minutes later. During the attack, the rear gunner opened fire, using 150 rounds, scoring hits. The U-boat was attacked at 2018 hrs and fifty minutes later when Isted returned to the scene of the attack two very large patches of oil appeared on the sea. The attack was successful and U623 sank in position 4868N 2915W. U623, a Type VIIC U-boat, had been built by Blohm & Voss in Hamburg. Commissioned on 21 May 1942, she was on her second patrol under the command of Oberleutnant zur See Hermann Schroeder when she was sunk with all hands. The convoy SNO detached two of the escorting warships following the attack but they found nothing but two large oil slicks and her loss was reported by the commander of the second U-boat, U91. A successful U-boat hunter, Isted had attacked and damaged U465 earlier in February whilst flying from Iceland.

No 1402 Met Flt began to re-equip on 21 February. For some time the unit had been operating Spitfire Mk Vs alongside its Gladiators, Blenheims and Hudsons. These Spitfires were now to be replaced by the Spitfire Mk VI. The first of the Mk VIs, EN176, arrived on 21 February. The Met Flt was also suffering from a shortage of Hudson Mk IIIs and it was decided to replace these with Hampdens. The first Hampden, P1196, arrived on 23 February.

On 23 February, a Fortress was tasked with a search for the survivors of a missing aircraft crossing the Atlantic but had no success. Jack Colman was also airborne in a 120 Sqn Liberator tasked to a convoy escort:

"We are off again to find a similar convoy, ONS167, even further south at 4731N 2927W. We are given two extra crew, partly for operational training and partly to keep an extra lookout for long range aircraft from Brest. At 4740N 2845W we find an abandoned merchant ship – a very slight list but otherwise it seemed OK. We circle around but see no sign of life so rattle of a few rounds of gunfire along its side to see if this brings anyone in sight, but it seems entirely deserted. We take some photos (with our German Leica camera) and press on. It must have been abandoned during the night, perhaps because it had been hit and its steering damaged, or maybe its engines broke down. It looks, however, as if the convoy may be in trouble. At the appointed meeting point there is no sign of the convoy so we commence a 'moving square search'. After four hours searching we eventually find it, miles off its intended position – this was confirmed when they gave their new position. Radio silence was being maintained but they gave us their new course, it had been altered because they had been attacked during the night. We reported the ship we had seen and went off to search ahead but soon we were recalled to Aldergrove, due to weather, so had to leave just before dark. Nearly back at Aldergrove we were told to divert to St Eval due to fog affecting nearly all the country. This was going to run us a bit fine so we kept the nav lights off and cut over the Irish Free State, making a beeline for St Eval. Once again we were in a Modified IIIA in which the fuel gauges bob up and down like a yo-yo due to the flexibility of the self-sealing tanks. As we were crossing the Bristol Channel, the level kept bobbing right out of sight at the bottom of the long glass tubes and at the best of times they are supposed to over-read by 36 gallons each tank, but we felt that as long as there was some bob up at all there must be a bit left. Freddie maintained he was confident by his calculations that we were OK. Nobody said very much but it was funny how everybody decided it was getting cold and put on their Mae West for a bit of warmth. I saw a light, which must have been on a boat and for a moment took it for a star and felt we must have gone into a steep turn, but soon got my orientation back. St Eval control were great, such a contrast to Benbecula, they had their Sandra Lights on so we could head straight for the airfield, gave us landing conditions without being asked and cleared to land. We did not need the SBA and landed after 16 hours and 45 minutes. Once again, top marks to a top Flight Engineer.

An Airman Flies on His Stomach

F/S John F Waite served with No 120 Sqn during 1942-43 and recalls the early attempts at providing suitable rations for the aircrew to eat on the long range Liberator sorties:

"In the early days of 120 Sqn we did try cooking various meals and we had a stove supplied in the galley room, but this practice did not last very long as the job was far too time consuming. So, we were issued with individual metal containers, one for each crew member, and these, like a good many other bits and pieces, had to be collected and placed on board the aircraft prior to take off. Very large flasks of coffee were also provided. The packaged meals nearly always comprised assorted sandwiches, hard boiled eggs (in shells), nuts and raisins, one bar of chocolate and spearmint chewing gum."

A Consolidated B-24 Liberator of No 120 Sqn at dispersal. Whilst at Aldergrove the Squadron maintained a detachment of aircraft in Iceland and in common with many other units the crews would often start their patrols at one base landing at another. Many 120 Sqn sorties starting in Iceland would end at Aldergrove and vice versa. *(120 Sqn).*

Before leaving St Eval on the 25th for a cruise up to Aldergrove we learned that the first convoy we had been to had lost fourteen ships over four days after they left our area and the second one had also been attacked. It all seemed so frustrating, we hadn't seen a bloody U-boat yet let alone attacked one and now the weather had eased up they were sinking ships again as fast as ever."

By March, the Fortresses of No 220 Sqn were ranging far and wide in the hunt for U-boats and in addition to patrolling from Aldergrove were also operating from Benbecula and from Reykjavik in Iceland. On 2 March, Fortress M/220 saw a fresh oil patch with pieces of timber floating in its centre and later a raft which was unoccupied. There was no sign of any survivors or the cause of the oil.

Jack Colman's sojourn at Aldergrove came to an end at the beginning of March when he and his crew returned to Iceland:

"After a day or two at Aldergrove doing air tests and landing at Nutts Corner to do compass swings we were delighted on 2 March to be off back to Reykjavik, in a Mk I, L for Leo. We had seven passengers, including a Wing Commander on his way to take up a job at Iceland HQ and a load of spares and equipment. At the last minute it was decided that we would do a short 'sweep' on the way to help round up a convoy – SC120 – south west of Iceland, which had become scattered due to bad weather and U-boat attacks. One of our chaps was out there from Iceland but needed some help as the

Liberator Mk I AM916 L for Leo with Jack Colman's crew. Left to Right: Ginger, Ron, Freddie, Joe, Fred, 'Little Titch', Norman and Jack Colman. This Liberator was used by the squadron from December 1941 until September 1943. It was finally sold in August 1946. *(120 Sqn).*

convoy was so split up. We found some ships and a couple of escorts around 6030N 2815W – Ginger was picking them up like flies on flypaper and we buzzed around signalling their bearing and distance to regain the main convoy. They were ploughing their way through a pretty heavy sea but it wasn't at all bad in the air. It was a damn nuisance having all these bods with us though – they kept getting in our way, some of them were sick and a Squadron Leader (non-flying type) kept putting 'his oar in'. It was only a short trip as we did not have full tanks and after nine hours we were pleased to see Reykjavik again after four weeks away."

No 220 Sqn were to see action on the 7th when three aircraft of the squadron carried out a parallel track offensive sweep. Two of the Fortresses returned to base without incident but Fortress Mk II FL459/J, captained by F/O W Knowles, flying at 2500 feet sighted the track of a U-boat at five miles distance at 0928 hrs. Knowles continued on course then turned to port and dived to attack from 80 feet dropping seven depth charges 12 seconds after the U-boat submerged. The depth charge straddle landed ahead of the swirl and shortly after the last depth charge had exploded a dark object, possibly the stern of the U-boat, appeared for about five seconds, followed by considerable quantities of oil. The aircraft remained in the vicinity of the attack until it reached its fuel limit and returned to base. The attack was made on U633 which was thought to have sunk at position 5714N 2630W. (Recent research has cast doubt on the identity of the U-boat and it is suggested that U641 was, in fact, the target and was not sunk). U633 was sunk three days later – rammed by the SS Scorton. Knowles returned to Aldergrove via St Angelo, where he landed to refuel.

Another shot of the crew of L for Leo. Left to right: Jack Colman, Freddie Payne, Harry Harrison, Fred Thorpe and Ron Babel.

Aldergrove Control Tower in wartime configuration. The tower, much modified, is still in use today.
(G Briggs via Geoff Gardiner).

Later the same day, at 1613 hrs, another Fortress sighted a U-boat in the 'Rovik 1' patrol area. The Fortress dived to attack, opening fire with its machine guns but the U-boat managed to crash dive before a suitable attack position was reached.

On 11 March, it was No 120 squadron's turn to battle the U-boats. Liberator Mk III FK214/H, captained by S/L Isted, was on convoy patrol when, at 1015 hrs, a fully surfaced U-boat was sighted. The U-boat dived before an attack could be made but the attack was pressed home with the depth charges, unfortunately, overshooting the target. Just twenty minutes later, a second U-boat was sighted partly submerged. Once again the U-boat was able to submerge before the Liberator could get into an attack position. A marine marker was dropped to mark the last known position of the U-boat and the Liberator continued on patrol. Forty minutes later, a 'V' shaped wake was spotted. Presumed to be a periscope, the Liberator closed on the target but it disappeared before a closer investigation could be made. The Liberator's eventful patrol continued and at 1222 hrs another U-boat was observed. This one was fully surfaced and H/120 attacked, dropping two depth charges. Although no wreckage was observed, a long streak of oil covering an area three miles long and sixty yards wide was observed. Yet another U-boat was sighted at 1328 hrs but Isted was unable to attack it as all of their depth charges had been expended on the other targets. The U-boat was not aware of this however, and immediately crash-dived. On completion of the patrol, H/120 returned to base safely.

A fine airborne shot of AM916:OH-L of No 120 Sqn. This aircraft was scrapped at Balado Bridge, Fife.
(No 120 Sqn)

Liberator Mk I AM929:H of No 120 Sqn on patrol. AM929 served with the squadron from August 1942 until December 1943 before being converted to a transport. She sank five U-boats. *(No 120 Sqn)*

The Liberator-equipped No 86 Sqn arrived at Aldergrove from Thorney Island in March 1943, the whole squadron being in place by 18 March, and was soon in the thick of things. On 11 March a Liberator of No 86 Sqn, FL930:R, captained by P/O BF Gaston, sighted a fully surfaced, stationary, U-boat whilst on convoy patrol. The U-boat was lying ahead of the Liberator and it dived to attack. The U-boat, however, submerged too quickly and the attack was aborted.

By this period of the 'Battle of the Atlantic', the U-boat fleet was being severely harassed by the long range Liberators and Fortresses. The range of these aircraft operating from Ulster, Scotland and Iceland was such that, coupled with similar aircraft patrolling from the United States and Canada, U-boats had to take increasing risks to remain on the surface during daylight to close with and attack convoys. While this hectic battle with the U-boats was going on, the main party of No 86 Sqn, which had been operating its Liberators from Aldergrove since February, arrived. The airmen had to be accommodated at Nutts Corner due to a shortage of accommodation caused by the delay in moving No 220 Sqn out. The WAAF contingent was accommodated at Aldergrove.

On 12 March, less than a month after arriving from Ballykelly, No 220 Sqn began to move out to Benbecula leaving the Liberators of Nos 86 and 120 squadrons to continue the fight from Aldergrove. On 17 March, Liberator FL931/M of No 86 Sqn, captained by F/O CW Burcher was

Liberator X of No 120 Sqn *(No 120 Sqn)*

The Very Long Range (VLR) standard Liberators

VLR standard Liberators were issued to Coastal Command squadrons in three versions; the Mk I (VLR), Mk IIIa (VLR) and Mk V (VLR). In order to provide this extended range all armour protection was removed from the rear of the aircraft.

A maximum range of 2,300nm at 4,000ft with 2,650 Imperial gallons of fuel was possible but this was only possible in the Mk I with normal tanks. The Mk IIIa was required to carry two additional bomb cell auxiliary tanks to attain this range. For the MK V, up to serial number FL971, the same tankage was fitted as for the Mk IIIa. From FL971, the fuel was carried in the main tanks, auxiliary wing tanks and one bomb cell auxiliary tank.

The weapons load for each mark varied as follows:

Mk IIIa & Mk V fitted with rear turret –	8 x 250lb Depth Charges (DC) or 2 x Mk 24 Mines and 3 x 250lb DC or 2 x 600lb Anti-Submarine (AS) bombs and 4x 250lb DC.
Mk V without rear turret-	10 x 250lb DC or 2 x Mk 24 Mines and 5 x 250lb DC or 2 x 600lb AS bombs and 4 x 250lb DC.
Mk V without rear turret and fitted - With Leigh Light	8 x 250lb DC.
Mk V without turret or Leigh Light - Carrying RP	8x 25lb head rocket projectiles (RP) and 5 x 250lb DC.

The standard crew for the VLR Liberators was 8 and each mark was equipped with a Mk III low level bombsight. The gun armament for the VLR version was as follows:

Nose gun -	1 x 0.5in with 500 rounds
Mid-upper turret -	Removed
Beam guns -	A single 0.5 in in each beam position with 500 rounds or twin 0.303in guns with 1,000 rounds per gun in each beam position or twin 0.3in guns with 500 rounds per gun in each beam position.
Tail turret -	4 x 0.303in with 500 rounds per gun, except in Mk V's fitted with ASG III radar, where the turret was removed.

The beam gun position of a Liberator Mk III (looking aft). *(No 120 Sqn).*

The gunner of a No 120 Sqn Liberator Mk III sighting from his mid-upper turret. *(No 120 Sqn)*

The Long Range (LR) standard Liberators

The Long Range (LR) marks of the Liberator were the Mk V(LR) and MK VI(LR). The Mk V had a crew of eight and a range of 1,900nm at 4,000 feet with full main tanks and outboard wing auxiliary tanks. The weapons load was as follows:

Without Leigh Light -	10 x 250lb DC or 2 x Mk 24 Mines and 5 x 250lb DC or 2 x 600lb AS bombs and 5 x 250lb DC.
With Leigh Light -	8 x 250lb DC.
With rocket projectiles (RP) -	16 x 25lb head RP and 5 x 250lb DC or 16 x
And Leigh Light	25lb head RP 1 x Mk 24 Mine 3 x 250lb DC.

The bomb sight used in this mark was the Mk III Low Level bombsight.

Gun armament was as follows:

Nose Gun -	1 x 0.5in with 500 rounds.
Mid-upper turret -	2 x 0.5in with 400 rounds per gun.
Beam guns -	1 x 0.5 in in each beam with 400 rounds per gun Or 1 x twin 0.303in in each beam with 1,000 Rounds per gun.

The Liberator Mk VI version had an increased crew of 10 and a shorter range of only 1,600 miles at 4,000 feet. This was obtained by using full main tanks and outboard wing auxiliary tanks. The weapon load was as follows:

With/without Leigh Light -	8 x 250lb dc or 1x Mk 24 Mine and 6x 250lb DC.
With RP and no Leigh Light -	16 x 25lb head RP and 3 x 250lb DC or 16 x 25lb head RP and 1 x Mk 24 Mine.

As with the Mk V, the Mk VI was equipped with a Mk III Low Level bombsight. The gun armament was as follows (figures are for a Mk VI without a Leigh Light. (When the Leigh Light was fitted the ammunition per gun was halved):

Nose Turret -	2 x 0.5 in with 500 rounds per gun.
Mid-upper turret -	2 x 0.5in with 400 rounds per gun.
Beam guns -	1 x 0.5in in each beam with 800 rounds per gun.
Tail Turret -	4 x 0.5in with 1,000 rounds per gun.

The tail turret of a Liberator Mk III of No 120 Sqn. *(No 120 Sqn).*

Liberator Crew Positions

F/S JF Waite GM of No 120 Sqn has provided a useful description of the various crew positions in the Liberator:

"These varied little between the Mk I and subsequent versions of the aircraft. In the Mk I we had a galley and crew room situated immediately behind the bomb bays and the rear portion of the aircraft. The radio operator was situated adjacent to this compartment in a small elevated office immediately over the bomb bays (complete with carrier pigeons) – not one of the best positions to be in, particularly when being fired upon! The navigator's position in the Mk I was behind the pilot and he had a table where he could set out his plotting maps, etc. He also did a certain amount of work in the nose compartment, which was rather cramped, mainly sextant work, where he had a small astrodome. It might not be appreciated on first thought, but the only way through to the nose of the aircraft when in flight was by crawling under the flight deck on hands and knees. This was a bit of an ordeal, particularly at night and one very often became hooked up on one of the many wires and electrical motors, etc., that seemed to be very abundant in this area. In the later models of the Liberator, the nose of the aircraft became more elongated and the navigator was permanently housed there. The radio operator was then brought from the back of the aircraft on to the flight deck, where he could operate the radio and radar equipment and pass information on to the pilots."

Another view of the tail turret of the Liberator Mk III. *(No 120 Sqn)*

The cramped interior of the Liberator Mk III tail turret. *(No 120 Sqn)*

The spacious flight deck of a Liberator. *(No 120 Sqn).*

on convoy escort when a U-boat was sighted at 0922 hrs and immediately attacked. Four depth charges were dropped and although M/86 remained in the area for thirty minutes nothing further was seen of the U-boat. At 1035 hrs, another U-boat was sighted and once again M/86 dived to attack. The U-boat quickly submerged but the Liberator pressed home the attack with the remaining depth charges. After the attack, an oil patch about 40 feet in diameter was seen in the swirl caused by the explosions. On the return leg, M/86 had to divert to Eglinton due to poor weather at Aldergrove.

The same day, Liberator Mk III FK225/G, piloted by F/S Stowes of No 120 Sqn, was tasked with a convoy escort and, whilst carrying this out, spotted a U-boat in position 5136N 3014W. Stowes dived, attacking it with four depth charges. The U-boat crash dived twelve seconds before the Liberator reached the swirl and the depth charges were dropped from 60 feet straddling the U-boat's track 150 feet ahead. A light oil patch appeared in the explosion area. Later, a second U-boat's periscope was seen and Stowes made a steep diving turn but the attack failed due to the depth charges failing to release.

F/O SE Esler was also on patrol in a No 120 Sqn Liberator that day. Flying Liberator Mk III FK224/J, Esler and his crew sighted a U-boat ten miles off the starboard bow at 2005 hrs. On the run up to attack this U-boat, another was spotted on the bow at a range of ten miles. As the first U-boat submerged, Esler attacked the second dropping five depth charges from 100 feet eight seconds after the U-boat had submerged. The depth charges landed 80 feet ahead of the swirl and the U-boat re-surfaced in the explosion area, bows first at a steep angle. The conning tower broke the surface for a few seconds and the U-boat appeared almost stationary before submerging. Esler was in luck this day and sighted three more U-boats forty minutes later. Selecting

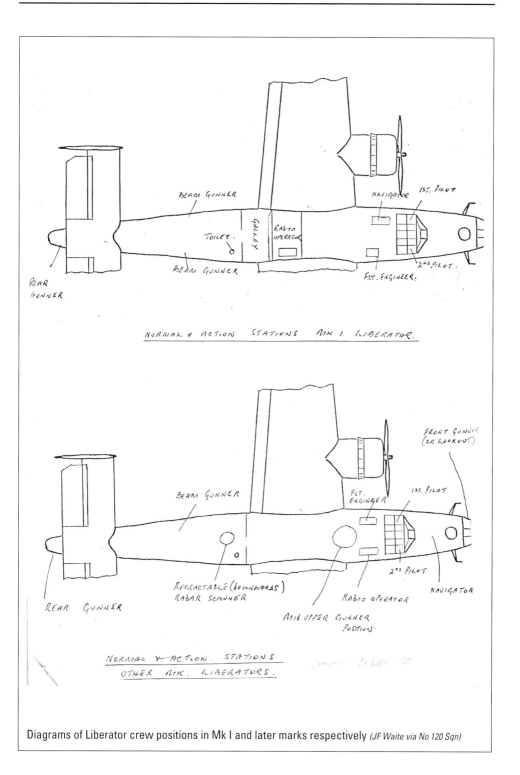

Diagrams of Liberator crew positions in Mk I and later marks respectively *(JF Waite via No 120 Sqn)*

No 1402(Met) Flight in Spring 1943. *(K Lunn).*

the centre U-boat he attacked from 200 feet with the remaining depth charge. The depth charge entered the water and exploded at the still surfaced U-boat's stern. Esler's gunners opened fire on the submarine for thirty to forty seconds before departing. A sixth U-boat was sighted and attacked with machine gun fire and marine markers scoring hits all around the conning tower. One of the marine markers scored a direct hit and a sailor on deck was probably killed. The U-boat quickly submerged after the attack and the Liberator left for Benbecula.

While all of this frantic activity was taking place over the Atlantic, another drama was taking place at Aldergrove. Warrant Officer BDL Gillman had taken off from Port Ellen en route for Aldergrove in a Lysander of No 1 APC only to crash at Hillside, near Whiteabbey. Gillman and his crew, LAC DE Winterton and AC AB Douthwaite were killed.

On the afternoon of 18 March, Liberator Mk III FL913/E of No 120 Sqn, captained by F/O JK Moffat, sighted a U-boat whilst on convoy patrol. The U-boat was attacked with four depth charges but, owing to the rough seas, it was impossible to estimate the damage. Four hours later, Liberator Mk III FK214/B of No 120 Sqn, sighted another U-boat on the surface and attacked with two depth charges. No results were observed but forty minutes later a further U-boat was located by P/O AW Fraser and crew and attacked with the remaining depth charges. Again, no results were observed. B/120 was to sight yet another U-boat at 2138 hrs. The 750-ton U-boat was fully surfaced but no attack could be made as they had expended all of their depth charges.

SE 'Red' Esler as a Flt Lt later in the war.
(No 120 Sqn).

Liberator Mk III FL913:E of No 120 Sqn *(No 120 Sqn)*

Liberator N/120 was also patrolling on the 18th and sighted a U-boat whilst trying to contact a convoy. The U-boat submerged but later the top of a conning tower was seen. Unfortunately, this also disappeared before an attack could be made. A third Liberator, Mk III FK228/M of No 120 Sqn, captained by S/L Isted, was on patrol over a convoy at 2107 hrs when a surfaced U-boat was observed. Isted dived from 900 foot and attacked with six depth charges, dropping them at 75 feet. The stern was still visible at the time of the attack. The first depth charge exploded 55 feet ahead of the conning tower swirl, the remainder overshot. The tail gunner reported seeing the stern at a steep angle before diving.

On 18 March, Jack Colman and his crew were out on patrol again when they were told to divert to Benbecula and thence to Aldergrove the following day:

"Although we had the whole Squadron here now – except for some ground staff based at Aldergrove for carrying out major servicing, trips seemed to be coming up pretty

A fine view of a No 120 Sqn Liberator in flight over Iceland. *(No 120 Sqn)*

A Liberator of No 120 Sqn taxying in the snow. *(No 120 Sqn).*

thick and fast. You seemed to jump about four places up the 'Mayfly' list every day. We were trying to cover all convoys from about 40 degrees West, at least during their daylight hours, until they came within reach of the UK squadrons, provided they were routed far enough north. It still meant a gap west of 40W, as there were no VLR aircraft yet operating from the Canadian side. In theory we could even close this gap but it would have meant that the time we could spend with the convoy would be too short to be considered worthwhile. On convoy escort we are just thinking about setting off home when we receive a signal, 'Divert to Benbecula'

The following day we were told to take Leo to Aldergrove as Iceland was still unfit and Leo was almost due for a major service. So, a pleasant little two-hour trip down the coast of Scotland to Aldergrove. At Aldergrove we were surprised to find that some of the Squadron were still there – we thought they had all come to Iceland – but it seemed the Squadron strength was to be 20 aircraft and there were another five aircraft and some crews getting ready to come and join us. 'Big Mel', the Flight Commander I had spoken to before about getting my own crew was also there so I had another go at him, reminding him that I was not one of those second pilots who had come straight from GR School but I had done an Operational Training Course and also checked out on Libs. He seemed much more receptive than the other Flight Commander, old Jimmy with the big 'tash.

Next morning I felt I may have made some impression on Big Mel as he sent for me to go with him on an Air test – a Mk IIIa which had just come out of major service – and as I made to get into the second pilot's seat, he beckoned me to get in the left hand seat, taking the second pilot's seat himself. I very deliberately went through the cockpit checks – told him what to do as second pilot and soon we were taxying out. More very deliberate, exaggerated, checks and soon we were away and I am telling him to raise the undercarriage and bleed up the flaps.

We fly around for an hour or so, checking that the engines and all the systems are working OK, whilst the Flight Engineer made notes. We cut and feather each engine in turn and do a mock drop on a target in Lough Neagh before coming in for the landing, which went off OK although the runways at Aldergrove seemed very narrow.

In the afternoon we did another air test, this time in a Liberator Mk I and Freddie came with us as Flight Engineer, also a couple of the groundcrew. The routine was as before but we finished by doing some Range flying on the new Radio Range at Nutts Corner and a couple of landings on the SBA at Nutts Corner before returning to Aldergrove. The only calamity was when taxying back in at Aldergrove. Big Mel pointed out a very narrow taxyway as a short cut back to dispersal so I followed his directions as he knew Aldergrove better than I did, but soon I found I was needing more and more power to keep moving and in spite of the power we came

Jack Colman, the co-pilot of Liberator AM916 L for Leo. *(No 120 Sqn)*

to a halt. On looking down at the wheel on my side, I could see it had sunk into the tarmac and had pushed up a bank of tarmac in front of it – it was the same at the other side – so we had to cut the motors and leave the aircraft to be pulled away backwards. This new taxyway was not supposed to be used by Libs.

The next day it was another air test in the morning, some practice dropping with Big Mel in the afternoon, followed by some night take offs and landings at Aldergrove and at Nutts Corner using their SBA. I felt pretty sure that these two days of hectic flying were not just to help him do air tests, but to check me out as a possible Skipper. However, the following day we were off on another trip, to meet what was left of convoy HX229 and then carry on back to Iceland.

For this trip we had an addition to the crew – a shy young Pilot officer, straight from GR School to act as third pilot. We christened him 'Titch'. He had no experience on Libs. Compared to the rest of us wearing our 'diversion kit' of creased battledress, roll neck pullovers or silk stockings as scarves and flying boots he looked like a tailor's dummy in his new, well pressed, best blue uniform, new flat hat, leather gloves and Van Heusen semi-stiff collar. Norman persuaded him to change his gear before we set off. At briefing we learned that two convoys – SC122 and HX229 – or what was left of them, had now closed up. Between the 16th and 19th they had lost 21 ships. One U-boat was thought to have been sunk by one of our Libs and many more suffered damage from Navy escorts. Two had probably been sunk but attacks were still taking place in the dark, after the air cover had left. Fortresses from Benbecula were also to join us and some Catalinas. 'Leo's' service was completed, so we were pleased to be taking a Lib I back to Iceland. In the three days since we were last with HX229, she did not seem to

Liberator Mk III 2-N of No 86 Sqn seen at Nutts Corner (possibly FL943). *(No 120 Sqn).*

have got very far. It was now over two weeks since the ships in the slow convoy had left the Canadian coast and they still had several days to go. This made us realise what a hell of a time the merchant seamen and naval chaps have – all that time tossing and rolling about in diabolical weather, being trailed by U-boats, explosions during the night as ships are torpedoed and the constant likelihood of their ship being blown from under them and pitching them into the cold, wet, black roaring sea – provided they survived the initial explosion. Our job was a piece of cake in comparison, 14 or 15 hours, then back to a cosy bed on firm dry land – those chaps at sea could not get a night's sleep for days and days on end. Without them the war would have been lost months ago, but do the folks at home give them much thought? I think very little.

We felt sure on this trip we would bag a U-boat to add to our 'possible', especially when we picked up a signal '512' from one of the other Libs, meaning he was going in to make an attack, but it was not to be. Both convoys were now nicely closed up together. We spent five hours sweeping on the south flank without any luck, but maybe we did some good without knowing it."

At 1550 hrs on 19 March, Liberator Mk III FK244/J of No 120 Sqn was requested to patrol ten miles astern of a convoy by the Senior Naval Officer (SNO). The patrol bore fruit for F/O Eslers' crew when a U-boat was sighted at 1916 hrs. Esler dived from 4,000 feet to 90 feet at 280 mph. Pulling up to 200 feet, the Liberator attacked with two depth charges. These appeared to straddle 350 feet ahead of the swirl thirty seconds after the U-boat disappeared. No results were observed. The Liberator continued to circle the convoy and, at the request of the SNO, investigated a persistent shadower to starboard. A fully surfaced U-boat was sighted and attacked at 0030 hrs in position 5417N 2124W. Esler dived in the moonlight but the attack was aborted when the bomb doors failed to fully open. The rear gunner, however, managed to fire 1,000 rounds at the 700 ton U-boat, many of which hit it in the area of the conning tower. At 0612 hrs on 20 March Liberator Mk III FL933/O of No 120 Sqn set out to find the convoy it was to escort. Several hours later, the SNO reported the sighting of two Heinkel He 111s and the Liberator crew, captained by F/L McEwen sighted them 700 yards away and 2,500 feet lower. The rear gunner fired two five second bursts at them but no hits were observed. Ten minutes later, two FW 200s were reported ahead of the convoy and, lacking adequate defensive armament to deal with them, the Liberator took to cloud cover. On its return to base, O/120 lost two engines on one side and warned base to prepare for an emergency landing. The Liberator managed to land safely on two engines.

F/O EC Hammond and crew in Liberator Mk IIIa FK222/U were also on patrol on 20 March providing escort to convoy SC122. At 2330 they were diverted to Benbecula but Hammond found himself to be considerably west of his assessed position due to a change of wind. At 0350 hrs, their estimated time of arrival at Benbecula, there was no sign of land. Hammond decided to jettison the depth charges to save weight and they finally made landfall at 0530 hrs. Two and a half hours after their planned ETA, their position was still undetermined and Hammond circled until dawn. Fuel was now running short and at 0615 hrs one of the engines cut. Thirty minutes later, dawn broke with 10/10ths cloud cover. Hammond endeavoured to find a landing place clear of cloud and at 0745 hrs found a possible landing place and force landed the Liberator on Eglinton Marshes.

On 25 March, one of the Met Flt's newly acquired Hampdens was lost when Sgt Collins swung off the runway on a local flying exercise and broke the back of Hampden P1314. No 86 Sqn entered the fray again on 28 March when Liberator Mk IIIa FL932/ H, piloted by F/O CW Burcher, sighted a Type 517 U-boat on the surface, ten miles from convoy HX230 during an escort patrol and attacked it with depth charges. Two of

Liberator Mk IIIa FK222 prior to being coded U and serving with No 120 Sqn. *(No 120 Sqn)*

YEAR 1943		AIRCRAFT		PILOT, OR 1ST PILOT	2ND PILOT, PUPIL OR PASSENGER	DUTY (INCLUDING RESULTS AND
MONTH	DATE	Type	No.			
—	—	—		—	—	—
MARCH						TOTALS BROUGHT
"	17	LIBERATOR	FK244	SELF SGT HAYNES P/O WILLIAMS	P/O GOODALL F/SGT KEMPTON " WALLACE P/O BAKER & CREW	OPS: A/S ESCORT. TO Co HX229 · 33·10W · 51·50N A 2 U/BOATS SIGHTED 4 MERC LANDED BENBECULAR
"	18	LIBERATOR	FK244	SELF	" CREW	BENBECULAR To KINNERR CONTINUATION OF SORTIE
"	19	LIBERATOR	FK244	SELF F/ SGT EDWARDS	P/O GOODALL F/SGT KEMPTON " WALLACE SGT KAMMDANAN " BLAIR P/O BARKER	OPS: A/S ESCORT TO Co SC122. SIGHTED U/BOAT + SIGHTED FURTHER U/B + M escorted for S30 L on mean To BALLYKELLY.
"	22	LIBERATOR	FK233	SELF F/SGT EDWARDS	P/O GOODALL " CREW	
"	26	LIBERATOR	FK233	SELF SGT HAYNES	P/O GOODALL F/SGT KEMPTON	AIR TEST + COMPASS Su
"	29	LIBERATOR	FK244	SELF SGT HAYNES	P/O GOODALL F/SGT KEMPTON SGT WALLACE SGT KAMMERLING " BLAIR	OPS A/S ESCORT. TO CON SIGHTED U/BOAT

		Summary for MARCH		1. LIBERATOR
		UNIT 120 SQDN		2.
		DATE 31· 3· 43		3.
		SIGNED		4.

GRAND TOTAL [Cols. (1) to (10)]

1304 Hrs 32 Mins.

TOTALS CARRIED FO

A page from Esler's logbook showing the sorties on 17th and 19th March 1943 during which he made attacks on U-boats. *(No 120 Sqn)*

SINGLE-ENGINE AIRCRAFT			MULTI-ENGINE AIRCRAFT							PASS-ENGER	INSTR CLOUD FLYING (In cols. (1) to (
DAY	NIGHT			DAY			NIGHT				
PILOT	DUAL	PILOT	DUAL	1ST PILOT	2ND PILOT	DUAL	1ST PILOT	2ND PILOT		ENGER	DUAL
(2)	(3)	(4)	(5)	(6)	(7)	(8)	(9)	(10)		(11)	(12)
25.10			12.10	872.5]	128.40	4.45	135.40	52.35		99.10	2.30
				10.95			8.00				
				1.45							
				5.45			10.00				
				8.20							
				1.30							
				10.50			4.10.				
			12.10	53.15.	4.10.		27.10	52.35		99.10	2.30.
		OPS	DAY 38.15.	NIGHT 27.10							
	NON OPS		8.00	NIL							
25.10.			12.10	904.27	128.40	4.45	160.20	52.35		99.10	2.30
(2)	(3)	(4)	(5)	(6)	(7)	(8)	(9)	(10)		(11)	(12)

Liberators at Aldergrove including FL933:O and FK228:M of No 120 Sqn and FL952 of No 86 Sqn. FK228 was struck off charge in July 1945 and FL952 was lost on 3 Sep 1943. *(No 120 Sqn)*

the four depth charges failed to release and, owing to the rough sea, they were unable to estimate the damage. On the same day, D/120 had to return to base having failed to find its convoy due to its D/F aerial being struck by lightning. J/120 was also on patrol and sighted a U-boat. A diving turn to attack was made but the U-boat was able to crash dive and escape. The run of bad luck for the new Hampdens continued on 30 March when P/O McGonigal landed after an altitude test and raised his undercarriage on the runway.

On 1 April 1943, the twenty-fifth birthday of the RAF was celebrated by the station with a parade. The unit personnel were given the rest of the day off as a holiday. No 120 Sqn also had a change of command when W/C RM Longmore OBE was posted in from No 612 Sqn. Five days later, Aldergrove had more to celebrate. On the morning of 6 April, Liberator T/120 was on convoy escort when a fully surfaced U-boat was spotted at 1045 hrs. This was attacked, just after it had submerged, with four depth charges from a height of 50 feet. About four minutes later, the U-boat momentarily broke the surface then disappeared. Nothing further was seen of it though Type IXC/40 U635 and all hands, captained by Oberleutmant zur See Eckelmann, went to the bottom. While this attack was taking place, F/O CW Burcher in Liberator Mk IIIa FL930/R of No 86 Sqn, had successfully made contact with convoy HX231 and sighted a large U-boat 18 miles from the convoy. Two attacks were made with depth charges. The first attack was made while the U-boat was on the surface. Only one depth charge was dropped, which fell a short distance astern of the U-boat. The four depth charges dropped during the second attack fell on track 100 feet ahead of the swirl caused by the submerging conning tower. A dark patch of oil was seen and later a dark object, thought to be one of the crew, was seen in the water. U632 and its crew had perished at position

A fine view of a 120 Sqn Liberator Mk III equipped with rocket pylons under the nose. *(120 Sqn).*

5802N 2842W. U632 was a Type VIIC U-boat and had been built by Blohm & Voss at Hamburg in September 1941. She was on her second war cruise under the command of Kapitanleutnant Hans Karpf when she was sunk south west of Iceland. Before her loss she had sunk two ships totalling 15,255 tons. Hoping to add to their success, the crew of R/86 attacked another U-boat at 2146 hrs. The U-boat was on the surface and they attacked with their remaining depth charges but no results were observed.

On 7 April, F/O EC Hammond took Liberator Mk IIIa FK234/W of No 86 Sqn out to continue the escort of HX231 and sighted a fully surfaced U-boat and attacked it. The depth charges failed to release on the first run and a second run had to be made. This time, the depth charges fell away and two dark patches of oil were seen after the attack. Three hours later at 1434 hrs a second U-boat, with its decks awash, was sighted and attacked but no results were observed. A third U-boat was seen at 1612hrs. This one crash-dived but the Liberator did not carry out an attack as they had expended all of the depth charges. A second No 86 Sqn Liberator, FK233/X, under the command of F/L JA Walker, was also roaming the seas in search of a target. Once again the convoy under the squadron's protection was HX231. At 1710 hrs, Walker's crew spotted a U-boat and turned to attack. Walker selected four depth charges for the attack but when released five fell away. After ten minutes of circling the target area no results were observed.

Although many of the Liberator attacks carried out during the Spring of 1943 showed little in the way of successful sinkings they did have a measure of success in that they forced the U-boats to stay submerged for long periods, using up their batteries and making it more difficult for them to shadow and close with the convoys, which were their targets. The advent of the long range Liberators and Fortresses was closing the

Atlantic gap and forcing the U-boats further into the Atlantic to search for convoys without aerial escorts.

On 12 April, F/L Walker was on patrol again in Liberator FL931/M. This crew had an experience which was to become all too common in the war against the U-boat. During a convoy patrol, a large U-boat of some 740 tons was sighted fully surfaced. As the Liberator levelled out to attack the U-boat opened fire with cannon and larger guns from the conning tower. The Liberator was forced to turn hard to starboard to avoid this fire. On the second attempt to attack, the U-boat remained on the surface and continued to fire at the Liberator. On the third attack attempt, the U-boat opened up with a heavier gun on the after deck and once again the Liberator had to take avoiding action. During these attacks, the SNO with the convoy was informed of events and headed for the scene of the battle. At 1210 hrs he was sighted approaching the U-boat's position. Half an hour later, the escort vessel opened fire on the U-boat, which quickly submerged making its escape. The same day, F/O Burcher patrolling in Liberator FK229/B sighted a fully surfaced U-boat at 2140 hrs, whilst escorting convoy HX232 and attacked it dropping four 250lb Torpex depth charges on track ahead of the swirl left by the submerging U-boat. The Liberator remained over the area of the attack for twenty minutes but no wreckage was observed.

The following day, the move of No 120 Sqn to Iceland was completed and Aldergrove soldiered on with No 86 Sqn, No 1402 Met Flt and No 1 APC. Liberator G/86 sighted the wake of a U-boat and attacked without result and the following day Liberator X/86 attacked another fully surfaced U-boat. As the Liberator approached to attack, it was fired upon from the conning tower. The depth charges failed to release and by the time the aircraft was in a position to attack again the U-boat had submerged. Whilst G and X/86 were busy in the Atlantic, the AOC in C Coastal Command, Air Marshal JG Slessor CB DSO MC visited Aldergrove. A third No 86 Sqn Liberator; L/86 was also on patrol over a convoy this day. At 0205 hrs, an ASV contact led to a U-boat which submerged before it could be attacked. At 0236 hrs, another ASV contact was picked up and led to another U-boat. Once again the U-boat submerged before an attack could be made. At 0337 hrs a third ASV contact once more led to a U-boat which crash dived. This time the Liberator attacked and dropped depth charges, which straddled the U-boat's path. Nothing further was seen but the SNO of the convoy later signalled to J/86, which had relieved L/86, "Your predecessor attacked and probably seriously damaged a submarine forcing him to fall to the rear."

On the night of 18 April, F/O RW Chadwick hauled his No 86 Sqn Liberator, FL952/L, off the runway at Aldergrove to give escort to convoy SC126. In the early hours of the 19th, he sighted a U-boat but was circling too far away to make an attack on its submerging swirl. An hour and a half later L/86 sighted a second U-boat and attacked with no observed results. Chadwick had relieved F/O Hammond in FK233/X, who, on the afternoon of the 18th, sighted a U-boat and made an attack run. The attack failed when all four depth charges selected failed to release and the U-boat submerged before a second attack could be made.

Jack Colman would make one more trip from Iceland to Aldergrove on 18 April escorting a convoy in atrocious weather:

"The gale force winds seemed to go on and on, several times whipping up so much that we had day and night sessions sitting in aircraft with engines running to keep them from being blown about. Then, during a relative lull, we got away in an aircraft, which had not many hours to go before It was due for a major service, with instructions to land at Aldergrove and then bring another aircraft back, which had had its inspection, if and when the weather allowed. The job was to meet a convoy, ONS5, of 40 vessels, which had left the Irish Sea on the 18th but was already in trouble, not from U-boats, but from the weather. It had set off with an escort of a destroyer, a frigate and four corvettes, and was due to be joined by three ships and a destroyer from Iceland. It was encountering mountainous seas, one ship had been badly damaged in a collision and was making its way to Iceland for repair and another ship had lost contact. The first destroyer was low on fuel because of all the running around it had been doing at high speed trying to keep tabs on things and the weather was so rough that it was having difficulty in refuelling from a tanker.

We were to try to find it and do what we could. The weather was truly diabolical, you could hardly see the surface of the sea for flying spray and the angle of the ships as they rode enormous waves, was frightening. They seemed at times to be standing on end, rarely was a whole ships length visible at once, half the ship seemed under water or obscured by spray and when the bow was down I even felt my heart in my mouth as I thought it was going to dive right down to the bottom. With all this tossing about, I am sure they were almost hove to, they had made little progress in the five days they had been at sea. Fortunately the escorts were using R/T as it would have been almost impossible for us to have communicated by lamp in these conditions. The cloudbase was about 1,000 feet, except in patches where it came down to the deck and it was bloody rough, but seeing what was happening to those ships took our minds off how we were getting tossed and thumped around. It was yet another trip where we had to keep the speed well up above the optimum for maximum endurance, as she could not be handled at low speed in this weather. This gave Freddie plenty to do in keeping tabs on the fuel consumption and, as usual, he looked pretty ill. The others were bearing up very well. There was no question of looking for U-boats in this sea – it was a matter of trying to locate the ships and report their positions to the escort. I felt sure some of the smaller, older looking ships were going to sink – God, who would be a sailor. The corvettes seemed to ride the waves and troughs pretty well but the destroyer – God knows, it was covered in spray most of the time and at the most incredible angles. For us it was only a short trip and after 10 hours we were jolly glad to be cutting the motors at Aldergrove. Next morning we learned that there would not be an aircraft ready to go back to Iceland for at least a week and later in the day the Station Commander informed us we may as well have 7 days leave."

F/S JA Bookless in FL930/R of No 86 Sqn sighted and attacked a U-boat in the early hours of 21 April whilst en route to convoy ONS4. The U-boat was at conning tower depth and attacked with four depth charges. No results were observed and the Liberator continued on to meet the convoy. The SNO informed the Liberator that a destroyer was on the way to the scene on the attack and ordered the aircraft to carry out a square search. This was done without result. At 0454 hrs the relieving Liberator, Mk V FL954/Z, captained by F/L Walker, met the convoy and at 0737 sighted a U-boat with its decks awash. A depth charge attack was made but no results were observed. Twenty minutes later, another U-boat was seen, fully surfaced. This U-boat dived and with the rough seas it was impossible to pinpoint the swirl and make an attack.

That same day, the Station Medical Officer (SMO) and the ambulance crew were called out to attend the crash of an American Liberator which had crash landed near the shore of Lough Neagh. One of the eight crewmembers was killed; the other seven had moderately severe injuries and were transferred direct to Langford Lodge.

On 25 April, F/O R Moreland took off in Gladiator N5576 of No 1402 Met Flt to carry out the evening Gladiator ascent. On his return, the winds were gale force and he was blown off the runway on landing and the Gladiator turned over in the mud. The aircraft was badly damaged but Moreland was fortunately unhurt. The following day, the staff of the Station medical centre had to deal with the body of Sgt Woodruff. He was a member of a Beaufort crew operating from Long Kesh whose aircraft had crashed into Lough Neagh during bombing practice. His body was washed up near Antrim and after being conveyed to Aldergrove was returned to Long Kesh the following day.

With No 120 Sqn departed, there was room at Aldergrove for another squadron and on 27 April W/C GCC Bartlett, Officer Commanding No 59 Sqn visited to discuss the move of the squadron to Aldergrove. No 86 Sqn began the month of May with a hectic sortie for F/L Walker and his crew in Liberator Mk V(LR) FL952/L. Walker was ordered to carry out a square search for survivors of a merchant ship, MV Port Victor that had been torpedoed. At 0859 hrs, they sighted a sloop in the search area and informed them of the allocated task. At 1025 hrs, the Liberator sighted wreckage and an extensive oil patch. Just under a quarter of an hour later, red smoke markers were seen and these led the Liberator to the six lifeboats, all roped together and drifting with the wind. There were 20-30 men in each boat and Walker signalled them, 'Help on way. Will stay with you for six hours'. The Liberator then left the lifeboats to contact the rescue ship and whilst en route spotted the conning tower of a U-boat. The U-boat submerged before it could be attacked. Once the rescue ship was contacted it was given the position of the lifeboats and the U-boat and Walker turned the Liberator back towards the survivors. Walker dropped Thornaby Bags to the survivors, which they picked up, and he continued to patrol around the lifeboats to deter the U-boat. At 1637 hrs, the Liberator set course once again for the rescue ship dropping aluminium marine markers. Contact was made with the ship when it was forty miles from the lifeboats and Walker turned the Liberator for base. The sloop picked up 120 survivors.

On 4 May, Liberator Mk V(LR) FL955/P of No 86 Sqn piloted by P/O JC Green, escorting convoy HX236 north-east of the Azores, sighted a fully surfaced U-boat and attacked it with four depth charges. The depth charges straddled the U-boat, two exploding to port and two to starboard, just forward of the conning tower. As the plumes subsided, considerable wreckage was seen consisting of bright coloured planks, one black cylinder about two feet by two feet and two white cylinders about twelve feet by eighteen inches. A large oil patch was also observed. The German Navy had just lost U109 in position 4722N 2240W. U109 was a successful U-boat up to this point. The Type IXB had completed eight patrols sinking 14 ships totalling 86,606 tons and damaging another. Her commander Oberleutnant Joachim Schramm went down with his crew. Success almost became disaster on the return to base when the Liberator was fired upon by a merchant ship, possibly the Denbighshire. Fortunately, the ship missed.

A spell of bitterly cold weather hit the station on 6 May. Many of the camp buildings were flooded and the winds reached gale force at times. The advance party of No 59 Sqn arrived from Thorney Island on 7 May and by 11 May, five of the squadron's Liberators had arrived at Aldergrove. The squadron had originally been equipped with Liberators at the end of August 1942, whilst based at Thorney Island. By October, they had placed a detachment at St Eval, but after only five months of operations with the Liberator it was decided to re-equip the squadron with Fortresses. By March 1943, the squadron was taken off operations to re-equip once again with the Liberator at Thorney Island and by May they once again had a detachment at St Eval for operations. On completion of the remainder of the squadron's conversion they were ordered to move to Aldergrove.

As the Liberators arrived they immediately began operations. On 7 May, S/L WW Cave DFC, who was new to the squadron, flying Liberator Mk V FL791/J, was diverted to Aldergrove from St Eval from an anti-submarine escort. The diversion message was acknowledged at 1713 hrs but the Liberator was never heard from again. S/L cave and his crew, P/O Summers, F/O Galbraith, and Sgts G Tsitselis, B Sainthouse, PG Polkinghorne, JHS Joanette were all lost. They had been one of four crews sent out from St Eval to escort the 'Queen Mary' in atrocious weather. By 1650 hrs, all of these aircraft had been recalled to base. F/O Murray Charlton and crew in M/59 acknowledged the recall and set course for base but were then diverted to Aldergrove. Unsure of their position they eventually landed at the first airfield they were certain was not in Eire and put down at Ballyhalbert. They remained there for two days and were well looked after by the fighter pilots based there. F/O Wally Allen in B/59 was diverted to Beaulieu but decided to press on to Thorney Island, which they were more familiar with. (They also knew that the accommodation at Beaulieu was not completed!) and just managed to arrive before the weather closed in. The Officers' Mess barman was called out of bed to supply rum and beer! The crew of K/59, captained by F/O Pete Wright, did not pick up the recall signal and managed to get R/T contact with the convoy, however they had to turn for base, short of fuel, before sighting it. On their return, they found every airfield in the south closed down by the weather and turned north eventually baling out over Lancashire. All of the crew landed safely though Pete Wright suffered cracked ribs and a fractured finger. They were picked up by the local home guard, who were quite unperturbed by their arrival as this was the thirteenth crew to bale out in the district. The crew was royally entertained in the local hospital before being released, all except for Pete Wright who remained for ten days. F/ O Neville Barson took off in X/59 as the others were returning, but after an uneventful trip in atrocious weather and not having found the convoy, returned safely to St Eval. The Squadron ORB recorded the day thus: 'Not a very fortunate start on operations on Libs again.'

Ernest E Allen and his crew photographed outside No 59 Sqn HQ building. *(M Allen)*

Two of the Liberators detached to St Eval to carry out escort patrols for the troopship Queen Mary departed at 0900 hrs followed by a second pair at 1100 hrs. Pilot Ernest E Allen was one of those airborne on this sortie and he takes up the story:

"Henry had picked up diversion of other aircraft to Aldergrove, Northern Ireland, so we felt that the weather must be expected to be above the landing limits there. On descent, at about one thousand feet, we broke out of cloud and identified an island near Land's End. This meant that we had a ground speed of over 300-mph, which meant we were in an area of hurricane force winds. We contacted St Eval – the field was closed – weather. Visibility was good under the cloud over the Irish Sea and we decided to go up to Chivenor, North Devon, where we had operated from with the B-17s. We were in touch with Chivenor by radio and he was reporting acceptable weather. Then, when we out only about 25 miles, Chivenor called to say that a fog had just rolled in and they were zero-zero in fog. We circled while making another decision. Henry intercepted messages that Aldergrove aircraft were being diverted to Gibraltar. Henry contacted Group on the alternate. They suggested Beaulieu, just west of Portsmouth. We knew Beaulieu; it was almost completely surrounded by balloons and to try to approach through the balloons in the dark, was something we'd rather not do. These balloons were put up to menace German aircraft if they came below 5,000 feet. The balloons were attached by cable to the ground. An aircraft hitting the cable usually crashed. However, Thorney Island was in the same direction as Beaulieu, so we decided to climb to 5,000 feet and try for Thorney. At 5,000 feet we were icing up pretty badly and it cut off our radio reception as well, so we climbed and finally got on top of the cloud and out of it at 12,500 feet.

I should mention that in the modifications to the Liberators they had removed the nose and top turrets, among other things, to reduce weight to carry more fuel and bomb load, and had removed the entire oxygen system. Now, flying at over 10,000 feet, it was accepted that crewmembers might do unusual things. We pass out, get overly aggressive and other unknowns. We discussed this as a crew and that we should watch one another for signs of trouble. I told Tommy that if he saw signs that I was in trouble, he was to take over and get the aircraft down to at least 8,000 feet, and I mentioned that if I saw signs of him getting aggressive, I would take the removable hydraulic hand pump, which was between the two pilots, and thump him on the head. Al Henry was on the radio set just behind the pilots and he told us later that Tommy and I sat there head to head eyeballing each other.

We were navigating blind but hoped to get radio bearings to Thorney when we got closer in. One of the pieces of emergency radio equipment we had was called a Darkie set. This had a very low powered transmitter and the procedure recommended that

Ernest Allen and his Liberator crew of No 59 Sqn. Left to Right: George LaForme, navigator; Al Henry, WOp/AG; George Flieger, rear gunner; Ernie Allen, pilot; Tommy Thomas, co-pilot; Lloyd Woods, gunner; Bart Barton, gunner. *(M Allen)*

when a crew were uncertain of their position (lost), they could call out 'Darkie, Darkie, please respond'. Thus the station that responded, and was heard by us, had to be within 25 miles of our position. We discussed whether we should declare an emergency.

We called Darkie and RAF Boscombe Down responded. We knew we were within 25 miles of Boscombe Down – La Forme gave me a course alteration and we proceeded easterly. The cloud tops continued to rise and we got up to 16,500 feet – still no oxygen. Eventually, while we were trying to get a radio bearing from Thorney, through a hole in the cloud we could see a set of runway lights. This was good enough for me. I pulled off all power and steep turned in a rapid descent through this hole, got below the cloud about one thousand feet above the ground, found the identifier beacon for this airdrome and found it was a fighter base called Ford.

From there it was only about fifty miles to Thorney Island and, when in range, called the Thorney Island tower for permission to land. The tower said that the field was closed on account of high winds. I informed him that we had declared an emergency a half hour previously so he gave us an OK to land at our own discretion and turned the runway lights on. He was reporting winds of 90 knots with gusts on our approach. We touched down, used almost no runway and parked the airplane on a dispersal point. I think a prayer of thanks went out from all the heathens on board.

A transport picked us up and took us to the Ops room for debriefing. My concern now was for the other crews, particularly Pete Wright's, as he had taken off at the same time we had. I went to the Ops controller, found he had no idea what was going on. He didn't even know 59 Sqn aircraft were in the air. I told him I thought Pete would try to get into Thorney and if he called in for bearings to be sure he was given them in plain language. These were usually coded so German intruders couldn't intercept – but as I told the controller, with the worst storm in twenty years raging outside, German pilots would not be over England tonight. We then went to the Officers' Mess for our rum ration and bacon and eggs. Some of the crew had ear troubles because of the rapid descent from 16,500 feet so we got the Squadron doctor out of bed and, besides doing what he could do to help those with ear trouble, he ordered our rum ration doubled.

I was still troubled that the ops controller wasn't taking this situation regarding the other crews seriously enough. W/C Bartlett, the Sqn CO, had his room in the mess building so I went up, got him out of bed, gave him a quick briefing, told him I wasn't satisfied the Ops controller was going to do what needed to be done and would he go over to ops immediately and see if there was anything he could do to help the other crews. Bartlett went to the ops room immediately, but before he got there Pete's operator, Rocky Livingston, had called in for a bearing and the stupid b.s..d's had not only sent the bearing in code; they sent it in the wrong code. The code changed at midnight. Ops coded the bearing in the code in force before midnight, which when Rocky tried to decode it using the after midnight code, it was nothing but garble. This was the last straw for Pete and his crew. They had been in turbulence all day and several hours above 10,000 feet without oxygen. Pete put the aircraft on autopilot on a westerly heading and they all walked out. All survived unhurt. Rocky Livingston landed in water, thought he was in the Irish Sea, inflated his personal dinghy and started to paddle. A minute later he bumped against a wall! He was in a static water tank in Blackpool!

The two aircraft who took off at 1100 hrs didn't fare well either. The second tour crew were never heard of again. Barsen and Charlton, co-captains of an Australian crew had tried for Aldergrove, but the Aldergrove weather had closed in and they ended up doing a crash landing on a little private airstrip on a small island on the Irish Sea side of Ireland. I suspect most of the aircraft is still there.

Thus, of the four aircraft that set out to escort the Queen Mary in the middle of the Atlantic (a completely unnecessary escort with the Queen doing 24 knots) we lost three aircraft and eight experienced crewmen. It wasn't a good start for the 59 Sqn VLR Liberators. Anyway, after briefing Bartlett, I joined the rest of the crew at rum and breakfast. As a crew we got together after lunch. Everyone looked and felt like death. The doctor looked us over and said 'You guys are all grounded until I say you can fly.' Nobody complained.

The next day, the rest of the crews, those who had aircraft, left for Aldergrove where the Squadron was to be based indefinitely. An aircraft was left for us and it was a week later that the doctor cleared us as fit to fly. We flew over to St Eval to pick up our kit that we had left there and then went on to Aldergrove to rejoin the Squadron. Aldergrove was just outside Belfast and at the first opportunity, having heard that the restaurants in Belfast had steak and eggs and all the trimmings, having not seen a steak since we left Canada; "this was some treat."

On the 12th, F/O Samuel, flying Liberator Mk III(LR) FL930/R of No 86 Sqn on a convoy patrol for a convoy code-named 'Thermos' sighted a U-boat with its decks awash. Samuel was unable to get his aircraft into a favourable attack position due to fire coming from the U-boat and made a weaving approach to within 80 yards of the U-boat. Samuel pretended to fly away but quickly returned as the U-boat began to submerge. Unfortunately, the swirl was lost in the rough seas. Two other aircraft, Liberator MK III(LR) FK229/B and FL916/N, captained by F/L Wright and F/L Bland both sighted and attacked U-boats on the 12th. Both whilst escorting convoy HX237. At 1313hrs, Wright sighted and attacked a U-boat, using a Fido homing torpedo he delivered a crippling blow to the U-boat, which later surfaced. The convoy escort SNO was informed and a destroyer, HMS *Opportune*, was subsequently directed onto the U-boat. The commander of U456, Kapitanleutnant Max-Martin Teichert, a Knights Cross holder, decided to take a chance and dive rather than face the destroyer and the U-boat was lost with all hands. At 1736 hrs, Bland sighted the second U-boat attempting to shadow the convoy and attacked with no evidence of damage. A third 86 Sqn Liberator, FK231/K, piloted by F/O Burcher, arrived to continue the escort of HX237 and at 1915hrs sighted a U-boat. The 517-ton U-boat was attacked but no results were observed.

Whilst No 86 Sqn were out in force battling the Atlantic 'Wolf Pack', the main party of No 50 Sqn had arrived at Aldergrove by road. The squadron would take a week to settle in before flying its first sorties from Aldergrove. One of the units administered by Aldergrove was the flying boat mooring at Sandy Bay. On 12 May, a Norwegian manned Sunderland landed at Sandy Bay and promptly submerged, luckily the crew escaped with no injuries.

On the night of 13 May, P/O GD Gamble in Liberator Mk III(LR) FK226/G of No 86 Sqn was escorting convoy SC129. At 2226 hrs, he sighted and attacked a U-boat and six minutes later sighted another 517 ton U-boat which he also attacked. No results were observed.

Less than an hour later at 0026 hrs on 14 May, S/L DF Wykeham Martin DFC took off from Aldergrove to relieve Gamble. One minute later, Liberator FK234/W crashed on take off. The Liberator came down at Hill Close, Aldergrove killing six of the crew, including the captain, and seriously injuring two others. Four members of the crew, F/Ss MF Burney, HL Carter, WC McGhee and Sgt JM Leslie were killed outright. Sgt H Little was recovered from the wreckage with a fractured skull and other injuries from which he later died. S/L D Wykeham Martin, the aircraft captain, was also found alive but unconscious also with a fractured skull and multiple injuries. He survived a further thirty-six hours before he too succumbed to his injuries. P/O S Neal and F/S A Cowan both had extensive injuries but recovered. Later that day, P/O Gaston took B/86 on patrol and managed to sight and attack a U-boat at 1633 hrs. U403 escaped the attack with no damage. Just a half-hour later, he sighted another U-boat but this one submerged before he could get into an attack position.

On 16 May, F/O Burcher re-entered the fray in Liberator Mk III(LR) FK229/B, whilst escorting convoy AT424. At 0834hrs he attacked a fully surfaced U-boat and, whilst circling the attack area, sighted a second U-boat at periscope depth. Just over three hours later, he sighted a third U-boat but no attack was made. The Liberators were making it increasingly difficult for the U-boats of the 'Wolf packs' to make their

No 15 Group Units based at Aldergrove – 10 May 1943		
Unit	59 Sqn	86 Sqn
Aircraft type	Liberator Mk V (VLR)	Liberator Mk IIIA & V (VLR)
Establishment	12+3	12+3
Strength	14	15
Available	1	8
Remarks	Partly Operational	

attacks on the convoys of vital supplies and equipment, which were so sorely needed by the Allies.

The next day sick quarters had to deal with another crash when a Tiger Moth from Ballyhalbert, N9127 of No 231 Sqn, crashed in Lough Neagh. Luckily the two crewmembers were uninjured and were not detained. Jim McGarry was among those who quickly went to the aid of the stricken Tiger Moth:

"Some accidents were as a result of very calm mirror-like conditions on the Lough surface, causing miscalculation of height above water, particularly when pulling out of a dive manoeuvre during imitation dog-fight exercises. One of these instances happened within 500 yards of where we were salvaging a Sunderland flying-boat near Rams Island in May 1943. A small Tiger Moth aircraft, on its way to a distant airfield with some tools, came down to have a closer look at our operation on this hot and dead calm day – and gently flew straight into the Lough, having lost concentration above the mirror surface.

A dash by our crew in an attendant boat secured the two crewmembers, who were taken ashore immediately. The salvage barge was released from the Sunderland and taken over to the new crash site where Charlie MaGee, the resident diver, donned his heavy canvas suit, copper helmet and lead weighted boots and secured the lifting crane sling to the propeller boss in 30ft of water. When the Moth was winched to well above water, the barge proceeded ashore carrying the Tiger Moth

The salvage barge operated by Henry McGarry from Ardmore Boatyard. (Photo taken in 1980)
(N McGarry).

like a tiger carries its cub. After leaving the Moth on shore, there was sufficient daylight left to return to the Sunderland salvage job and carry on working. Such was the trend during those war years; the job in hand had to be completed in good weather conditions regardless of hours worked and 36 hours at a stretch was not uncommon."

No 59 Sqn entered the fray from Aldergrove on 20 May. Liberator X/59, captained by F/O Geoff Lynch, sighted two fully surfaced U-boats and attacked the first with four depth charges. A few minutes later they observed an oil patch. The patrol was continued and just over three hours later another fully surfaced submarine was sighted. Lynch attacked it with his two remaining depth charges. The U-boat captain elected to remain on the surface and fight it out. As Lynch made his attack the U-boat opened fire and the depth charges overshot the target. Leaving this U-boat on the surface, he continued his patrol and an hour later spotted another U-boat on the surface. He dived to attack but the submarine dived beneath the waves. This had been the Squadron's most successful trip since its days flying Hudsons on shipping strikes from North Coates and had a great effect on morale.

Liberator Mk V(LR) FL954/Z of No 86 Sqn took off from Aldergrove on the night of 20 May and the crew soon sighted a fully surfaced U-boat. The submarine crash-dived before an attack could be made but in the early hours of the following day a Liberator, piloted by F/O Limbrey, came upon a fully surfaced U-boat. Due to very rough seas and poor visibility Limbrey was unable to attack the crash diving submarine. Two hours later, one of the gunners spotted a U-boat immediately below the Liberator but after circling the crew were unable to relocate it.

No 59 Sqn began to settle in at Aldergrove and Ernest Allen and his crew flew some training flights before their first operation from Aldergrove on 23 May:

"We did a few more practice bombing and air firing flights and then on May 23rd did another convoy escort, which La Forme's logbook shows at sixteen hours 'air time only'. It should be mentioned that until the VLR Liberators were put in operation, 59 and 86 Squadron's in Ireland and an RCAF squadron in Newfoundland, there was a six hundred mile gap in the Atlantic in the middle of which aircraft from neither side could give convoys coverage and the U-boats had been having a field day.

On this May 23rd trip out to mid-Atlantic we caught up to a Sunderland who was going in our direction. Sunderlands were notoriously slow and we were feeling sporting, so we lowered our wheels and flaps (so we could fly at his speed), pulled alongside him and flashed him a message on the Aldis lamp, 'Put it in second gear!' We got a very rude unprintable response from him, so we pulled up our wheels and flaps, resumed normal speed and left him disappearing behind us."

On 23 May, Liberator Z/86 was again on patrol. This time, the captain was S/L Fleming. A U-boat was sighted at 0723 hrs and attacked. The U-boat stayed on the surface and returned fire with cannon as the Liberator approached. As Fleming attempted to close with the U-boat it countered with gunfire and tight turns to port. Fleming finally attacked it on his third attempt. Fleming followed up this attack with another on a second U-boat at 1057 hrs. This U-boat had already been attacked by a

Swordfish, which had been on the scene. Orbiting the area where the U-boat was last seen only a large swirl was apparent. Earlier, a second 59 Sqn Liberator, S/59, piloted by F/O HAL 'Tim' Moran had arrived over the convoy and were 'disgusted' to find the FAA Swordfish attacking 'their' submarine!

On 24 May, it was announced that F/O Roy Neilson of 59 Sqn had been awarded a DFC. This was celebrated by a prolonged party, reported to have been of gigantic proportions. The hilarity continued the following day when an entry appeared in Daily Routine Orders:

"Warning To Airmen Working On Aircraft In Gum Boots. – An unfortunate incident has recently occurred when an airman wearing gumboots slipped off the hull of a Catalina and fell on his head, causing injuries from which he died. The attention of airmen is drawn to the caution necessary when walking on aircraft. Airmen falling off Liberator aircraft are strongly advised not to fall on their heads!"

The Wireless Operator on Roy Neilson's crew was Herbert Tuckwood, a native of Madawaska, Ontario. Tuckwood recalled many of the sorties carried out by 59 Sqn during this period:

"On one of our Liberator patrols we pick up the convoy we were to escort. We were asked by Aldis lamp if there were any stragglers, so we flew back on the path the convoy had been and found one lonely French (Free) ship. The code at that time was international and we were asked where the convoy was, so we flew over the ship showing the direction it was to go. We always felt sorry for this ship, so defenceless.

Our Scottish navigator was one of the best and you had to be good away out over the ocean and know where you were. We always threatened him that if we got lost we would turn the radar dish on him and make him sterile. It had a high frequency of 278 kilocycles.

At Aldergrove on Liberators we had rockets fitted under the wings. The procedure was to go into a 30 degree or so dive and fire these rockets in the water. All went well until we started to pull out. It took the two pilots to bring the plane back out. However, the action so affected the plane it never flew again.

When taking off from Aldergrove one night in a Liberator, we had a new co-pilot, and he had his procedure to carry out on take off. He forgot to bring the landing flaps into position and we couldn't gain any height. We were heading directly to some buildings when our pilot saw what was wrong, corrected the fault and we just cleared that building. A couple of times we were sent out to find crews of aircraft that had ditched. Unfortunately we had no luck.

On one patrol over the Atlantic and flying at 4,000 feet all four engines cut out and we dropped like a stone. The flight engineer, whose job it was to switch petrol tanks when running low, forgot, but managed to do so right away. Too close for comfort.

Radar was very good as time went on. We could come up the west coast of Ireland and see all the coastline. This in darkness. On one trip back to Aldergrove, we did just that, knowing when to make a turn to base, coming over Lough Neagh and then gradually circling lower and lower and breaking cloud at 300 feet right in line with the runway." (Herb Tuckwood was posted as an instructor to Nassau in the Bahamas at the end of his tour and died in 2002.)

F/O Limbrey took J/86 out on patrol on the 26th and early morning on 27 May sighted a U-boat. When he turned to attack, the U-boat took evasive action and opened fire with machine guns on the conning tower. Limbrey experienced great difficulty in lining up for an attack but finally managed to drop a 600lb depth charge. The U-boat escaped. F/O Neville Barson of 59 Sqn was also out on convoy escort and, after an uneventful sortie he returned to Aldergrove in Liberator N/59. On landing, the nose wheel of the Liberator began to shimmy and eventually gave way destroying the aircraft's nose.

F/O Roy Neilson and his 59 Sqn crew.
(HF Tuckwood via H Coles).

Lough Neagh was the scene of another tragedy that day when a Beaufort crashed into the Lough exploding on impact on 28 May. F/O Broadbent from Sick Quarters was despatched to the scene but nothing other than wreckage was found.

No 59 Sqn sent out Liberator Mk V FL984/S on 29 May, captained by F/O HAL 'Tim' Moran. On the passage out to a convoy he found a U-boat and attacked it as it was in the act of diving. Four depth charges straddled the submarine, which came back to the surface apparently out of control, with the bows breaking the surface at a steep angle. Moran attacked again with a further four depth charges but these overshot and the U-boat managed to get underway, remaining on the surface for nearly an hour before submerging. Whilst on the surface men appeared on the deck of the U-boat and calmly proceeded to open fire on the Liberator with light anti-aircraft fire. The squadron diary recorded of this incident that: "They're tough, mighty tough out west". The U-boat was U522 on her 12th war patrol. She survived to become a training boat, having limped into St Nazaire on 13 June. In her 14 patrols she had sunk 31 Allied ships.

On May 31st, the British Prime Minister, Winston Churchill was en route to America on board the Queen Elizabeth and S/L Evans flying X/59 was detailed to escort the ship part of the way. On arrival over the ship they were signalled to send 'Vs' by Aldis lamp, which they duly did, but their binoculars were, unfortunately, too weak to observe Churchill returning the salute with his fingers.

On 2 June, a Beaufort from Long Kesh crashed near Aldergrove village. The crewmembers were uninjured and, after treatment for shock at Aldergrove, were transferred back to Long Kesh. Also on 2 June, Ernie Allen and his 59 Sqn crew came across a target, which turned out not to be quite what they expected:

"We set out to escort a northbound convoy in a location a few hundred miles west of Portugal. It was a dawn or first light escort and when it was just getting daylight we saw what appeared to be a U-boat, just awash, dead ahead. So 'bomb doors open', we roared in and dropped six depth charges. Just too late we realised it was a WHALE. We weren't the only stupid ones. An Aussie crew from 59 coming down to relieve us four

Wireless Operator, Herbert Tuckwood, of 59 Sqn.
(HF Tuckwood via H Coles)

or five hours later went through the same exercise – 'bomb door open' and dropped another six depth charges on the whale. They had the decency to admit that the whale was already dead. This convoy turned out to be all oil tankers escorted by the American Navy. Shortly after we got on patrol, the SNO of the convoy called us and ask that we investigate a radar contact he had about forty miles astern. As we had no friendly shipping other than this convoy showing on our Green Sheets, this definitely sounded like action, so we headed out. We soon picked up the radar contact on our set and started homing in on it. There was broken air fog in the area. We couldn't get below it but it was broken enough to verify our altitude above the water, though we had no forward visibility. Al Henry was on the radar and when we were within five miles, we went into the 'bomb doors open' routine. As we went below the one-mile on the radar, we were flying about thirty feet above the water, still no forward visibility, when it suddenly occurred to me that if this was a ship instead of a U-boat, we were going to fly right into the side of it. A little back pressure on the stick and we were on top of this fog bank and there was a damned big freighter, just hose-piping tracers at us. Ah – a blockade runner we thought and there's the US Navy back there a few miles, so we headed back to the convoy, called the SNO and told him what his radar contact was and that it was UNFRIENDLY. In a very broad southern accent, he said 'Well, you stay here and look after my chickens and I'll take a couple of the boys back and look after him'. We stayed until our relief arrived, the one that had depth charged our dead whale – then we took off for home. We got to the end of the story when we got to our ops room. Our 'blockade runner' was one of our own fast freighters, who was over two hundred miles out of position. It took the dullness out of our life for that day – that and the whale!"

The second aircraft was C/59 flown by Neville Barson. The 'blockade runner' was in fact a friendly liner – the Rembrandt.

Around this time, the 59 Sqn engineering officer, F/O Dave Winton was observed going around looking 'something of a wreck' as he and his men had been up all night digging a Liberator out of the mud. It had been put there by F/O Taylor who, after landing on the short runway, swung off to avoid hitting the boundary fence. Taylor was new to the squadron and this was his final navigation trip prior to being placed on operations. The CO of 59 Sqn, W/C GCC Bartlett also found out, by unusual means, that he had been awarded the AFC. A member of 86 Sqn noticed the award in the Daily Telegraph list of Birthday Honours and thought that 59 Sqn should know about it. The announcement of the award was excuse for a party in the Officers' Mess to celebrate. The 59 Sqn diary recorded: 'never has so much been drunk by so many in so short a time; in fact, a good time was had by all'.

On 7 June, F/O Dennis Kelvin had flown W/C Williams from Coastal Command on a sortie during which they provided an excellent meal of bacon, eggs and steak on a stove they took with them. W/C Bartlett and crew were less well fed, however, on 10 June, when they carried out a 16-hour sortie without any rations due to a mistake in the flying canteen. The crew got very little satisfaction from the Horlicks tablets in the emergency packs.

On 9 June, F/O Lynch and crew of 59 Sqn and several other, set out from Aldergrove in an elderly Fortress Mk I for Northolt and thence to interviews at HQ Coastal Command and the Air Ministry. On the way they landed at Leconfield with a burst oil tank in the No 1 engine. One of the fitters at Leconfield recognised the machine and informed the passengers that he had serviced and almost rebuilt the aircraft in Egypt eighteen months previously after it had been shot up twice!

Convoy TA48 came under the escort of 86 Sqn on 12 June when F/O CW Burcher

The one that got away. The first attack by Neville Barson on the U-boat on 29 May 1943.
(VPI International/E Pratt).

arrived in Liberator Mk III FL932/H. At 1300 hrs, the crew sighted a grey, 517 ton U-boat and Burcher dived to attack, crossing over the conning tower from the starboard bow. Depth charges were released but overshot. Heavy, though inaccurate, fire was experienced from the U-boat, which remained on the surface, apparently undamaged. Burcher circled the U-boat endeavouring to make an attack with the aircraft's guns but tight turns to port and starboard by the U-boat made an attack difficult. However, on two occasions, Burcher closed with the U-boat and hits were scored. Just over half an hour later, the combat ended with the departure of H/86. Burcher informed the convoy of the attack and returned twenty minutes later to attempt a further attack on the U-boat but found no trace of it.

Also on 12 June, a No 86 Sqn Liberator lost one of its crew when on patrol in the Bay of Biscay escorting the same convoy. A surfaced U-boat elected to stay on the surface and fired at the Liberator, FK226/G, with cannon. The dark brown U-boat had been sighted at a range of 2 ½ miles on the starboard quarter and F/O Samuel altered course, crossing over the U-boat at 1,500 feet. No attack was made at this point and the U-boat opened fire with intense and accurate fire while Samuel circled 1,500 yards away endeavouring to make a head on attack. This was prevented by the U-boat's manoeuvres. After circling for ten minutes with the U-boat circling inside the aircraft, Samuel closed to attack making a weaving approach and with nose guns firing. The Liberator passed over the submarine at 90 degrees from the starboard beam forward of

The Queen Elizabeth heading for America with the Prime Minister, Winston Churchill, on board. Photographed by X/59 on 31 May 1943. *(VPI International/E Pratt).*

the conning tower and released the depth charges. The explosions were not clearly seen but the last depth charge was sufficiently near for the U-boat to be in the explosion swirl. During the attack, a fire broke out in the aircraft caused by fire from the U-boat. The crew swiftly dealt with this but unfortunately WOp/AG F/O JW James was struck in the chest by an exploding cannon shell which killed him outright. The Liberator also suffered a damaged fuel tank and bomb bay.

There was a bit of a 'flap' at Aldergrove on 13 June when all available crews were put on standby. It was thought that the German battle fleet might break out and the Liberators would be sent out to shadow them. The Liberator crewmen did not think much of their chances if they were called upon to do more than shadow the fleet and the 59 Sqn diary records their thoughts with the terse comment: 'At least we hope that's all'.

On 16 June, F/L EE Allen and crew in Liberator Mk V FL973/C of No 59 Sqn sighted three surfaced U-boats in position 4322N 1413W. Allen attacked two of the U-boats in the face of concentrated anti aircraft fire. The Liberator was hit and most of the cockpit instruments were damaged. No casualties were suffered, however. Allen attacked the centre U-boat with six depth charges, which overshot by 50 yards. The Liberator suffered four hits from anti-aircraft fire and the rear gunner managed to obtain hits on the conning tower in retaliation, firing 120 rounds. Allen followed up this attack with an attack on the starboard U-boat of the group thirty seconds after it submerged. Ernie Allen recalls this memorable sortie:

We set out at 0200 hrs to do an anti-sub sweep down through the Bay of Biscay in a parallel sweep with two other 59 Sqn aircraft. Our aircraft had the inside, or easterly, of the three tracks. At briefing we were given the story about intense air coverage on the Bay of Biscay both day and night. (Wellingtons equipped with Leigh Lights were the night aircraft, but of course in June the hours of darkness were very short). This intense coverage was resulting in more and more U-boats staying on the surface and fighting it out with the aircraft. By this time, all U-boats had a four cannon 88mm turret mounted behind the conning tower. This weapon was well respected by attacking aircraft. A Sunderland had been shot down the day before in the area we were to patrol. About 150 miles west of the north-western tip of Spain,

It was with these instructions that the crews at Aldergrove would patrol the Atlantic searching for the elusive U-boats in future. Again with Al Henry covering the radar and radio set, we picked up a radar contact suspected to be a U-boat. We were flying at 5,000 feet above a broken cloud, relying on the radar on the assumption that this U-boat was outbound into the Atlantic, we turned away to the west to manoeuvre so that we would be attacking head on, on our approach. We came busting out of the base of the cloud at about one thousand feet and there, a mile and a bit ahead of us was not one, but three U-boats. We had been briefed that we might find three to five U-boats together on an 'anti-aircraft patrol' and that if we did, we should circle and call in the two other aircraft for a combined attack.

I momentarily considered whether to do this, but it appeared we had the element of surprise in favour of our pressing our individual attack so that's what we did. The three U-boats maintained their Vic formation until we were in range of their flak and then turned away so that all three could get their 88's to bear on us. Soon we had a rattling sound like gravel on a tin roof; it was the shot going through the metal skin of the aircraft. We had built up so much speed in our dive; I had to pull the power off to avoid building up too much speed. It was very difficult to control direction at high speed, and needless to say, accurate direction was necessary to track over the U-boat.

COASTAL COMMAND TACTICAL INSTRUCTIONS

On 12 June 1943, the AOC in C of Coastal Command, Air Marshal JC Slessor, issued a new set of tactical instructions to his crews for the conduct of operations. These instructions included orders and advice on visual lookout, ASV radar lookout, heights to fly whilst on patrol, anti-submarine weapons capabilities, methods of attack, points of aim, when and when not to attack, actions in the event of a U-boat remaining surfaced during an attack, actions to be taken after an attack, 'baiting' tactics, photography, signals procedures and observation and reporting of attack results. The section dealing with surface U-boats fighting back makes interesting reading:

U/Boats Fighting Back

It is evident that U/Boat Commanders are now tending, increasingly, to remain on the surface and fight back with their gun armament when attacked by aircraft. It is in fact, known that they have received orders to adopt these tactics if surprised on the surface, in such a way as to be unable to dive to a safe depth before the aircraft can deliver its attack. When a U/Boat remains on the surface and fires at the attacking aircraft, the decision as to the method of attack must rest with the Captain of the aircraft who will take into consideration his armament, the degree of surprise achieved, the presence or otherwise of A/S surface vessels and the extent to which he is committed to the attack when the U/Boat opens fire. In general, however, he must remember that the primary reason for his existence is, for the time being, to kill U/Boats and that a U/Boat on the surface presents a much better chance of a kill than one submerged. It is no coincidence that recently, by far the larger proportion of certain or probable kills have been U/Boats which stayed on the surface and fought back.
It should also be borne in mind that even a big aircraft properly handled and using its guns well presents a difficult target for the gunners in the necessarily cramped positions of a U/Boat, which in any sort of sea is a very poor gun platform and especially so if the sea is beam-on. While, therefore, the tactics to be employed must be left to the Captain's judgement the attack should, whenever possible, be pressed home at once, preferably from dead ahead, making full use of the front guns to kill the U/Boat's gun crews or at least to keep their heads down.
If, however, the Captain of the aircraft considers the direct form of attack undesirable, alternative tactics are to circle the U/Boat at such a range as to bring accurate fire to bear, flying an irregular course with constant variations in height and firing with as many guns as possible, until the U/Boat's gunners are disabled or the U/Boat begins to dive; when the aircraft must be prepared to make an immediate attack. While adopting these tactics, a very careful watch through binoculars should always be maintained to ensure that the earliest possible warning is received of any intention on the part of the U/Boat to submerge.

LaForme would have killed me if I didn't put us in the right place for him to drop his depth charges. Also, knowing we would want a lot of power after the drop, I had pressed forward the little metal bar that pushed the little electrical toggle switches which advanced the propeller pitch. Just as I was doing that there was a yell from Tommy in the co-pilot's seat – 'I'm hit!' By this time we were pretty close to the target and I was 'busy'. I remember thinking somewhat cynically, 'What the hell does he think I can do about it?'

A Liberator Mk III of No 59 Sqn. *(M Allen).*

I managed a good track over the leader of the three U-boats and as soon as we passed over our target, I called LaForme on the intercom and asked if he thought we had hit the target. (We were barely fifty feet in the air, so I didn't see how we could miss). The answer was 'Look out of the left window and for Christ's sake get weaving.'

I looked out and there was a shower of little, mean looking black puffs closing in on us from the left side – I 'got weaving'. I had pushed the throttles pretty well wide open on seeing the flak closing in and became aware that we were getting a lot of vibration. I looked at our engine instruments and there was no evidence of the expected increase in power and the tachometers were indicating widely different prop speeds. I asked for and got a course for the nearest land in expectation we would not long remain airborne.

I had swung into a left turn as soon as we were out of range of those two remaining U-boats. For some reason I couldn't figure out, given the engine power the instruments were indicating we were staying in the air with a reasonable airspeed on the gauge. We still had six depth charges on board. Tommy seemed to have had a miraculous recovery from being hit. It turned out a shell had gone through the AC junction box, distorting its shape which flung its cover off and it was this cover that had hit Tommy.

" **E**VERY time I surface for a breather, I seem to catch a packet." —By Neb.

A cartoon by 'Neb' from a wartime newspaper printed after the incident recounted above pasted into the 59 Sqn diary. *(VPI International/E Pratt)*

About this time, somebody shouted that one of the U-boats was diving so we turned in to drop our remaining depth charges on it. The gen was that to get a 'kill' on a diving U-boat, the depth charges had to be dropped within thirty seconds of the conning tower going under. It was looking like we'd be late on that timing when we noticed the third one had started to dive, so we switched our attack to it. We had no trouble dropping our depth charges within the thirty seconds and George reported a good drop.

There was a lot to think about for a few moments. I sorted out the engine vibration; the engine pitch was all out of synchronisation. The engine instruments were not indicating it because they worked on AC power and the hit on the junction box at Tommy's elbow had put that out of action. Should we circle and attempt to call in the other aircraft? We reviewed the signals that Al had transmitted during the attack. We knew the other crews would have monitored our transmissions and our position had gone with each message, so they were in a position to make their own decisions and as we were well within range of the Ju 88 fighters on the French coast, who could home onto us if we made lengthy transmissions. I didn't have any trouble getting a crew consensus that we should get up into the layer of cloud above us and stay in it until we were long past Brest as we headed for Aldergrove, with the option of going to St Eval on the way if we found aircraft damage to justify it. No serious damage was found. A shell had cut the actuating rod for the bomb doors just behind the navigator's position and we had to wind the bomb doors manually – no big deal. This and losing our AC power was the most serious damage we had. The ground crew counted 192 holes in the aircraft when we got back, but apart from the cover of the AC junction box there was no serious damage.

The Operations controller was quite critical of our decision not to call in the other two aircraft and to make the attacks ourselves. We defended our decisions and told the controller that if he wanted to make the tough decisions he'd better be on the aircraft. The good news came the next morning, a signal from Coastal HQ congratulating the Squadron and the crew. We had been given a 'kill' 'assessment on the first U-boat attacked and a probable kill on the second one. The crew had an evening out in Belfast to celebrate."

Shortly after the trip of 16 June, Ernie Allen was ordered to report to the Station Commander. He reported with some trepidation:

"Someone came to my room and told me I was to report to the Station Commander immediately. I thought, 'My God, what have I done now to be on the carpet in front of the Station Group Captain.' Needless to say, I went. It turned out it was the Group Captain's pleasure to tell me that I had been awarded the DFC. The citation was the usual blarney about setting a high standard for the Squadron and pushing attacks against the enemy over and above the call of duty. He congratulated me but confirmed that he hoped I would not take this as a signal that I should ease up.

I felt this should have been a citation for the whole crew, but the RAF didn't do things that way.

A few weeks earlier, the Group Captain had taken an anti-sub patrol in the Bay of Biscay with our crew. It made us all very nervous having him on board but we got through the trip. At one point Al Henry picked up a radar contact which we treated as a U-boat contact and homed in on it with the bomb doors open. He stood up between and behind the pilots on the run in. Visibility was very poor. It turned out the contact was on some boards fastened together floating. And he was very impressed that our radar could pick this up."

The following day, F/O Dennis Kelvin was returning from a night trip and became confused by the lights of Nutts Corner and Aldergrove. In an attempt to establish which was which he flew over

The three U-boats attacked by Ernest Allen of 59 Sqn on 16 June 1943. The photograph was taken by the 2nd pilot, *(M Allen)*.

one of them calling Aldergrove and asking if they could hear him overhead. When they replied that they could he landed safely. He had been airborne for 18 hours 35 minutes. On the same day, F/O Geoff Lynch in Liberator MK V FL975/B sighted three U-boats in a 'vic' formation after homing on an ASV contact. The lead and port U-boats dived and the third, larger U-boat took violent evasive action and remained on the surface to give covering fire. Lynch circled the area at a range of ½ to ¾ of a mile with the U-boat turning inside and firing all the while. Lynch turned the Liberator to port and the U-boat crash-dived. Before departing, Lynch homed Liberator Y of No 86 Sqn to the scene to continue the patrol.

Incidents like this one were often the case. Not only were many attacks thwarted by the prompt actions of the alert U-boat crews, who were extremely vulnerable to attack on the surface, but many Coastal Command crews flew very many hours on patrol never sighting, much less attacking, a U-boat.

That evening, a party was held in the Officers' Mess to say farewell to G/C Hampton, as the Station Commander was posted away. The 59 Sqn diary notes that much alcohol was consumed. Two days later the CO of 59 Sqn, W/C Bartlett and the new station commander, G/C IE Brodie OBE gave talks on tactics to all the available aircrew. New instructions were issued that in future the Liberators would carry six A/S bombs and only two DCs. Thirty minutes after the lectures

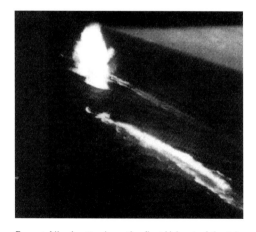

Ernest Allen's attack on the first U-boat of the trio encountered on 16 June 1943. The depth charges can be seen exploding around one U-boat whilst a second U-boat and its wake are visible in the foreground. *(M Allen)*.

this order was countermanded. There was also much discussion about forward firing guns, which the crews had been demanding for some time. They were notified that the squadrons would be allowed to carry out their own modifications to effect this.

The ditching in the mid-Atlantic of another No 86 Sqn Liberator on 21 June followed this. The pilot, F/O Samuels escaped without injury, Sgt Hollick was killed in the crash and later buried at sea. The remaining members of the crew, P/O Musker, F/Ss Buller, Bunny and Hopkins and Sgt Hollinson were all injured and the final crew member Sgt Fast was missing. The crew were picked up by HMS *Faulkner* of Force H after ditching and transferred to Gibraltar.

Ernie Allen's 59 Sqn crew were also airborne on 21 June:

"On another convoy escort we sighted another two U-boats, but they dived well before we could get in an attack."

F/L J Wright DFC and crew took off from Aldergrove in Liberator Mk III FK231/K on the morning of 23 June to escort two convoys, WS31 and KMF17. At 1154 hrs, they sighted three 517 ton U-boats on the surface and attacked them. Over six hours later, Wright came across three more U-boats sailing in a 'vic' formation. The leading U-boat was dark brown and of the 740 ton type. The others were 517 ton U-boats. The port U-boat dived immediately whilst the other two remained on the surface and opened fire. Wright circled his Liberator to gain an attack position and, whilst doing so, the other U-boats began to submerge. Wright flew his Liberator into an immediate attack on the leading U-boat dropping one 600lb anti submarine bomb. There was a large explosion but no results were seen. U650 commanded by Oblt zur See Ernst von Witzendorff, on her first war patrol had, in fact, been damaged in the attack. She was out of action until December and was finally lost to unknown causes in the Channel, returning from her seventh war patrol in January 1945.

June 27th saw F/O Pete Wright of 59 Sqn at the controls of a Liberator for the first time since his bale out over Lancashire. Unfortunately, whilst attempting to taxi from the dispersal to the hangar, the Liberator's undercarriage sank through the tarmac. Following these incidents, Wright commented that when he went on 'rest', he wanted to join the Pathfinders! Two days later, Wright, F/O Lynch and S/L Sissons were detached to Davidstow Moor for operations in the Bay of Biscay.

The first six months of 1943 had been highly successful for the Aldergrove squadrons. With the new long range Liberators and Fortresses equipped with ASV, the U-boats were finding it increasingly hard to hide from the marauding aircraft. The tempo of operation from Aldergrove was increasing and No 59 Sqn carried out 53 operations in June alone. Sinkings were few in number but the fact that a surfaced U-boat could come under sudden attack kept many of them submerged, coming to the surface only to recharge their batteries. Having to remain submerged cost them speed and made it all the more difficult to close with the convoys. Many of the U-boats were now crossing the Bay of Biscay area and many aircraft were detailed for anti-submarine sweeps in this area to meet the new situation caused by the apparent withdrawal of U-boats from the northern portion of the Atlantic. The Liberators of No 59 Sqn had been flying almost unarmed and had to have the guns replaced for operations in the Biscay area. The Aldergrove squadrons were only just beginning to reap the harvest.

By the middle of 1943, the Kriegsmarine had lost the Battle of the Atlantic. The early months of 1943 had seen some of the worst shipping losses for the Allies but the extension in range provided by the Liberator and Fortress left no place

Liberator 'B' of No 59 Sqn. *(M Allen)*

for the U-boat to hide and Aldergrove was in the forefront of the battle to finally defeat this menace.

One of the tactics used by the U-boat hunting aircraft was to carry out a procedure known as 'baiting'. After an attack, where the U-boat was not definitely confirmed as sunk, or when the aircraft had been spotted by the U-boat before an attack could be developed this tactic would be adopted. The Coastal Command Tactical Instructions issued in June 1943 laid down the procedure.

BAITING TACTICS

In adopting "baiting tactics" the aircraft will set course from the position of the attack to a distance of at least 30 miles and will remain outside this range for not less than 30 minutes. The aircraft should then return to the scene of the attack, taking full advantage of cloud, sun and weather conditions for concealment, in the hope that the U/Boat will have again surfaced.

Chapter 9

JULY 1943 – DECEMBER 1943

The first week of July saw the Liberators regularly patrolling although some sorties were recalled due to adverse weather conditions. No 59 Sqn detached aircraft to Davidstow Moor for operations, which continued throughout the month. The squadron was to concentrate its efforts in the Bay of Biscay area throughout July.

On July 1st, F/L Knowles carried out his first operational trip on an anti-submarine patrol known as 'Seaslug'. The patrols were very long and boring and Knowles returned reporting a sighting of the 'original seaslugs' – two dolphins! The following day, 59 Sqn carried out liaison exercises with a British submarine in the Irish Sea. Whilst F/O Neville Barson was carrying out his exercise he took violent evasive action which caused the rear hatch to blow open. F/O Dick Massina, his rear gunner, was very amused to see a parachute bag sailing back behind them, until on landing he found that it was his own!

No 59 Sqn was notified on 3 July that their CO, W/C Bartlett was to be posted as Chief Instructor at the Liberator OTU and he was to be replaced by W/C Gilchrist, the CO of No 120 Sqn. The squadron was very sorry to see him go.

On 7 July, F/L Kelvin took Liberator P/59 on patrol and at 0805 hrs observed the firing of a 2 star cartridge. Kelvin proceeded to investigate and soon an aircraft dinghy was sighted. Flame floats were dropped to mark the position but due to the rough seas the crew lost sight of the dinghy. Kelvin continued the search for another hour and sent a sighting report to base. The Liberator continued with its patrol and returned at 1203 hrs to recommence the search. Twenty-five minutes later the dinghy was found again and two survivors were seen to occupy it. The Liberator crew dropped an improvised Thornaby Bag containing emergency food boxes, tins of water and a Verey pistol and cartridges. The improvised bag fell within 500 yards of the dinghy. Once again the Liberator crew lost sight of the dinghy and, being at the limit of their endurance, set course for home. This day also saw a change of command for No 59 Sqn when W/C PA Gilchrist DFC replaced W/C GCC Bartlett AFC, who was posted to No 111 OTU as CFI. The following evening a 'Smoking Concert' was held in the Flying Canteen to say farewell to the CO. Large amounts of alcohol were consumed and the crew's chief worry was how it was going to be paid for!

On the 9th, Liberator Mk V FL972/E on convoy escort, captained by F/O Charlton, sighted a U-boat on the beam at a range of six miles in position 4347N 1425W. The U-boat began to submerge as the attack was made and Charlton dropped four depth charges 1 ½ to 2 swirl lengths ahead of the diving U-boat. Following the attack an oil streak and turbulence within the U-boats diving swirl were observed.

On 13 July, S/L Walker in Liberator G/86 sighted a U-boat in position 4600N 1340W and attacked it. Just over an hour later the crew spotted an aircraft approaching out of the sun and, fearing it was a German fighter, Walker made for cloud cover. Ten minutes

The British submarine, which exercised with 59 Sqn on 2 July 1943, photographed by F/O Neville Barson. *(VPI International/E Pratt)*

later he elected to jettison his bomb load to lighten the Liberator in the event of an attack but the intruder turned out to be Liberator A/86. The following day, P/O Gaston in Liberator Mk V FL952/L of 86 Sqn sighted a U-boat in position 4457N 1200W which he attacked. He followed this up with a sighting of a U-boat periscope feather at 4302N 1100W. The U-boat was directly below when it was spotted and Gaston circled to make an attack but he considered that the submarine had been submerged too long to make a successful attack.

On 16 July, a Spitfire from High Ercall being delivered by F/O J Clarke of No 3 Delivery Flight overshot the end of the runway on landing. The pilot was shaken but unhurt in the incident. The following day, the Met Flt received a request for trial flights to be carried out using Gladiators at Midnight each night. S/L Heaphy in N5900 carried out the first Midnight Gladiator climb the following night. On the 20th, S/L Heaphy informed No 15 Gp that in his opinion night climbs in Gladiators were impracticable with the present wireless equipment and proposed the fitting of VHF radios to the Gladiators. Ten days later, No 15 Gp agreed to a trial installation of VHF radios.

On 19 July, Liberator Mk V FL977/H, captained by F/L Allen, sighted a fully surfaced U-boat in position 4514N 1640W. Allen closed on the black painted 750 ton U-boat, which opened fire with cannon and began violent evasive turns to port when he was at 1,000 feet. The Liberator gunners returned fire and hits were observed around the conning tower. The Liberator sustained damage to the wing during the attack. Pulling up to 3,500 feet, Allan dropped his depth charges in a stern to bow attack with one depth charge, which overshot by 75 yards. Pretending to leave, he turned for a second attack with machine guns. During this attack the rear gunner, F/O AW Henry was hit by bullet and shell fragments. He later had a large fragment of shell and pieces of his patella removed from his wound. The Liberator passed ahead of the U-boat at 75 feet and dropped the remaining depth charges 100 feet ahead of its bow. After the second attack the Liberator turned for home and left the U-boat still on the surface. FL977 had suffered ten hits during the attacks.

Ernie Allen recalls this sortie:

"We did a number of A/S patrols and convoy escorts and a fair number of air practice flights until 19 July 1943 when we got 'some more excitement'. This was an anti-sub patrol straight west from Aldergrove into mid-Atlantic. By this time our bomb load had been changed from 12 depth charges to six depth charges and two 'homing torpedoes'. These homing torpedoes, when dropped reasonably near a U-boat, or ship for that matter, would home acoustically on engine sound and detonate on contact. This was a 'secret weapon' and we had been briefed that these torpedoes could not be dropped on a surfaced U-boat, the reason being that there were problems with them, in that sometimes when dropped, something malfunctioned and the thing would just run in ever decreasing circles until it stopped and the information was that if the Germans captured one of them they could quickly figure out how to neutralise the homing feature of the weapon and it would become useless. We were briefed that any Captain who dropped one of these on a surfaced U-boat would be court martialled. Also, any crew found to have discussed the weapon other than with his own crew would be court martialled.

At almost the westerly limit of our patrol we located a U-boat on the surface and started in on an attack 'depth charge'. At extreme range we were hit on the leading edge of the left wing, so, thinking discretion would be the better part of valour, we broke off the attack, expecting we would persuade him to dive and then we would get him with our homing torpedo. We tried every trick in the book to get him to dive, but no dice. He stayed on top. After about an hour of playing games we were running out of time – our fuel required we leave soon or run out before we got home. We decided we would have to attack with our depth charges. Knowing the effectiveness of the four cannon turret behind the conning tower, we tried to manoeuvre to get an attack in from the bow. He manoeuvred to prevent this. Our final tactic was to go into a steep turn around him trying to get ahead of his conning tower. We tried left and right turns –he could turn direction and turn faster than we could.

Tommy Thomas had, by the date of this flight, gone on a Captain's Course and his replacement was a very shy little English pilot. At one point we were close in on a right hand circle and the flak was coming pretty close. Al Henry was on the beam gun trying to shoot their gunners and this second pilot had the big F-24 camera up trying to take

The U-boat attacked by Ernest Allen on 19 July 1943, during which his WOp/AG, Al Henry was wounded. *(M Allen).*

Another photo of the 19 July U-boat attack by EE 'Wally' Allen. *(VPI International/E Pratt).*

pictures. I was getting pretty frustrated by this time and I snarled at him to get rid of the camera and tell me what was going on on the deck of the U-boat. We ended up in a left-hand turn and by getting in close we were moving up toward the front of his conning tower. We were taking as lot of flak and I could see Al was knocking down some of his people on the deck of the U-boat. There came a time when I figured I could level out and bomb across ahead of the conning tower. As soon as I committed to this, he must have thrown both engines into reverse and we tracked across in front of him. I thought, 'my God, we are going to have to do this again.' Then somebody called that the depth charges had gone off ahead of the U-boat. It turned out that LaForme had figured we were going to splash and had released the depth charges as we crossed in front of the U-boat. We pulled away and someone called that Henry was hit and they needed bandages and morphine. LaForme was the nearest thing we had to a medic and he went back and did a first call job. We set course for home with Henry having enough morphine in him to kill all pain.

We had no nose gun. Crews had been bitching for them for months. The engineering had been done but someone had decided they would only install the guns as the aircraft came in for routine overhaul inspection. It was something over six hours back to Aldergrove. By the time we arrived I was really steamed up about not having a nose gun. We had radioed in that we had wounded on board, so there was a reception committee on arrival. 59 Sqn had a new CO by this time, a W/C Gilchrist. The ambulance people took Al to hospital. Gilchrist and the Station Gp Capt asked me to ride back to Ops with them. During this ride I really exploded about the stupidity of not having the nose guns installed. They were quite tolerant of my outburst and when I went to breakfast the next morning, found that orders had gone out for both 59 and 86 Sqns that no ops were to be done by the Liberators until the nose guns were installed. Somehow I felt better, but Al had a bad knee for the rest of his life and he was gone from the crew.

Before we did another trip, LaForme was the only one left of the original crew. Woods and Flieger went on rest. Barton went to a Canadian flying boat squadron. Tommy had already gone on his Captain's Course. LaForme and I went on leave and came back to start to train our new crew of Englishmen. The fun had gone out of the Squadron. By this time all of the North Coates crowd had gone on rest."

Also on the 19th, Liberator Mk V BZ772/J of No 86 Sqn, piloted by F/L W Roxburgh DFC, homeward bound from a 'Seaslug' patrol sighted an attacked two U-boats. The

---

LONDON GAZETTE – 10 SEPTEMBER 1943

ALLEN, Flight Lieutenant Ernest Ellwood (J5295) RCAF – No 59 Squadron - Distinguished Flying Cross

F/L Allen was born in Ontario in 1921 and enlisted at Hamilton, Ontario on 21 August 1940. After training at No 1 ITS, No 4 EFTS and No 8 SFTS he was commissioned in 1941. Allen was invested with his award at Buckingham palace in December 1943.

Flight Lieutenant Allen has proved himself to be a most determined and capable captain of aircraft. By his gallantry and fine fighting spirit he has contributed much to the morale of his squadron.

Willis Roxburgh's 86 Sqn crew at Aldergrove in late 1943. L to R: Joe Griffith (Observer), Douglas Ely (WOp/AG), Willis Roxburgh (Pilot), Jack Churchill, Richard Thomas, Jock Rimmer, Ray Simpson (all WOp/AG), in window Floyd Meech (co-pilot). *(J Griffith via J Meadows).*

U-boats were together on the surface in position 4710N 1410W. While Roxburgh circled the starboard U-boat dived, screened by fire from the other U-boat. A few minutes later the second U-boat began to submerge. On the run in, the Liberator crew opened fire with machine guns scoring several hits. The Liberator dropped depth charges ahead of the swirl but both U-boats submerged leaving no evidence of damage.

On 22 July, Wally Allen's damaged Liberator H/59 was taken to Prestwick, complete with 16 bullet holes, for repair. On the social side, the rivalry between the squadrons

Dinghy drills in the pool at Aldergrove, 24 July 1943. *(VPI International/E Pratt)*

The dinghy drill races. Left to right the crews of F/O Henson, F/L Moran and F/L Barson of 59 Sqn. *(VPI International/ E Pratt).*

continued and 86 Sqn defeated 59 Sqn at football. Further competition ensued on the 24th when an 'organised' dinghy drill in the pool turned into a race between the squadrons. The victorious crew in the race was that of F/L Neville Barson of 59 Sqn.

In the week leading up to 26 July, No 59 Sqn began to receive new aircraft in the shape of the Liberator Mk VIII, four of which had arrived. During this period, the squadron was rife with rumour that it would soon be on the move to Ballykelly.

On 27 July, Liberator Mk III FK241/Y of No 86 Sqn, captained by F/O Green, escorting convoy MEF19, was attacked by a Junkers Ju 88 which registered several hits on the Liberator, damaging the hydraulics. Green managed to escape and on return to Aldergrove made a tail down forced landing. The following day, Liberators FL990/A piloted by F/L Knowles and F/59 under the command of F/O Lawson, were on escort duties. They met the convoy at 1005 hrs just as an attack by enemy aircraft was developing. They observed several enemy aircraft bomb the convoy and one of the ships was hit. F/L Knowles attempted to intercept the enemy aircraft jettisoning his depth charges to lighten the Liberator. The enemy bombers, FW 200s, were operating at a considerable height and Knowles was unable to reach them. The seven enemy aircraft continued to make attacks on the convoy until 1225 hrs when they left. A/59 and F/59 left the convoy at 1400 hrs to return to base.

On 29 July, F/L Knowles of 59 Sqn arrived over a convoy to find that it was being shadowed by seven FW 200 Condors. Contacting the SNO, he was ordered to circle the convoy whilst the Condors carried out their leisurely bombing runs. They sank one ship and damaged another before the SNO ordered Knowles to climb to 10,000 feet and get up among them. Knowles jettisoned his DCs and proceeded to climb into the enemy aircraft, but no damage was inflicted by either side. When he arrived back at base his report caused a terrific 'flap' and the squadron proposed to Coastal Command that a 'battle flight' should go out the next day and wait for the enemy to arrive. Coastal Command agreed and four Liberators from 59 Sqn and two from 86 Sqn went out. Bad weather prevented the enemy from reaching the convoy, though four had been plotted on their way. On the last day of the month, a swimming gala took place in the pool. The competition was between SHQ, 59 Sqn, 86 Sqn and 23 MU. 86 Sqn won fairly easily, though F/L Barson of 59 Sqn and three of his crew won the four seater dinghy race easily.

During August 1943, No 59 Sqn detached aircraft to St Eval, Gibraltar and Iceland carrying out 56 operations in the 'Seaslug' (later 'Percussion') and 'Moorings' patrol areas. The 'Moorings' patrols were in the vicinity of the Faroe Islands under No 18 Gp control.

F/L Murray Charlton took Liberator Mk V BZ719/K out on patrol on 1 August with orders to hunt a submarine in position 4724N 1212W and at 2147 hrs Sgt EW Harris, the second pilot, sighted a fully surfaced grey painted, 517 ton U-boat four miles ahead. Charlton turned to starboard, down sun and wind, losing height. When at right angles to the U-boat and four hundred yards ahead, he turned ninety degrees and attacked up track from the bow. When the Liberator was within 200 yards, the U-boat turned hard to port. The U-boat opened fire with multiple machine guns as Charlton attacked with depth charges. The navigator, F/O FR Short, released two depth charges with a third hanging up. As the Liberator passed over the U-boat, the rear gunner opened fire. The first depth charge exploded approximately 95 yards from the U-boat bow and the second 65 yards from the bow. During the attack the Liberator gunners exchanged fire with the U-boat and thick black smoke appeared on the starboard side of the conning tower and fire from the U-boat temporarily ceased. Excellent manoeuvring by the U-boat prevented further attacks and Charlton continued to circle the U-boat until his fuel state forced him to leave for St Eval in Cornwall.

At Aldergrove, No 1402 Met Flt carried out the VHF trials in the Gladiators and on successful completion of the trial it was decided that TR1133 radios would be fitted in future to allow the night climbs to be undertaken. The sporting calendar continued

No 15 Group units based at Aldergrove – 23 August 1943

Unit	59 Sqn	86 Sqn
Aircraft Type	Liberator Mk V (VLR)	Liberator Mk IIIA & V (VLR)
Establishment	15	15
Strength	16	16
Available	6	6
Remarks	59 Squadron's availability was much improved since May 1943. The overall establishment and strength of both squadrons was also much improved.	

LONG RANGE METEOROLOGICAL FLIGHTS

Kenneth E Lunn served as a WOp/AG with No 1402 (Met) Flt at Aldergrove, arriving from OTU at Maghaberry in the spring of 1943. He provides a valuable insight into the routine, but extremely hazardous, task of obtaining meteorological information, which would be passed on to the various Commands, for the purposes of operational planning.

"When in early 1943 I found myself posted to 1402 Met Flight RAF Aldergrove I was none too pleased. After all I was just 20 years of age. I had served two years of training as a WOp/AG and qualified in all other modern radio aids such as ASV.

I was even more upset when I discovered that the squadron consisted of about five Hampdens and three Hudsons plus one Spitfire. There were ten crews, four per aircraft, excluding the Spit pilot who daily soared to heaven.

Accommodation was good compared to many other RAF stations and a lot of time was spent on training – getting used to the two types of aircraft we were flying, Hudson and Hampden. Not as much spare time as my logbook might indicate – we did, however, enjoy the free time spent in Belfast. The only time during the war I had plenty of food to eat and pints of 'Porter' – poor man's Guinness took me to 14 ½ stone – heaviest weight ever.

Contrary to belief most crews had just left OTU. It came as something of a shock when we started out first Met flights – taking off at 0400hrs for what was known as Positions 6-7-8. No doubt records will show exactly where these positions are; to us they were a long way out in the Atlantic. Flying at 50 feet in big Atlantic swells frightened the life out of us (well, it did me).

To get the Hampden up to 18,000 feet took us at least 30 minutes, largely due to the worn out state of the engines. The aircraft was completely unsuitable for the job. It should be remembered that the lower and upper gun positions were fitted with twin Vickers K guns (pan ammunition). The Perspex cowling only partly covered the gun platforms. The only heating being a large flexible tube which you pushed up your trouser leg in an effort to keep warm. We had to wear so many layers of clothing that you could hardly move. My logbook shows the longest flight in a Hampden as 7hr 45 min. The only food was a dry corned beef sandwich. Tea in a flask froze. The toilet was a football inner tube with a spout. In these conditions you may wonder how we ever sent Met information back via the appropriate W/T station.

There was no MAO (Meteorological Air Observer). The navigator had received basic Met training and was expected to carry out this work in addition to navigating the aircraft. I believe this system accounted for the loss of a number of aircraft. The navigator spent a lot of time on Met work, especially translating his information into code for the wireless operator to send to base. As for myself I realised why I had received such extensive training – we had no ASV but we did have the standard Marconi transmitter/receiver. This had obviously been installed as an afterthought, long after the aircraft was designed. It was impossible to service in flight. The working table for transmitting lengthy, coded Met reports was about 18" by 10" including the Morse key. Frozen stiff and bumping about over the Atlantic it was a very demanding job.

The Hudson had a duration of just over 7 hours because some clever individual had the idea of putting a long range tank in the belly of this very rounded aircraft (designed for carrying passengers). The tank looked like a large version of the cold water tank you see in the roof of the average house. It held many gallons of petrol – pipes and levers everywhere – smell of petrol nauseating. They were absolute death-traps – although, if you discarded the danger of being fried alive, you travelled in considerable comfort compared to the Hampdens.

It is perhaps worth remembering that at this stage of the war Coastal Command was still the 'Cinderella' of the service. The war at sea, especially in the Atlantic, had taken a turn for the worse and losses of shipping reached alarming proportions. We later learned that this was due to more modern and larger U-boats. Also the German 'Enigma' codes had become more sophisticated and the code establishment at Bletchley Park had problems in breaking the new codes. The movements and whereabouts of U-boats were therefore unknown.

This state of affairs obviously interfered with the gathering and reporting of Met information. We would be briefed for a Met flight – then be diverted to assist a convoy in trouble and search for missing aircraft, or search for a U-boat sighted on our track. All very exciting, especially at night. It was all too easy to be fired at by U-boats on the surface recharging batteries of naval types who assumed all aircraft as anti-social. One can imagine the frustration at the Air Ministry Met Office at this time. 'Bomber' Harris was at last receiving four-engined aircraft in numbers, which enabled him to plan big raids on Germany. What he did not have was good Met information. I doubt there was an ops room in the country that did not give the Met briefing officer a hard time. Perhaps it was good-natured banter, but the truth was the information was not available for reliable Met forecasting. Also at this time 1402 was losing too many aircraft. As an example, on 23 July 1943 we took off from Aldergrove in Hampden AD736. Some three hours into the flight, whilst attempting to reach a height of 18,000 feet to take various Met readings, the aircraft lost power and went into a spin. The bomb bay door flew off hitting and damaging the tail fins and other parts of the aircraft. Ammunition pans came adrift and everything was chaos until the pilot got the aircraft out of the spin at about 3,000 feet. With engine and airframe trouble we were likely to ditch some 450 miles west of Ireland.

Somehow, amidst the ammunition pans I was able to send an SOS. The excellent work by HQ Western Approaches at Liverpool nursed us home. A Sunderland was sent to help us but, thank goodness, we did not need their help. Perhaps the sad end to this story is that the ATA sent a pilot to take Hampden AD736 to Hawarden MU to be dismantled. Control of the aircraft was lost on landing. It hit a building and the pilot was killed.

About August 1943 our pilot, F/S Taylor, was unable to fly. We were asked to fill in with other crews who were short. My fellow WOp/AG, Paddy Hopkins, lived in Belfast and was due to fly with another crew on the night he had a date with his girlfriend. Asked if I would swap with him, I did – and yes I am still around – poor Paddy did not return. A spin of a coin ended in my favour."

F/L Barson and his victorious crew. *(VPI International/E Pratt).*

through August and on the 2nd a sports meeting was held during which 86 Sqn triumphed, winning among other events the six-a-side football against 59 Sqn. The 59 Sqn groundcrew XI took the Station Cup. The same team lost a match against 86 Sqn for the best dispersals at Ballykelly to which it had been confirmed both squadrons would move in early September.

The weather in the Atlantic during August was a major factor and between the 8th and 12th several sorties were abandoned or diverted. A good example of the difficulties encountered is F/L Murray Charlton's efforts to carry out sorties. On the 9th he had to abandon a sortie due to the weather and return to Aldergrove, having taken off from St Eval. This sortie followed one in which they were diverted to St Eval. The previous day F/L Barson abandoned his sortie and landed at Beaulieu and on the 12th, F/O Lynch and F/O Duplooy were diverted from 'Moorings' patrols to Benbecula and Reykjavik respectively.

No 59 Sqn were in the thick of it again when Liberator Mk V FL984/S, captained by F/L Moran, sighted a FW 200 at a range of 8 miles on 14 August. The Condor did not see S/59 approaching and the Liberator closed to attack opening fire at two to three hundred yards with the nose turret 0.5 in machine guns. No hits were seen and the Condor opened up its throttles and passed across the Liberator's nose to starboard. S/59 turned to follow and the port beam gunner opened fire with a burst of twenty rounds from a range of 500 yards, observing some hits. By this time the enemy aircraft was returning fire from about 1,200 yards but failed to hit the Liberator. Suddenly, the Condor dived steeply and disappeared into cloud before S/59 could close for another attack.

Liberator P/59 bombing a towed target in Lough Neagh on 3 August 1943. *(via 206 Sqn)*

Two hours earlier, Liberator Mk V FL954/Z of No 86 Sqn escorting two convoys, OS53 and KMS23 had been informed by the convoy it was escorting that a FW 200 was shadowing the convoy to starboard. P/O GD Gamble turned the Liberator to investigate and soon sighted the Condor on the starboard beam of the convoy. The Condor took evasive action by flying towards cloud cover. Gamble followed and opened fire with the front guns from a range of 650 yards. The Condor turned to starboard with Z/86 following in a steep turn. Z/86 closed on the Condor again and opened fire from 300 yards. This time, the Condor was hit and smoke was seen to come from one of the engines before the Condor escaped into cloud cover. A further Condor and a Heinkel He 111 were sighted, but not engaged, by Liberator F/59, flown by F/L Murray Charlton that same afternoon. The Liberators shadowing the convoys were doing a good job, not only in keeping the U-boats submerged and away from the convoys, but also seeing off any Luftwaffe patrol aircraft and bombers brave enough to close with the convoys.

The Liberators continued to patrol the Atlantic sea-lanes and FL932/H of No 86 Sqn under the command of F/O CW Burcher on an anti-submarine patrol code-named 'Moorings' sighted a U-boat at periscope depth on 16 August. Burcher dived to attack but unfortunately the U-boat submerged before an attack could be made. He then directed an escort group of four destroyers to the scene. It is believed they sank the U-boat.

By 17 August, four of 59 Sqn's crews had been diverted to Reykjavik; Duplooy, Wright, Lynch and Moran. An attempt was made to return to Aldergrove in formation the following day. Three of the four managed to get off and struggle back in bad weather, the fourth, Moran, burst a tyre on the runway and remained behind.

Date	Hour	Aircraft Type and No.	Pilot	Duty	REMARKS (including results of bombing, gunnery, exercises, etc.)	Flying Times Day	Night
					Time carried forward :—	145·15	10·40
JULY 20·7·43	1000	HAMPDEN P2139	F/S. Taylor	WOP	Air Test	·15	
20·7·43	1435	HAMPDEN P2139	F/S Taylor	WOP	D. T. C.	2·00	
21·7·43	1055	HAMPDEN PS333	F/S Taylor	A/G	⑤ BASE — POS.7 — Base	5·20	
23·Y·43	0505	HAMPDEN AD 736	F/S Taylor	WOP (A/c in s.s.c. bent)	⑥ BASE — POS.8 — BASE (6·15)	5·45	·30·
25·Y·43	1135	HAMPDEN PS333	F/S Taylor	WOP	Air Test	·15	
26·Y·43	1100	HAMPDEN PS333	F/S Taylor	WOP 200 RNDS	⑦ BASE — POS. 8 — BASE.	6·10	
28·7·43	1105	HAMPDEN PS333	P/o Roberts	A/G	⑧ BASE — POS. 8 — BASE	6·20	
30·Y·43	0520	HAMPDEN P1717	P/o Roberts	WOP	⑨ BASE — POS 8 — BASE(6·40)	6·10	·30

Summary for JULY 19 43
Unit. 1402 MET. FLIGHT.
Date 1·8·43
Signature K Lunn

Aircraft Types.
1. HUDSON .... | NIL |
2. HAMPDEN ...... | 32·15 | 1·00 |
4. TOTAL .... | 54·55 | ·00 |

OPS HOURS ON UNIT.

SIG .... A.D.Heaphy. S/L
O/C 1402 MET FLIGHT.

TOTAL TIME ... 177·2· | 11·410

Ken Lunn's logbook for July 1943. (K Lunn).

Several Liberators went out on patrol on 20 August and F/59 failed to return. F/O
Bill Taylor's Liberator had last been heard of about one and a half hours from base at
2029 about 150 miles west of Ireland. The weather that day was good and no reason
for their loss was found. The following day, two aircraft were sent out to search for the
Liberator but with no success. The air battles over the convoys continued and Liberator
FL952/L of No 86 Sqn, captained by F/O BF Gaston, exchanged machine gun fire with
two Ju 88s at 0910 hrs on 25 August. The Ju 88s were spotted approaching from the
direction of the Spanish coast making for L/86. One Ju 88 attacked from the port
quarter while the other approached from astern. The port Junkers opened fire at 700
yards. The Liberator scored several hits on one of the Ju 88s, which made a sudden
turn with smoke coming from the starboard engine. The Ju 88 dived towards the sea
and then was lost to sight. The other Ju 88 did not fire and also broke away to port.
L/86 fired two-second bursts from the rear turret at the Junkers and turned slightly to
port. The Junkers formated and returned to make two further attacks, during one of
which they failed to open fire. Gaston's crew returned fire during each attack. Several
more attacks were made by the Junkers, but to no effect. L/86 fired at one of the Ju
88s and saw strikes, after which the Junkers made a sudden turn to starboard, with
smoke coming from the starboard engine. The Junkers dived towards the sea and was
not seen again. The second Ju 88 attempted several more attacks but did not open fire
due to effective evasive action by Gaston. L/86 sustained only one hit during the fight;

Date	Hour	Aircraft Type and No.	Pilot	Duty	Remarks (including results of bombing, gunnery, exercises, etc.)	Day	Night
		No. 1402		MET FLIGHT	Time carried forward :— 177·30 11·40		
AUGUST 3·8·43	0530	HAMPDEN P1265	Sgt. Buswell	WOP	(10) BASE - POS. 8. - BASE	6·30	
7·8·43	0550	HUDSON V9068	Sgt. Buswell	A/G	(11) BASE - POS 3. - BASE. D.N.C.O. N/T·Y/E	2·35	
10·8·43	1140	HUDSON V9068	Sgt. Collins	WOP	(12) BASE - POS 6 - BASE	5·10	
18·8·43	0410	HAMPDEN P1265	Sgt. Bartlett	A/G 200 Rnds	(13) BASE - POS. 8. BASE (Y·0)	6·10	·50
20·8·43	1000	HUDSON AE686	Sgt. Collins	WOP	(14) BASE - POS. 7. BASE	7·05	
24·8·43	0405	HAMPDEN AD756	Sgt. Bartlett	A/G	(15) BASE - POS 8. - BASE (7·45)	6·15	1·30
26·8·43	1055	HUDSON V9068	Sgt. Bartlett	WOP	(16) BASE - POS 6 - BASE	5·35	
29·8·43	1000	HAMPDEN P.5333	Sgt. Scott	WOP	BASE - A/C. U/S. - BASE	·25	
29·8·43	1105	P. 5333	Sgt. Scott	WOP	(17) BASE - ST. ANGELO. STB. ENGINE U/S 1·40		
29·8·43	17.25	P. 5333	Sgt. Scott	WOP	ST. ANGELO - BASE	·35	
AUGUST 1402 MET FLIGHT 1-9-43	43			HUDSON HAMPDEN TOTAL nrs	HOURS	20·25 21·35 46·55	2·20
					TOTAL TIME ... 219·30	14·00	

Ken Lunn's 1402 (Met) Flight logbook entry for August 1943. *(K Lunn).*

a small calibre cannon shell penetrating the port beam window. Twenty minutes later, two more Ju 88s were sighted followed by another fifteen minutes later. None of the Ju 88s came to fight.

Over 20/21 August, the 59 Sqn groundcrew produced a 'Review' which was enjoyed by all and was said to have put the 'professional' Aldergrove 'Blue Coastals' in the shade.

On 27 August, Liberator Mk V BZ802/V of No 86 Sqn on an anti-submarine patrol in the 'Percussion' area passed a weather report to base from position 4906N 1130W at 1926 hrs and was never heard from again. F/O RH Kildea and his crew, F/O DW Roberts, F/O CF Cropper, Sgt WH Harris, Sgt JS Rippon, Sgt GL Plume and Sgt EBH Wells were all killed when the Liberator crashed on the return journey near Kenmare River, Eire. The Luftwaffe was out in force during this period and on 29 August, Liberator B/86 sighted a Ju 88 and three other unidentified aircraft during the course of its patrol.

September saw changes once more at Aldergrove with No 86 Sqn departing for Ballykelly on the 4th. On 8 September, the Met Flt lost Hudson 'N' when Sgt Bartlett and crew failed to return from a 'Bismuth' sortie. The second Liberator squadron, No 59, also moved out to Ballykelly on 13 September, the ground party having departed on the 11th. The following day, Aldergrove once more came under the control of No 17 Gp and on the 20th, No 1402 Met Flt learnt that the Bismuth sorties from Aldergrove were to be halted and the two Hudsons were to be detached to Tiree and absorbed by No 518 Sqn to carry out 'Mercer' sorties. Fourteen groundcrew were to be sent to Tiree with the aircraft and these left Aldergrove on 23 September. Hudson 'K' departed for Tiree on 24 September with aircrew and the remaining groundcrew and was followed on 30 September by Hudson 'Q'. Many of the Met Flight pilots were posted to No 518 Sqn on 1 October to convert to the Halifax. Meanwhile at Aldergrove, Sgt Whitney made a forced landing on 6 October. He was undertaking his first solo in Gladiator N5900 when he had to force land at Nutts Corner, unfortunately he hit some trees on the approach and damaged the aircraft which had to be sent to Short & Harland in Belfast for a major overhaul. The Met Flt received a new Gladiator, N5575, from No 8 MU at Little Rissington to replace N5900 on 25 October.

Once again, Aldergrove was left with No 1 APC and No 1402 Met Flt sharing the airfield with No 23 MU. One other unit was at Aldergrove during this period; a detachment of No 547 Sqn from Thorney Island arrived during October to convert to the Liberator and remained until January 1944. During this period, the MU was busily preparing and storing Wellingtons in the main. In addition, Ansons, Fleet Air Arm Corsairs, Oxford and Stirlings passed through the MU.

A new unit formed at Aldergrove on 10 October 1943 in the shape of No 1674 HCU. This unit had been preceded the previous month by the Liberator Conversion Flt of No 1 OTU, which had arrived from Beaulieu on 6 September in anticipation of the formation of the HCU. This unit also took over responsibility for Boeing Fortress training for Coastal Command from No 1 OTU. Just over a week after forming, the HCU moved to Longtown. The HCU would return to Aldergrove in 1944.

S/L Heaphy of No 1402 Met Flt relinquished his acting rank on 22 November with the disestablishment of the S/L post and reverted to F/L. He was posted to No 105 OTU on 10 December and awarded an AFC for his work on the Met Flt on 4 January 1944. A new CO, F/L PE Daniels, took his place.

The last month of 1943 saw the station take a well-deserved holiday on Christmas Day and Boxing Day. After the fierce battles of the Atlantic convoys during the year they deserved it.

Chapter 10

JANUARY 1944 – JUNE 1944

No 1 APC control room on 12 February 1944. *(206 Sqn)*

No 1 APC and No 1402 Met Flt continued their armament training and meteorological flights in the new year of 1944 and on the third day of the year a Liberator of No 59 Sqn, piloted by F/L Cooke DFM, attending the APC, ran off the runway and was damaged. On 25 January, the Met Flt establishment was increased with the arrival of another Gladiator, N5576, which brought the Flight up to full strength.

On 5 February, No 1674 HCU returned to Aldergrove with Liberators and Halifaxes and began training crews for Coastal Command. The Fortress elements of the unit went to Longtown. The following day, F/S JG Parkinson took off for the evening THUM flight in Gladiator N5637 and immediately flew into a flock of birds. He managed to complete a circuit and landed back at Aldergrove. Luckily the only damage was a crack in the port front windscreen. On 19 February, ACM Sir William Sholto Douglas, the AOC in C Coastal Command visited Aldergrove with AVM Sir LH Slatter, AOC No 15 Gp. During the visit they inspected the Met Flt. On the same day, F/S GA Rich of the Met Flt experienced severe engine trouble on take off in Spitfire BR298. The throttle lever had ceased to operate and he was forced to make a dead stick landing with the switches cut. The landing was successful but the Spitfire obstructed the runway for fifteen minutes delaying the departure of the C in C. The Spitfire required an engine change after this incident. On 24 February 1944, a deputation of Air Ministry officials and representatives from Pan American Airlines visited the APC and examined its facilities with a view to using Lough Neagh as a diversion base for Trans Continental Airways flying boats. The facilities were explained to the deputation and this was followed by a tour of the target quadrants and mooring area at Sandy Bay. In the afternoon the alighting area was inspected from a marine tender and Mr Crossman of the Air Ministry viewed the Lough from one of the APC Martinets. The first Transatlantic Ferry Service Coronado flying boat arrived at Sandy Bay on 18 May 1944.

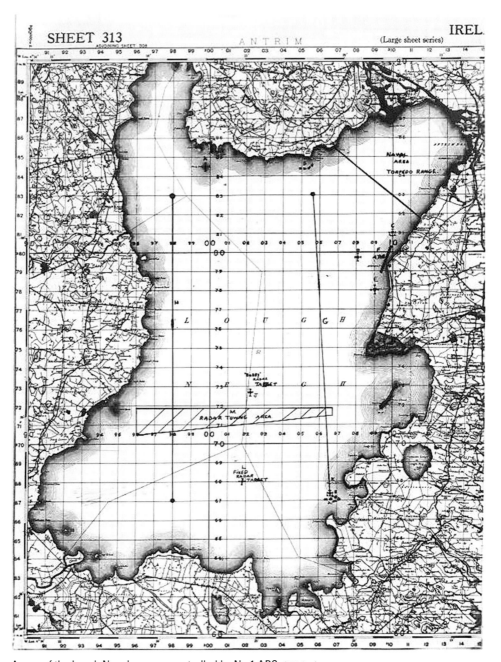

A map of the Lough Neagh ranges controlled by No 1 APC. *(206 Sqn).*

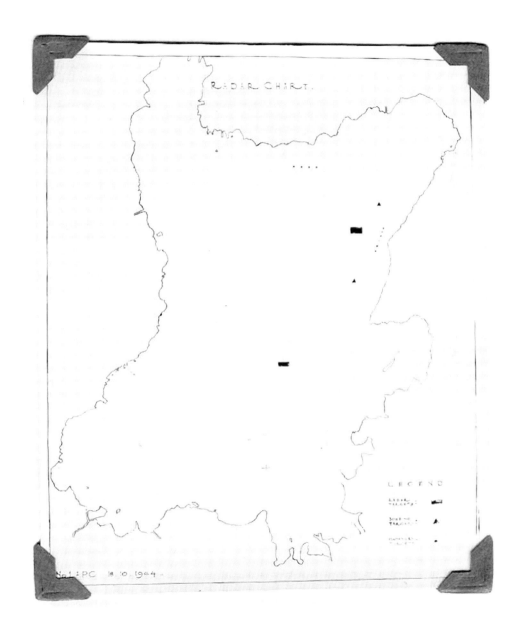

A radar chart of the Lough Neagh ranges controlled by No 1 APC, 18 October 1944. *(206 Sqn)*

On 10 March, Wellington Mk II W5385, flown by a crew from No 16 FPP, crashed at Aldergrove. In March 1944 the Met Flt increased its sortie rate by introducing a second Prata flight each day from the 20th. The establishment of the Met Flt reduced by one Gladiator on 7 April when N5902 departed for 521 Sqn at Bircham Newton but the sortie rate continued to increase with the introduction of another THUM sortie at midnight each night from 10 May.

The Leigh Light installation on a Coastal Command Liberator.

By May 1944, No 1674 HCU was training ten strong crews in Leigh Light operations with Liberator Mks V and VI. In June, repairs were made to the North-South runway at Aldergrove and the Met Flt detached two Gladiators to Nutts Corner from 5 to 7 June. On the 19th, No 1674 HCU received a new Chief Instructor when W/C WH Ingle was posted in. By the end of June, Aldergrove had a unit strength of 280 officers and over 1,600 other ranks.

Chapter 11

JULY 1944 – DECEMBER 1944

O n 1 July No 1402 Met Flt were informed by Coastal Command that they would shortly be receiving Hurricane Mk IIc's to replace the Gladiators but that the Gladiators would be retained until the pilots had been fully converted to the Hurricane. On 15 July two Hurricane Mk IIc's, PZ754 and PZ756 were delivered to the Met Flt by the ATA and the following day the CO, F/L Daniels was the first to begin conversion to the type. On 24 July the Station lost another aircraft when Halifax DT642 crashed shortly after take off. All nine of the crew were killed. The midnight THUM sortie introduced on 10 May was discontinued on 24 July and the following day the CO, F/L Daniels was posted. F/O Hicks assumed command of the Met Flt. On 8 September he in turn was replaced as CO by F/L RG Brown AFC.

The re-equipment of the Met Flt continued in September with the first Spitfire Mk VII being delivered on the 10th. The Spitfire was fitted with a Merlin 64 engine and trials were carried out in connection with re-equipping the Flt for Prata sorties. The first Spitfire trial being flown the following day.

No 1674 HCU had been carrying out training course for Liberator crews since its return and by October it was starting the third Liberator (Leigh Light) Course. Seven crews began this course alongside the third Liberator (Acclimatisation) Course comprising two crews and one pilot, W/C BO Bias on a captain's course. In addition to the Liberator course the HCU was also training Halifax crews and three crews were converting to the Halifax on No 12 Halifax Course, one crew to the VLR role and the other two destined for Met Squadrons.

The changes of command within the Met Flt continued with F/L EJ Woosley RAAF taking over on 6 October. On 18 October a further two Hurricanes arrived in the shape of PZ759 and PZ799 and the following day a third, PZ774, was delivered by the ATA. Two further Hurricanes, PZ815 and PZ805 were delivered on 20 October bringing the unit up to full strength. With a full establishment of Hurricanes the Gladiators began to be ferried away and N5637 and N5575 were disposed of.

Halifax JB963 of No 1674 HCU was lost on 23 October. The aircraft was being flown by a crew of No 12 Course under the instruction of F/L D Evans when it dived into the ground on a training flight. The crew, F/S JH Saunders, F/O MLM Gillis, and Sgt RL Dixon were killed alongside the instructor. F/S Kevan Smith, who was WOp/AG on the crew captained by F/S Keith Proverbs was a witness to the crash. Proverbs had come from the West Indies and was about to start his second tour. Smith recalls the training on 1674 HCU and the crash:

"Roy Cartwright trained in Canada as I did and he was a Wireless Operator mechanic (WOM). After Canada he went to the Coastal Command OTU at Nassau in the Bahamas, as I did. We trained on Liberators there and afterwards went back to Montreal to a holding depot in Lachine. My crew were transferred to Atlantic Transport Command and after some more training at Dorval we flew a Lib to Scotland via Bermuda and the Azores.

'MET' PILOT

Ralph Schenk left his home in Ontario, Canada in February 1942 to enlist in the RCAF. After training on Fleet biplanes and Ansons he gained his 'Wings' in April 1943 and the following month was posted overseas. He continued training at Peterborough, Cambs flying Masters. Because of his small size he was able to obtain a waiver and a posting to single engined aircraft. Most of his colleagues were posted to bombers. Loaned to the RAF for the duration he spent five months as a staff pilot at CGS flying from Sutton Bridge and Catfoss before being posted to the OTU at Dyce, Aberdeenshire and promoted to Pilot Officer. After training on photo-recce Spitfire Mk IVs he was posted to a P-51 squadron on the Continent. Unfortunately he came down with tonsillitis and on recovery he found he was posted to No 1402 Met Flt at Aldergrove.

"I hated to miss the action in France, but you go where you are told! I reached Aldergrove on 30 July 1944 and had my first flight on 6 August in Tiger Moth 206 with F/O Hicks. The Moth made a fool out of me, as I hadn't flown anything like it since the Fleet 16 at EFTS in December 1942! I couldn't slow it down for a proper landing. On 11 August I made my first flight in Gloster Gladiator N5592. Later on I would make the last sortie of a biplane fighter in the RAF in this airplane on 7 January 1945.

I would make eight practice flights in Gladiators before my first Met-recco on 26 August. I loved the old Gladiator. Great for aerobatics and easy to fly. A crosswind was difficult to deal with and would keep you on your toes. This was due to the narrow landing gear and high centre of gravity. These 'THUM' (Temperature and Humidity) flights lasted about one hour and ten minutes on average. A wet and dry bulb thermometer was attached to the 'N' strut, large enough to be easily read. For night flying a spotlight on the side of the fuselage would illuminate the thermometers. We also made flights for radar calibration, search and rescue and general reconnaissance.

By 8 January 1945 we exclusively used Hurricane Mk IIc's for 'THUM' ascents. I made my first flight in a Hurricane, serial PZ754, on 1 September 1944. I loved the Hurricane. It didn't have the glamour of the Spit, but a good, solid airplane, a grandmotherly appeal. She was easy to handle, good visibility for landing, take-off and taxiing. In bad weather she would get you home. I don't recall the exact levels that out 'THUM' readings were taken, but I think it was every three to five hundred feet. We would climb to 30-35,000 ft. On our right knee was strapped an information board to write down all the info. We were always under radar and radio control. We were 'Belljar Sqn' and my callsign was 'Belljar Niner Zero'. On 15 November 1944 I began to use the Hurricane Mk IIc for 'THUM' ascents and still did some trips in Gladiators. On 16 November I checked out in my first Spitfire since leaving Scotland, a Mk IV, BR298, which was being used for 'PRATA' (Pressure at Altitude) climbs. On 1 December 1944 No 1402 Flt was moved to Ballyhalbert, CO Down, right on the Irish Sea. Here I would continue to fly Hurricanes and the terrific Spitfire Mk VII at high altitude with a pressurised cabin.

I loved Aldergrove as we lived like kings there. Nice, luxurious officers quarters and mess. The food was the best yet and we were close to Belfast for time off. I have many happy memories of Ulster and fell in love with her. I almost got married to a colleen from Portavogie but her parents nixed it. I had a tall, handsome civilian man as my batman and a WAAF as well. They spoiled me rotten! I never had it so good, before or after. The big Irishman would take me by Jeep anywhere I wanted to go. I found the Ulster people just great and the girls – Wow! I met some gorgeous young ladies in the Belfast Officers Club. The weather, however, was the worst I have ever seen. Most of our flights were instrument flying all the way. I always made above average grades in instrument flying and it paid off. We had great controllers and radar men that kept us alive.

The CO was S/L 'Slim' Woosley, an Australian and I recall F/L Hicks and F/O Bob Bramley. I recall one incident when we were at the Officers Club in Belfast and one of our pilots and an American officer were arguing the merits of the Spitfire and P-38. They arranged to have a match over Aldergrove some evening and we all stood outside the Officers Mess and watched it. Our pilot got on the tail of the twin boom P-38 and just stayed there. The yank should have known that no twin engine fighter could out-manoeuvre a single engine fighter! He was impressed by the Mk VII Spitfire.

Post-war, Ralph Schenk would move to America and become a doctor. In 1990 he returned to Aldergrove to visit the station and flew around the old airfields he had flown from.

The intention was that we take it on to India but the RAF in its wisdom handed it over to another crew at Prestwick and we scattered to various reception centres in the UK.

I went to Brighton, which was the Australian Centre. I got sick there and when I recovered my crew had been sent off to operate out of the Azores and I was a loose cannon! My short visit to the Azores showed me that it was the pits so I wasn't really sorry to miss the posting.

It took a long while for the system to catch up with me but when it did I was posted to the Heavy Conversion Unit in Aldergrove to convert to Halifaxes and there I met Roy with Keith Proverbs and the rest of the crew. I had my first flight with 1674 on 8 August.

Before we started flying we went into Belfast one day and bought a shillelagh as a lucky charm. A lovely knobbly stick painted a bright green! We carried it on our first long night navigational exercise on 15 October and for the first half of the trip everything was fine, even though there was heavy cloud above us and continuous rain. Eventually McMillan, the navigator, asked me to get him some positional radio fixes to check his navigation as he only had his dead reckoning to go by. Mac didn't believe the result of the fixes, which showed us heading off into the wide blue yonder where we certainly should not have been. Roy checked the fixes with me and we decided they were correct and that Mac was a dud navigator. He agreed that something was wrong and that we had better head home before it was too late, as we were many miles from where we should have been. It looked as though we should head for Tiree rather than Aldergrove due to fuel considerations so I asked Tiree for a course to steer to reach them and we turned onto it and abandoned our exercise.

About this time, Mac discovered that he had inadvertently picked up the previous day's Met reports instead of the current ones and had been navigating with the wrong wind speed and direction. He never made that mistake again and turned out to be an ace navigator. On the way to Tiree, the pilot opened his side window and with our universal blessing, consigned the shillelagh to the Atlantic. That was our worst experience at Aldergrove, but others weren't so lucky.

Just before lunch one day I was walking around the perimeter of the airfield with Keith Proverbs and we watched a Halifax taking off. It didn't gain much height before the pilot turned and came in for a landing. The plane was fully laden with depth charges and fuel and before it was properly lined up it suddenly dived into the ground and exploded.

We ran to the wreck but found nothing but a hole surrounded by charred fragments and one boot. We flew our last trip the following day. A while later, after the relatives had arrived, there was a parade and a formal funeral with the appropriate number of weighted coffins. We never did find out why the plane crashed.

Before lunch each day we used to meet in the Mess and have a drink. The place was usually full with a wide variety of uniforms of a lot of nationalities. We had Free French, Polish, Czech, Dutch etc. On this occasion as we sat down to lunch we remarked on the fellows further down the table from us and tried to guess their nationality. After lunch these fellows (we discovered later that they were dressed in Luftwaffe uniform) went to the control tower and declared that they had captured it and then to the CO's office and 'captured' him. They spent the afternoon wandering around at will. An alert guard at the gate finally challenged them as they were leaving. They were actually Air Force security testing the security of Aldergrove. As you can imagine it tightened up after that – and we had a crash course in foreign uniforms!"

The following day, No 2 Liberator (Leigh Light) Course was completed and three of the crews, captained by F/O HE Miskiman, F/O H Nixon and F/L AR Wilcox were posted to Iceland. F/L RCC Pratlove and crew went to No 224 Sqn. P/O RW Ridler was posted with his crew to No 547 Sqn and F/L JJ Gubbings took his crew to No 206 Sqn. Two crews of No 3 Liberator (Acclimatisation) Course also completed training on the 24th and were posted to No 220 Sqn along with W/C BO Bias. No 11 Halifax Course, which should have ended the same day, was extended for a week due to bad weather and aircraft unserviceability delaying the end of the course. The next day, No 4 Liberator Course commenced training with seven Leigh Light crews and one Acclimatisation crew. No 13 Halifax course commenced alongside the Liberators with five crews. The course was planned to last three weeks. On 31 October, under a reorganisation of the Station, No 1674 HCU, which had been an independent unit, became, Training Wing with a role similar to an OTU.

A second Spitfire Mk VII was delivered by the ATA for No 1402 Met Flt by the ATA on 1 November. Unfortunately, it sustained minor damage on landing due to the failure of the tailwheel-locking device. On 2 November, F/L Woosley learned that he had been promoted to S/L with seniority backdated to 1 July 1944. Another of the unit's Gladiators, N5575 left for No 226 MU and disposal on 7 November. A third Spitfire Mk VII, MB159 arrived on 9 November and Hurricane and Gladiator movements continued throughout the month with Hurricane Mk IIc PZ853 arriving on the 19th followed by PZ756 departing to No 22 MU for disposal on the 20th. The previous day, Gladiator N5637 was flown out to Cosford.

G/C JR Leggate, SASO No 17 Gp visited Aldergrove on 10 November and as a result of the visit changes to the organisation of Station accommodation were brought in. The WAAF Section was to be removed and Training Wing (1674 HCU) would take over the vacated accommodation. The radar Section would be incorporated into the training Wing in the reorganisation. One crew of No 12 Halifax Course, captained by F/O GE French, completed training on 14 November and was posted to No 517 Sqn. The other crew was delayed due to the suspension of five of the crew. No 3 Liberator (Leigh Light) Course completed training the same day. F/L D Richards, F/L Alexander and F/L GA Haggas took their crews to No 206 Sqn. W/C Selby and crew were posted to No 547 Sqn. S/L EA Johnston and crew went to No 224 Sqn and F/L DE Melliship and crew were posted to No 53 Sqn. F/L Mulheron's crew was taken over by F/O Rowley and recoursed to No 4 Liberator Course.

On 15 November, No 14 Halifax Course (VLR) commenced with three crews alongside No 5 Liberator Course comprising seven Leigh Light crews and one Acclimatisation crew. On 18 November, two aircrew from the station were killed in a flying accident to a Liberator at Tain. The station lost F/O SD Easterbrook and F/S JA Humphreys

On 22 November, one of the last Gladiators on the unit, N5576 sustained considerable damage when the pilot collided with a tree on the approach to land. The pilot managed to make a successful landing and the damage was repaired. The next day, No 1402 Met Flt learnt that it was to move to Ballyhalbert and the advance party moved out on 28 November, the move being completed by 3 December. With the Met Flt gone, Aldergrove soldiered on with No 1674 HCU, by now converting crews onto the Liberator Mk VIII and No 1 APC. During the previous months work on the North-South runway had been carried out and by the end of November a 400-yard extension to the south end of the runway was in use.

No 4 Liberator Course was completed on 6 December and the crews were posted away. Three crews went to No 120 Sqn, three to No 53 Sqn and one to No 224 Sqn. On 13 December, No 15 Halifax Course commenced with two VLR crews captained by F/O JB Goodyear and F/O W Atkinson and one Met crew captained by F/L DI Chapman. On 19 December, the station received plans for reconstruction for post war use. On 22 December, F/L Thomas and his crew completed their Liberator Acclimatisation Course and were posted to No 59 Sqn. The following day, No 14 Halifax VLR Course ended and the three crews were posted to No 58 Sqn.

By 28 December, it had been decided to resume Fortress (Met) training at Aldergrove. The unit would train two crews every six weeks and the No 1 Fortress Course commenced on the 28th with crews captained by F/O FA Hughes and F/S E Redman. No 16 Halifax Course commenced the same day with two VLR crews, F/L EL Holdon and F/O FW Mawdlsey and one Met crew, captained by P/O SN Howland.

An ASR buoy moored in Lough Neagh for search and homing training photographed on 13 December 1944. *(via 206 Sqn)*

On 30 December No 23 MU took over the airfield at Maghaberry and Aldergrove became responsible for certain Accounting, Equipment and Administration responsibilities. The last day of 1944 saw No 6 Liberator Course being extended until 3 January 1945.

DUCK SOUP

Canadian Ken G Hutson served as an Air Gunner on Liberators. Following initial training at No 111 OTU based at Sir Harry Oakes Field and Windsor Field in the Bahamas he was posted to Aldergrove for further training:

"I flew about 70 hours out of Aldergrove from 21 December 1944 to 20 January 1945 on Liberators of No 1674 HCU on No 6 Leigh Light Liberator Course. I have no pictures as someone stole my camera when I landed in the UK and I have little recollection of the base as we were flying often during daylight. S/L Barry Peck was our Officer Commanding. He had been awarded the DFC whilst flying with 120 Sqn. He sunk U470 on 16 October 1943 flying Liberator 120/Z, attacking at 100 feet.

Our duties were extensive training on radar, bombing and gunnery and our pilots were training on handling heavily laden Lib's. We had just come from operational training at No 111 OTU so this was duck soup (easy) for us.

A 'Bobby' buoy moored in Lough Neagh. These buoys simulated submarine targets. *(Via 206 Sqn)*

Another view of a 'Bobby' buoy in Lough Neagh. *(via 206 Sqn).*

Chapter 12

JANUARY 1945 – JUNE 1945

By 1945 the war in Europe was drawing to a close. The German army had made its last attempt to throw the Allies back into the sea at the Battle of the Bulge and had failed. On the Eastern front the Russians were advancing closer to Germany's borders every day and in the Atlantic the U-boats were increasingly on the run from the ships of the US and Royal Navies as well as the large number of long range patrol aircraft now operating from Scotland, Iceland, the American seaboard and Northern Ireland.

The U-boats had had a burst of activity in December 1944 but an increase in patrolling by 17 Gp units in the Cape Wrath – NW Ireland transit area and between Barra and Northern Ireland dealt with this threat. No 1674 HCU continued to train coastal crews throughout this period.

On 3 January, No 7 Liberator (Radar & Leigh Light) Course assembled at Aldergrove with eight crews. Two days later, No 15 Gp called upon the services of the HCU. A Mitchell had ditched and No 15 Gp requested an aircraft for ASR. A Halifax was prepared for a dawn take off but No15 Gp abandoned the search at 0715 hrs due to poor weather in the search area.

On the night of 12/13 January, a Mosquito from a base in England on a flight around Lough Neagh and back to its base went missing. Aldergrove's training aircraft were instructed to keep a look out on or near the Mosquitoes route. No trace of the aircraft was seen. Two days later No 15 Gp asked Aldergrove to provide aircraft for urgent operational sorties in the Irish Sea. Aldergrove offered two aircraft manned by pupil crews but, as these were not fitted with Leigh Lights and the Navy would not allow the use of flares in the area, the night sorties were cancelled and re-scheduled as dawn patrols. No 15 Gp cancelled the planned sorties when sufficient aircraft from operational squadrons were found.

No 5 Liberator course ended on 16 January and the crews were posted. F/O Hamilton and crew went to 224 Sqn, F/L Deleford and F/O Rowley to No 53 Sqn. F/O Frewen to No 120 Sqn. F/L Thorne and crew were posted to No 59 Sqn and the remaining crew to No 86 Sqn. The following day, No 17 Halifax Course commenced with three crews. Two crews were destined for the Met squadrons and the third to a VLR squadron.

No 15 Gp advised the station of a possible ASR task on the evening of 21 January. A Halifax captained by F/L McGonigal with a staff crew would take off at dawn to search for a ditched Halifax and its crew of eight. By midday on 22 January, the Halifax was still on the ground with its wings iced up and severe weather at Aldergrove. No 15 Gp cancelled the sortie but requested a stand by for a dawn take off on the 23rd. The next morning the sortie was again postponed due to bad weather in the search area. The aircraft and crew remained at readiness until 2100 hrs when No 15 Gp abandoned the search due to the weather. The same day No 15 Halifax Course completed its training and the crews were posted. The two VLR crews, those of F/O JB Goodyear and F/O

V Atkinson were posted to No 58 and No 502 Sqns respectively. The following day F/O Hughes and the officers of his crew on No 1 Fortress Course were posted to No 53 Sqn.

February saw a continuation in the training of Fortress, Halifax and Liberator crews and on 7 February, No 18 Halifax course assembled with two VLR crews and one Met crew. On 9 February, No 16 Halifax Course ended and two of the crews departed. F/L EL Holden's to No 58 Sqn and F/O FW Mawdsley's to No 502 Sqn. Five days later, No 9 Liberator Course commenced with eight Radar & Leigh Light crews.

On 16 February, the HCU lost a Liberator when EV954, captained by F/O PC Cox, flew into high ground. Cox, F/O JG Fenwick and Sgt W Howden were injured. The remainder of the crew, F/L KD Faulkner, F/O AL Whitney, F/O PG Sim, F/O ER Matthews, Sgt JE Morgan, Sgt HE Benwell and Sgt A Bladon were all killed.

Seven crews of No 7 Liberator Course graduated on 20 February. The crews of F/O HJ Oliver and F/O J Shelley were posted to 120 Sqn. F/L HE Addington's went to No 53 Sqn. F/L RJ Traill and F/O HC Kay's crews were allocated to No 86 Sqn and No 59 Sqn received F/O DG Reid and F/L CA Hobson and crews. A week later, No 17 Halifax Course ended with F/L D Chapman and P/O I Foy taking their crews to No 518 Sqn. F/O L Davey and his crew went to No 58 Sqn. The next day, the HCU continued on the treadmill of producing VLR and Met crews when No 19 Halifax Course commenced with four crews.

Training continued without incident until 19 March when Liberator KG896 crashed, fatally injuring all of the crew. The Liberator was captained by F/O WI Holmes and crewed by P/O AJ Pryde, F/O SFB Sargent, P/O RH Appleyard, F/O WD Cheyne, Sgt P McNeilly, Sgt RS Hook, Sgt RJ Edge, Sgt O Aston and Sgt DA Bates. The instructor, F/O CAJ Honey, was also killed. The next day, another four Halifax crews reported in and No 18 Halifax Course was posted out. P/O Foucard took his crew to No 518 Sqn whilst F/Os Rasmussen and Shackell took crews to No 58 Sqn. During the month the HCU had flown over 810 hours on the three types.

The war in Europe was now nearing its end with the Allies closing in on Berlin from all directions. The U-boat, however, was still a major threat to the convoys crossing the Atlantic and the shipping supplying the armies on the Continent. No 1674 HCU continued to train crews to defeat this threat and No 10 Liberator Course passed out on 18 April. The crews of F/O Chapple and F/L McCullough were posted to No 224 Sqn. F/L Nicholls took his crew to No 120 Sqn with F/O Lamont and crew. F/O Mason and crew were posted to No 53 Sqn. No 12 Liberator Course commenced on 19 April and three days later Liberator BZ880, piloted by F/L GB McDormand, was involved in an accident. The accident was not fatal however and McDormand took his crew to No 86 Sqn on posting three days later. The same day, the last crew of No 10 Liberator Course, captained by P/O Sarson, left for No 220 Sqn. No 2 Fortress Course had also ended and F/S Sedgwick took his crew to No 251 Sqn. Two new crews arrived to form No 3 Fortress Course the same day, captained by WO Fox and F/S Richards.

The second day of May 1945 saw No 22 Halifax Course, comprising the crews of S/L Piejus and F/S Buggy for Met training and F/O Smith and WO Robins for VLR training. The last day of the war in Europe saw No 11 Liberator Course posted out. Two days later, No 13 Liberator Course assembled, comprising F/L Pettman, F/L Seward, F/L Oughton, F/L Boyce, F/L Tuckett, F/L Petrie, F/L Bury, F/O Chave and F/L Moore and crews. The Japanese still had to be defeated.

On Monday 14 May 1945, the formal surrender of the U-boat fleet was taken by the C in C Western Approaches at Lisahally near Londonderry. A convoy of U-boats sailed from Loch Alsh to Londonderry escorted by a Liberator, Wellington and Sunderland of No 15 Gp. The surface escort was carried out by escort vessels of Western Approaches Command. The war in Europe was over and the scourge of the U-boat had been defeated, in no small part by the Ansons, Blenheims, Beaufighters, Whitleys, Fortresses and Liberators of the many Coastal Command squadrons to operate from Aldergrove. The war against Japan was not over however and Aldergrove continued to train crews for Coastal Command for some months to come.

With the end of the war against Germany, the Canadian and Australian personnel of the HCU courses were withdrawn from training and the crews of No 12 and 13 Liberator Courses were reformed to continue training. Re-organisation of the training within Coastal Command was inevitable with the shift in operational theatres to bring about the defeat of the Japanese and No 1674 HCU were informed that they would move to Lossiemouth on the Morayshire coast in July 1945. With the uncertainty of requirements for maritime operations against the Japanese No 22 Halifax Conversion Course completed training on 12 June and were sent on leave pending posting instructions. The Canadian Aircrew who had been withdrawn from training in May were posted to Bircham Newton on 24 June for repatriation to Canada. By the end of the month all of the Australians had also departed. With peace in Europe the RAF began to slowly return to something like a peacetime routine and during June an instructor from the RAF Central Band arrived on the station and a Military Band was formed. Around eighteen musicians from the station personnel volunteered and rehearsals commenced.

Chapter 13

JULY 1945 to DECEMBER 1945

On 5 July 1945 G/C TH Carr DFC AFC took over command of the station when G/C LR Briggs left on release fr,om the Service. On 17 July, the King and Queen, accompanied by Princess Elizabeth, visited Northern Ireland for a three day tour and Aldergrove accommodated, refuelled and serviced the fighter escort, comprising Mustangs flown by Polish pilots. The following day, an Investiture was held in Parliament Buildings at Stormont during which several station personnel received awards. W/C JB Grant received the DSO, S/L BE Peck and P/O SL McCaul the DFC. F/L G Davidson received the AFC and F/S JD Ackerman the MBE. During the royal visit, the Marine Craft Section on Lough Neagh stood by for ASR patrols during the flights to and from Londonderry. The patrols were marred by the death of AC1 Ashard who fell overboard from a pinnace and was drowned despite a gallant rescue attempt by AC1 McLoughlin. McLoughlin was recommended for a Mention in Despatches for the rescue attempt.

Prior to all the royal activity, No 1674 HCU had been preparing to depart and would leave the station for Milltown, Lossiemouth's satellite airfield. The planned completion date of the move was 14 August. While the HCU was planning to move out, No 1402 Met Flt was to return to Aldergrove from Ballyhalbert.

Another Liberator Conversion Course was completed on 25 July with the crews going to No 220 Sqn and five days later two crews of No 23 Halifax Conversion Course completed training. F/O Mitchell took his crew to No 520 Sqn and WO Amesbury left with his crew for No 518 Sqn. The last day of July saw Aldergrove once more transferred from No 17 Gp to the control of No 15 Gp.

The advance party of No 1674 HCU departed for Milltown by air on 1 August. The following day G/C MC Collins assumed command of RAF Aldergrove from G/C Carr, who had held the post for less than a month. On 7 August, the main party of the HCU departed, completing the move by 10 August. On 8 August, F/L RT Saunders brought No 1402 Met Flt back from its sojourn to Ballyhalbert. The Flt continued to carry out its planned sorties during the move and the rear party arrived from Ballyhalbert on 10 August.

A new unit arrived at Aldergrove on 12 August when the advance party of No 22 Aircrew Holding Unit (ACHU), comprising a F/L and seven other ranks arrived. They were followed by the main party the next day and settled into the station under the command of W/C RN Lambert. Three days later, the rear party of No 1674 HCU left for Milltown.

No 1 APC, a self-contained unit that had been at Aldergrove since the end of 1941, was disbanded on 1 September. The APC had controlled all of the armament practice areas on Lough Neagh and had played a large part in the success of the U-boat hunters of No 15 Gp. On 3 September, F/L Forbes-Clark DFC took over command of No 22 ACHU from W/C Lambert, who was leaving the service. On 7 September,

NORTHERN WING SEPTEMBER 29, 1945

BY L. RALPH BOSSENCE
'WING' STAFF REPORTER

R.A.F. "MET" MEN AT WORK

Flight with "met" boys from Aldergrove
After listening to the Commanding Officer of the R.A.F. meteorological squadron at Aldergrove yesterday tell how, with remarkably few casualties and accidents, Halifaxes have flown 2,500,000 miles during the War in all kinds of weather in order to forecast the weather, and how Hurricanes and Spitfires have roared six to eight miles into the stratosphere 8,600 times in order to do the same thing, I went for a half-hour spin about 800 feet over Lough Neagh and landed with a very severe gash indeed at the rear of my skull.

Criticism unjustified
The result is that I feel rather foolish – always keep your head lowered to about stomach level when you walk through a Halifax – and in no mood to join the critics of the Air Ministry weather forecasts we have had since the war ended.
Actually a lot of this criticism, I learned, is unjustified. The daily weather prophesies in the newspapers form an extremely small part of the meteorological squadron's work. No responsible "met" man would guarantee to forecast conditions accurately for longer than six hours ahead, and even then, he would be dealing with a restricted area. Nor does "fair" in meteorological language necessarily mean sunshine; it could mean simply a certain cloud condition.
So if you read that it will be fair and warmer in Northern Ireland to-morrow and it turns out wet, don't blame the 518 Squadron at Aldergrove. They wouldn't promise anything of the sort if it were left to them.

War service
It is pretty common knowledge that throughout the six years of war the information obtained by the squadrons at the four "met" stations in Great Britain and those in Iceland, Gibraltar and the Azores was of incalculable value to bombers, ack-ack batteries, U-boat hunters, transport ships and finally the invasion forces.
That great wartime organization has been immediately switched to the need of peace, and twice a day, still, at noon and midnight, Halifaxes make their triangular 1,500-mile, 10-hour flight from Northern Ireland over the Atlantic and back, while from the same station the 1402 Flight of Spitfires and Hurricanes, which have been operating from Northern Ireland bases for nine years, fly miles up towards the stratosphere.

"All weathers"
At each 50-mile stage of the Halifax's journey "met" readings are taken and periodically radio operators flash messages back to Aldergrove. These in turn are forwarded to a

"clearing house" in England, where all the messages from weather reconnaissance planes are correlated and a complete picture arrived at.

Pilots engaged in flying long-range meteorological aircraft have to have plenty of experience. They must be equally expert in dodging 100ft waves at sea-level, and flying by means of instruments in dense fog. Significantly, only four sorties were cancelled during the War and then it was because ice and snow on the runways made it impossible to take off.

But such incidents only serve to vary the monotony of the daily routine, which, though dull and unspectacular, nevertheless is now in peacetime, and will be in the future, an invaluable service to humanity at large.

Reproduced from 'Belfast Telegraph' September 29th, 1945.

Climbs 38,500 Feet for Clear Weather

The Aldergrove Experts

Flying sorties covering more than two-and-a-half million miles in long-range expeditions over the Atlantic, and 8,600 Hurricane and Spitfire flights reaching almost to the stratosphere, combine to make a proud record for the meteorological Squadron No 518 of RAF Coastal Command, with which is incorporated No 1402 Flight.

Headquarters are now at Aldergrove, one of the four stations in the United Kingdom providing the Air Ministry with weather details, but claiming no responsibility for the manner in which the forecast is given to the general public.

The 'Met' section is one of the only two branches of the RAF still performing its wartime job, the other being Air-Sea Rescue, and it is destined to guard the highways of peace against the forces of nature. Its development has been one of the less spectacular tasks of the Coastal Command, but the prodigious feats performed by its personnel in the worst Atlantic and local weather have made possible the planning of bomber raids, the hunting and destruction of U-boats, the transport of men and material from America, and a hundred and one other operations. It was 'Met' which provided the date of D-Day.

HOW THEY MAKE RECORDINGS

No 518 Squadron was the first to operate long-range Halifaxes for weather recordings, and at that time flew from the Island of Tiree, in the Western Hebrides. Two trips are made by the big aircraft every 24 hours, one at midnight and the other at mid-day, and from the time the airmen pass over the Foyle until they reach land again they travel about 1,600 miles – half the way to Newfoundland and back.

In the extreme western position the aircraft climbs to about 18,000 feet (approximately 3 ½ miles), and then follows the hazardous descent to sea level, where at times the breakers reach a height of 100 feet. Violent turbulence makes aircraft control an exhausting struggle and only very experienced pilots are engaged on the expeditions, which provide a ten-hour endurance test. Observations are transmitted at intervals and are picked up by ground stations.

A tribute to the skill of these unsung warriors is the fact that throughout the whole period of the war only four sorties had to be cancelled. In each case the cause was ice and snow on the runways and cross-winds which made it impossible to take off. Three aircraft were reported missing and one 'ditched' in Northern Ireland, the crew being saved.

Throughout a period of almost nine years the No 1402 Flight (Hurricanes and Spitfires) personnel have made vertical ascents almost to the stratosphere from either Aldergrove or Ballyhalbert and during that time only twelve climbs have been missed.

MEN MUST BE VERY TOUGH

'Expert' must be written over every one of these pilots, who take the Spitfires to a height of 40,000 to 42,000 feet (eight miles) and the Hurricanes six miles. They have to be well above average in health and toughness to combat altitude troubles, such as 'The Bends' – air bubbles in the blood – which cause intense pain.

Their worst enemy is the weather they go up to record. Often they have to rely entirely upon instruments, taking off and landing in darkness and fog, but even the blizzards of last January did not stop them. They scraped ice and snow from the wings and took off from snow-covered runways. One of the most remarkable experiences fell to a Birmingham pilot, who took off in ten-tenths cloud and climbed to 38,500 feet before he came to clear weather.

Some outstanding records were set up by the Flight in the early years of the war when there was a shortage of pilots. For three months there were only three pilots in the Flight and they often flew twice daily. In fact one who had to bale out at midday was back again on the job in the evening. The record for all 'Met' flying in Britain was gained by a Bromley (Kent) pilot who made 647 day and night ascents in 18 months. In six months a former squadron leader made 254 ascents.

SENT TO LEAD FORTRESSES

So expert were these skymen in bad flying weather that during the war they were called upon to meet Flying Fortresses crossing the Atlantic in rain and low cloud, and lead them to airfields. Once one of them 'bumped into' two Forts without clues to get down, and made two journeys to bring both safely into Nutts Corner.

There have been a number of life and death dramas, but only one pilot has been lost during the history of the Flight. He disappeared completely, being last heard of at 23,000 feet.

These hazardous jobs are undertaken in a light-hearted manner by a body of brave men, determined to do their job well. Don't grumble too much next time you hear the weather forecast, but give a thought to the gallant lads who risk such dangers. The lowest temperature they have recorded is 70 degrees below zero (Fah.)

No 1402 Met Flt lost its independence when it was absorbed into No 518 Sqn. No 518 Sqn were due to arrive shortly and the Hurricanes and Spitfires of the erstwhile Met Flt continued to carry out THUM and Prata flights daily. The 15 September saw the commemoration of the Battle of Britain by the Station and the day started with church services and parades. In the afternoon, the Station opened to the public in the first post-war 'At Home Day'. Despite poor weather,

A Spitfire of No 1402 (Met) Flt over Ballymena
(R Robertson)

10,000 visitors arrived during the four-hour open day. This number is all the more remarkable considering there was an International soccer match in Belfast and Field Marshal Montgomery was receiving the freedom of the City of Londonderry. Additional buses and trains were provided during the day and remarkably 2,000 private cars were parked on the station.

No 1 hangar held a display of engines, dinghies, parachutes, flares, bombs and gun turrets and a vast array of aircraft, including a Lancaster, Fortress, Stirling, Halifax, Warwick, Spitfire, Hurricane, Corsair, Wellington, Anson, Martinet, Mustang, Oxford and the Commanding Officer's Tiger Moth were on display on the tarmac. The CO's Tiger Moth began the day in spotless condition but by the end had received some rough handling by the visitors. The Chief Technical Officer was optimistic that his staff would be able to replace the broken ribs!

The Operations Block was set up to display a typical day during the peak of the Battle of the Atlantic, but No 23 MU provided the' showstopper' for the crowd by allowing them to clamber all over an Anson, Wellington and Stirling which were due for write off. Long queues assembled for this privilege throughout the day. The day ended when the Adjutant forcibly evicted the last visitor –a small boy – from the tail turret of one of the aircraft!

The following day, a large parade was held in Belfast and the station provided three contingents comprising 50 Aircrew, fifty maintenance crew and fifty WAAF. Three Hurricanes of No 518 Sqn provided the flypast.

On 18 September, No 518 Sqn proper began to arrive from Tiree and Tain. The

A Met Observer in the nose of a No 518 Sqn Halifax. (R Robertson)

squadron was visited by the press on 28 September and the following day the Pathe Pictorial Film Unit arrived and began shooting film of Spitfires and Halifaxes in the air and on the ground and crews boarding and briefing. That same day, the Station provided another contingent for a parade in Belfast. Aldergrove was getting its share of publicity.

On 8 October, the first Warwick of a detachment of No 280 Sqn arrived, captained by F/L O'Reilly. The detachment would have responsibility for ASR in the area. A second Warwick, captained by F/L Jeffcott, arrived two days later. The final two aircraft of the detachment arrived on 11 October. The Station was involved in yet another parade on 13 October in Antrim followed by another on the following day in Crumlin. The public loved them but the CTO complained about the loss of manpower.

During the month, No 518 Sqn carried out 58 long range Met recces with their Halifaxes and 121 'vertical ascents' in the Spitfires. Among the more unusual sorties carried out by the squadron were those to fly supplies of chlorine from the mainland for water purification in Londonderry and Dublin. The squadron took umbrage at press reports stating that these sorties had been carried out by Transport Command. The sorties had been made necessary by the Dock Strike spreading to Northern Ireland.

The Station observed Remembrance Day on 11 November with a parade and church service for the first time since the outbreak of war. On 27 November, a sign that the Station was reverting to peacetime routines came when officers of Queens University Air Squadron arrived to arrange accommodation for the unit. Aldergrove would soon assume parent Unit responsibility for this unit.

On 29 November, the No 280 Sqn Warwick detachment saw action when Warwick 'F' was scrambled, captained by F/O O'Reilly, to search for an Anson missing on a flight from RAF Jurby, on the Isle of Man. A search was carried out on tracks east

The crew of a No 518 Sqn Halifax on return from a 10-hour 'Met' flight. *(R Robertson)*

A Halifax and Spitfire of No 518 Sqn formate over Ulster in 1945. Slemish Mountain, near Ballymena, can be seen between the two aircraft. *(RAF Aldergrove)*

and west of Wigtown Bay and at 0544 hrs red flares were sighted on the port bow. At 0602 hrs, a dinghy was sighted with the aid of markers and flares. The Anson crew were subsequently rescued in fit condition and returned to Jurby. During the month, despite very poor weather, No 518 Sqn managed to carry out 36 long range met recce sorties and 122 'vertical ascents'.

On 2 December, F/O MacLachlan of No 518 Sqn took off in his Spitfire for a 'Vertical Ascent' and when he was at approximately 25,000 feet the engine developed a Glycol leak which caught fire. MacLachlan made an extremely rapid descent and landed to have the fire extinguished in just over three minutes.

The war had been over for almost three months and the struggle against the U-boat for longer so it came as a surprise to F/O O'Reilly when he was scrambled in Warwick 'U' on 5 December to search for just such a vessel. The aircraft took off at 1019 hrs to search for the U-boat, which was unmanned and adrift, causing a danger to shipping. The danger was exacerbated by the fact that the U-boat was loaded with explosives. The U-boat was not sighted.

On 7 December, Aldergrove took responsibility for the Radar site at Ballywattick near Larne. On 12 December, an aircraft was reported to have crashed in the sea off Blackpool and Warwick 'F' of No 280 Sqn, under the command of WO Barnes, took off at 1302 hrs to carry out an ASR search. The Warwick worked in co-operation with a lifeboat but nothing was sighted.

On 17 December, a Court of Inquiry was convened to inquire into the absence of an airman. AC1 Cahan, a native of Eire, had gone absent, leaving a charming note in which he stated that he would not be returning to RAF Aldergrove as he felt his health was failing and food was so much better in the 'South' "Therefore," he went

This page and opposite page: Two views of a No 202 Sqn Halifax Met Mk VI crashed at Aldergrove by F/L Thorne on 29 Oct 46. Note the aircraft still carries the No 518 Sqn artwork on the nose.
(K Atkinson via Geoff Gardiner).

on. "after long and faithful service it is with regret that I tender my resignation from the Royal Air Force. Please send my medals to the above address and I shall be proud and happy to wear them."

Aldergrove took responsibility for Queens UAS on 18 December and on 22 December, the station closed down for the first peacetime Christmas break since 1938. No 518 Sqn continued to work at minimum manning and on Christmas Day, the officers and SNCOs served dinner to the other ranks. A free cinema show and a dance followed this. On the 29th, the station hosted a children's Christmas party and the last day of the year saw Aldergrove able to look back on a highly successful war. During the conflict the Station and its squadrons had had its share of success and, sadly, losses too. In the last year of the war practically every crew engaged in hunting U-boats and carrying out the vital task of Met Recce passed through No 1674 HCU and Aldergrove. The station had hosted almost all of the Northern Ireland based units for bombing and gunnery practice at No 1 APC from 1941 onwards and the ranges at Lough Neagh had been the location of many trials and experiments including low level attacks by night using radar homing and Leigh Light techniques. Aldergrove had had a hard war and now would enjoy the peace.

Chapter 14

ALDERGROVE POST WAR
JANUARY 1946 TO PRESENT

No 518 Sqn soldiered on at Aldergrove with their Halifaxes carrying out the routine of met sorties required by the forecasters, which were so essential to RAF operations.

No 502 Sqn was reformed at Aldergrove on 10 May 1946, equipped with De Havilland Mosquito B.25s, NF.30s and a single Mk III.

No 518 Sqn was renumbered No 202 Sqn on 1 October 1946 and retained the Halifax until it was replaced by another Handley Page product, the Hastings, in October 1950. A conversion flight began to train the crews in August 1950. On 18 August, No 22 Recruiting Centre, which was situated at Aldergrove, was redesignated No 4 Reception Centre. No 224 Sqn was reformed at Aldergrove on 1 March 1948 under the command of S/L Davidson DFC to complement No 202 Sqn in the meteorological reconnaissance role. No 224 Sqn was equipped with Halifax Mk VI.

In November 1948, No 502 Sqn relinquished its Mosquitoes in favour of Spitfires and then re-equipped with Vampire FB5s which it retained until 1953. This was not the last

F/L Thorne was involved in another incident in the summer of 1947 when the port inner propeller of this Halifax was lost on a Bismuth sortie. Note the No 518 Sqn badge on the nose almost a year later.
(G Briggs via Geoff Gardiner).

Halifax Met Mk VI Y3-A of No 202 Sqn pictured at Middleton St George in 1950. *(Geoff Gardiner).*

the station would see of the Mosquito, however, as the Station Flight would continue to operate the type, alongside Oxfords and Tiger Moths, well into the 1950s. The Mosquitoes were used for fighter affiliation and drogue towing for air to air gunnery. In January 1949, the station began a refurbishment programme for the Lough Neagh ranges to allow No 502 Sqn to carry out air to sea firing. September 1949 saw a detachment of No 617 Sqn with Lincolns from the 12th to the 14th.

Halifax Met Mk VI Y3-Q of No 202 Sqn pictured at Middleton St George in 1950. *(Geoff Gardiner).*

A Halifax Met Mk VI of No 202 Sqn takes off from Aldergrove in 1950. *(B Mitchell via Geoff Gardiner).*

By October 1949, the main aircraft being dealt with by No 23 MU were Ansons, Oxfords and Lincolns. Another unit operating from Aldergrove at this time was the RAF Northern Ireland Communications Flight equipped with Ansons and Proctors. This flight was renamed No 67 group Communication Flight in April 1950. On 20 February 1951 Canberra B.2 WD932 staged through Aldergrove en route to America for demonstration flights for the USAF. On 31 August 1951 another Canberra, WD940, arrived at Aldergrove to make an attempt at the Atlantic record. The aircraft completed the trip in the record time of 4 hours 19 minutes.

Hastings Met Mk I Y3-K of No 202 Sqn on patrol at low level. *(B Mitchell via Geoff Gardiner).*

A pair of No 120 Sqn Shackleton GR Mk Is formate over the sea. *(RAF Aldergrove).*

No 224 Sqn left Aldergrove in August 1951 but the Coastal Command presence at Aldergrove was soon increased with the arrival of No 120 Sqn, one of the station wartime squadrons, in April 1952. No 120 Sqn were equipped with Avro Shackleton GR.1s. 18 February 1952 saw an increase in the station aircraft strength when four Lancasters of No 210 Sqn and two RCAF Lancasters arrived to take part in an exercise until 21 March. On 26 August 1952, Aldergrove was once again involved in a successful record breaking attempt when Wing Commander Beamont flew a Canberra on a double Atlantic crossing from Aldergrove to Gander in Newfoundland and return in record time.

North American F-86 Sabres on delivery to the RAF often staged through Aldergrove. *(RAF Aldergrove).*

W/C Beamont's record breaking Canberra being refuelled at Aldergrove. *(RAF Aldergrove)*

In 1953, No 502 Sqn began to replace its Vampire FB.5s with Vampire FB.9s and retained these until disbandment on 10 March 1957. Lord Wakehurst KCMG presented the squadron with its Standard on 24 May 1954 in a ceremony at Aldergrove.   In December 1954, the Station Flight was redesignated the Target Towing Flight. In November 1955, the Target Towing Flight began to operate Vampires alongside the venerable Mosquitoes, Ansons and Oxfords. The last flights by Mosquitoes at Aldergrove took place in January 1956 and the following month the Target Towing Flight reverted to the title of Station Flight. No 120 Sqn replaced its Shackleton GR.1s with MR.2s in April 1956 and retained this type until moving to Kinloss in 1959. In June 1956, No 120 Sqn won the Aird Whyte Trophy for the highest proficiency in bombing and air gunnery in Coastal Command. On 14 February 1957, Aldergrove began to operate aircraft of No 1913 Light Liaison Flight to provide air

V9 coded Vampire FB.5s and Meteor T.7s of No 502 Sqn. *(R Spencer via Geoff Gardiner).*

A Hastings of No 202 Sqn departs from Aldergrove on a goodwill tour of the Far East and Singapore on 15 Oct 53. *(RAF Aldergrove).*

support for No 39 Brigade in operations against the IRA. The Flight was equipped with five Auster AOP aircraft. In July 1957, squadrons of Fighter Command began to be detached to Aldergrove for the defence of Northern Ireland. The first to arrive was No 74 Sqn, from Horsham St Faith. The squadron remained at Aldergrove from 8 July to 1 August. Another new arrival was a detachment of No 275 Sqn, designated 'F' Flt, equipped with Sycamore helicopters for search and rescue duties. The detachment arrived on 9 July. The next Fighter Command detachments to arrive were No 43 Sqn from Leuchars between 6 and 16 August and No 64 Sqn from Duxford from 20 to 30 August 1957.

In September 1957, No 278 MU, a maintenance Command Repair and Salvage Unit which was lodging at Aldergrove was absorbed by No 23 MU. No 23 MU now became an Aircraft Storage Unit and a Repair and Salvage Unit. With the formation of the Army Air Corps in September 1957, No 1913 Flt was renamed No 13 Liaison Flt, part of No 651 Sqn, and transferred to the operational control of the Army. On 6 September, No 202 Sqn was presented with its Standard by HM the Queen in a ceremony at Aldergrove. Fighter Command detachments continued with No 63 Sqn from Waterbeach arriving on 3 September and staying until the 23rd. They were replaced by the return of No 74 Sqn from 23 to 30 September.

On 5 October 1957, Aldergrove was granted the freedom of the City of Belfast and a ceremonial parade took place in the city. October saw the arrival of No 152 Sqn on detachment from Stradishall between the 1st and 14th and No 19 Sqn from Church Fenton from 15 October to 4 November. The next squadrons to arrive were No 25 Sqn from Tangmere from 4 to 22 November and No 263 Sqn from Stradishall from 25 November to 13 December. No 72 Sqn arrived on 2 January 1958 and remained until the 24th, returning to Church Fenton. This squadron was to figure large in the life of the station in years to come. No 56 Sqn from Waterbeach replaced No 72 Sqn between 28 and 31 January.

The station Target Towing Flight operated Mosquitoes in the early 1950s. *(RAF Aldergrove).*

No 671 Gliding School redeployed from Bishops Court to Aldergrove during January for a trial period of six months.

The next batch of Fighter Command squadrons to arrive on detachment at Aldergrove was No 56 Sqn from 1 to 11 February and No 153 Sqn from 11 to 28 February. March 1958 saw the arrival of No 1 Sqn on detachment from Tangmere from the 4th to the 25th. The Hunters of No 54 Sqn arrived from Odiham on 30 April and returned on 20 May. Prior to their arrival the station had hosted the Meteor NF.12 and 14s of No 64 Sqn from 15 to 29 April. No 85 Sqn was the next fighter unit to arrive on detachment in May remaining until 17 June. In June 1958, 'F' Flt 275 Sqn became 'B' Flt. No 19 Sqn arrived on detachment on 17 June remaining until 6 July. During July a Coastal Command squadron, No 42, was detached from St Eval for an exercise from 6th to the 16th. During the period 26 August to 26 September, No 85 Sqn was once again detached to Aldergrove with its Meteors. No 25 Sqn who stayed between 14 and 18 October replaced them. No 25 Sqn were to be the last of the detached Fighter Command squadrons and the Fighter Squadron Support section (Northern Ireland), which had been set up to support these squadrons was disbanded on 31 January 1959. In November, the airfield was closed to allow for resurfacing of the runway intersection and was reopened on 8 December.

On 1 April 1959, No 120 Sqn departed Aldergrove for Kinloss and two days later 'B' Flt No 275 Sqn ceased operating from Aldergrove and the detachment moved to Leconfield on 14 April

May 1960 saw the flight of No 228 Sqn which was based at Aldergrove for search and rescue duties with Sycamore helicopters re-numbered as No 118 Sqn. No 118 Sqn remained at Aldergrove until disbanded on 31 August 1962. A major change occurred at Aldergrove on 26 September 1963 when the airfield became Belfast Airport taking over the role from Nutts Corner, which had reached the limit of expansion. No 202 Sqn, which had been based at Aldergrove for eighteen years, was disbanded on 31 July 1964. No 23 MU remained at Aldergrove until 1978 when it disbanded.

During the 1960s several helicopter detachments operated at Aldergrove in support of

'F' Flight of No 275 Sqn operated Sycamores similar to this one.

the Army and from 1968, with the increase in tension in the province, No 72 Sqn was detached regularly with its Wessex helicopters. They were first based at Bishops Court, then to Long Kesh and then Ballykelly before relocating to Aldergrove on 17 August 1969. In March 1970, crews from No 18 Sqn supported the detachment. In December 1972, No 33 Sqn detached four Pumas to Aldergrove and in October 1978 a Royal Navy Wessex detachment arrived on the station. No 72 Sqn would become permanently resident in the province in November 1981. In November 1992 No 230 Sqn relocated from Germany to Aldergrove complementing No 72 Sqn with its Pumas. In January 1997, No 72 Sqn had one flight of Wessex replaced by Pumas and operated both types from Aldergrove. These had previously been part of No 18 Sqn. In addition to the RAF presence at Aldergrove there were numerous Royal navy detachments throughout the 80s and 90s and the Army Air Corps presently have a squadron of Lynx and a squadron of Gazelle aircraft operating from the station alongside a flight of Islanders.

Aldergrove has had a long and illustrious history with a wide variety of training and operational units based on the unit. The recent rebuilding programme hopefully ensures that the station has a long life ahead of it. For the RAF the station was 'Ours To Hold' for 90 years. It will however, have the chain which links it to the RAF broken with the departure of No 230 Sqn to England in 2008, leaving the military section of the airfield in the hands of the Army Air Corps. The station has a glorious history and the RAF can be justifiably proud of its record.

THE END OF AN ERA

Appendix I

STATION COMMANDERS 1939 –1945

Dec 38 – Oct 39	W/C HC Samard
Oct 39 – Dec 40	G/C CS Richardson MBE
Dec 40 – Mar 41	G/C GW Bentley DFC
Mar 41 – Oct 41	W/C WR Leftlay
Oct 41 – Jun 43	G/C HN Hampton DFC
Jun 43 – Nov 43	G/C IE Brodie OBE
Nov 43 – Jul 45	G/C LR Briggs
Jul 45 – Aug 45	G/C CH Carr DFC AFC
Aug 45 – Mar 46	G/C MC Collins CBE

Halifax Y3-H salvage after ditching in Lough Neagh in 1948. *(N MCGarry).*

Appendix II

FLYING UNITS BASED AT ALDERGROVE 1939 – 1945

No 1 Armament Practice Camp
5 Nov 1941 - 1 Sep 1945
Codes: None

Aircraft types used	Examples
Battle	L5590
Dominie Mk I	X7406
Lysander TT Mk1	R2591
Lysander Mk II	P9125
Lysander Mk III	T1446
Lysander Mk IIIa	W6957
Magister	
Martinet Mk I	JN679
Master Mk II	DK951

No 1 (Coastal Command) Engine Control Demonstration Unit
19 Dec 1943 - 21 Apr 1944
Codes: Individual Letters

Aircraft types used	Examples
Wellington	

No 1 Operational Training Unit Liberator Conversion Flight
6 Sep 1943 – 10 Oct 1943
Codes: Individual Letters or numbers

Aircraft types used	Examples
Liberator Mk III	FK219
Liberator Mk V	FL981

No 3 Air Observer School
17 Apr 1939 – 1 Nov 1939
Codes: None

Aircraft types used	Examples
Battle	L4995
Gauntlet	
Gladiator	
Hart	K3892
Henley Mk III	L3375
Heyford Mk II	K6904
Heyford Mk III	K5191, K5192, K5196, K5198, K6857, K6864, K6876
Shark	
Swordfish	
Wallace Mk I	K3657, K3906, K3908, K4017, K4018, K8901, K5080
Wallace Mk II	K6014, K8701

No 3 Bombing & Gunnery School
1 Nov 1939 - mid Jul 1940
Codes: Individual Numbers

Aircraft types used	Examples
Battle	K7646, L5011, L5129, L5136:8, L5386, N2228
Battle Trainer	R7384:9
Botha	L6288, L6123
Demon	K8196
Gauntlet Mk II	K5279, K5280, K5282, K5283
Gladiator Mk II	N5592
Henley Mk III	L3308
Heyford Mk III	K6857, K6885, K6864
Magister	P2402
Shark	L2377

Swordfish	L2799
Wallace Mk I	K3562, K3672, K5074, K5076, K5082
Wallace Mk II	K6083, K8696, K8699

No 4 Coastal Patrol Flight
1 Dec 1939 – 6 Dec 39
Codes: None

Aircraft types used	Examples
Tiger Moth Mk II	N6717, N6719, N6720 N6721, N6722
Hornet Moth	W5747, W5752, W9383, W9388

No 9 Operational Training Unit
7 Jun 1942 – 14 Sep 1942
Codes: 3 and 4

Aircraft types used	Examples
Beaufighter Mk Ic	T4655:4S
Beaufighter Mk VI	EL357L4L
Beaufighter Mk X	JM220
Beaufighter Mk XI	JM117:4T
Beaufort Mk I	N1014, N1038, N1096, N1161, N1175
Beaufort Mk II	JM574
Lysander Mk III	V9906
Magister	N3957
Martinet Mk I	HN863:3C
Master	
Oxford Mk I	ED177, NM748
Oxford Mk II	P8919
Tiger Moth Mk II	L6921

Commanding Officers

7 Jun 1942 – 14 Sep 1942	W/C Woodruff

No 15 Group Operational Practice Flight
Oct 1941 – 5 Nov 1941
Codes: None

Aircraft types used	Examples
Lysander Mk III	T1548

No 48 Sqn
Jul 1940 – 20 Nov 1940 (Detachment)
Codes: OY
Sep 1941 – 15 Oct 1941 (Detachment)

Aircraft types used	Examples
Anson Mk I	K6153, K6154, K6155, K6156, K6157, K6159, K6164

Commanding officers

Jul 1940 – 5 Nov 1940	W/C Findlay
5 Nov 1940 – 20 Nov 1940	S/L RH Harris
Sep 1941 – 15 Oct 1941	S/L Wherry

No 59 Sqn
7 May 1943 - 13 Sep 1943
Codes: 1 and WE

Aircraft types used	Examples
Liberator Mk V	BZ712: 1-D, BZ764:1-J, BZ781:WE-A, BZ821:WE-Q, BZ912:WE-Z, FL946:1-M, FL951:1-J, FL972:E, FL973:C, FL975:B, FL976:WE-N, FL977:H, FL981:1-B, FL984:S, FL988:WE-R,FL990:A

Commanding Officers

7 May 1943 - 7 Jul 1943	W/C GCC Bartlett AFC
7 Jul 1943 – 13 Sep 1943	W/C PA Gilchrist DFC

No 86 Sqn
3 Feb 1943 - 18 Mar 1943 (Detachment)
Codes: Individual codes
18 Mar 1943 – 4 Sep 1943

Aircraft types used	Examples
Liberator Mk IIIa	FK223:U, FK226:G, FK229:B, FK231:K, FK233:X, FK234: W, FK241:Y, FL907:F, FL916:N, FL922:Z, FL930:R, FL931:M, FL932:H, FL943:L
Liberator Mk V	BZ719:K, BZ724:E, BZ772:J, BZ788:W, BZ802:V, BZ870: S, BZ877:B, BZ919:T, BZ943:N, FL944:Y, FL952:L, FL954:Z, FL955:P,

Commanding Officers

23 Feb 1943 – 4 Sep 1943	W/C RD Williams

No 102 Sqn
Sep 1940 - 8 Oct 1940 (Detachment)
Codes: DY

Aircraft types used	Examples
Whitley Mk V	P4995:DY-P

Commanding Officers

Sep 1940 – 8 Oct 1940	W/C SR Groom

No 120 Sqn
14 Feb 1943 - 13 Apr 1943
Codes: Individual code

Aircraft types used	Examples
Liberator Mk I	AM916:OH-L, AM929:H
Liberator Mk III	FK214:H later B, FK220:K, FK223:T, FK224:J, FK225:G, FK228:M, FK233:J, FL913:E, FL928:R, FL933:O, FL943: N, LV340:X, LV345:G
Liberator Mk IIIa	FK222:U

Commanding Officers

14 Feb 1943 - 1 Apr 1943	W/C PA Gilchrist DFC
1 Apr 1943 - 13 Apr 1943	W/C RM Longmore OBE

No 143 Sqn
15 Jun 1941 – 5 Jul 1941
Codes: HO
14 Dec 1941 – 23 Apr 1942

Aircraft types used	Examples
Beaufighter Mk Ic	T3231, T3234, T3241, T3244, T3245, T3246, T3248
Blenheim Mk IV	N3531, N3533, N3603:HO-B, P4835, V5447, Z5731, Z5972

Commanding Officers

14 Dec 1941 - 5 Apr 1942	W/C GV Garey
5 Apr 1942 – 23 Apr 1942	W/C Thornhill

No 206 Sqn
1 Mar 1941 – 15 Apr 1941 (Detachment)
Codes: VX
9 Aug 1941 – 30 Jun 1942

Aircraft types used	Examples
Hudson Mk I	N7275:VX-R, N7311:VX-G, N7367:VX-E, N7402, P5120: VX-C, P5143:VX-M, P5178:VX-V, R4059:VX-R, T9288: VX-L, T9303:VX-V, T9350:VX-J
Hudson Mk II	T9383:VX-Q
Hudson Mk III	T9392:VX-R, T9454:VX-J, T9463:VX-Q
Hudson Mk IV	T9431, T9444:VX-A, T9453:VX-Q, T9458:VX-H, AE611, AE612:VX-O, AE620:VX-F, AE623:VX-P, AE629:VX-T
Hudson Mk V	AE648:VX-N, AM570:VX-P, AM587:VX-D, AM588, AM604 :VX-J, AM605:VX-K, AM613:VX-G, AM622:VX-L, AM664:VX-B, AM689:VX-P, AM706, AM711:VX-U, AM722:VX-R, AM734:VX-O, AM762:VX-S, AM788:VX-A, AM805:VX-W, AM875:VX-U

Commanding Officers

1 Mar 1941 – 15 Apr 1941	W/C CD Candy
Aug 1941 – Jun 1942	W/C AF Hards
Jun 1942 - 26 Jun 1942	W/C Cooke
29 Jun 1942 - 30 Jun 1942	W/C RJS Romanes DFC

No 220 Sqn
14 Feb 1943 - 12 Mar 1943
Codes: Individual codes

Aircraft types used	Examples
Fortress Mk II	FK186:S, FK206:K, FL459:J

Commanding Officers

14 Feb 1943 – 12 Mar 1943	W/C PE Haddon

No 224 Sqn
13 Sep 1940 - 10 Dec 1940
Codes: QX
1 Mar 1941 - 15 Apr 1941 (Detachment)
15 Apr 1941 –

Aircraft types used	Examples
Hudson Mk I	N7272, T9277, T9278, T9326, T9328
Hudson Mk III	T9416, T9417, T9419, T9420, T9425, T9426

Commanding Officers

13 Sep 1940 - 10 Dec 1940	S/L CFC Wright DFC
1 Mar 1941 – end 1941	W/C TC Curnow

No 231 Sqn
1 Jul 1940 – 15 Jul 1940
Codes: VM

Aircraft types used	Examples
Lysander Mk II	N1213, N1220, N1276, P9097, R2028
Mentor	
Oxford	
Tiger Moth Mk II	N9127

Commanding Officers

1 Jul 40 – 15 Jul 1940	S/L Humphries

No 233 Sqn
2 Aug 1940 -Sep 1940
Codes: ZS
7 Dec 1940 – 9 Aug 1941

Aircraft types used	Examples
Hudson Mk I	N7226:ZS-D, N7253:ZS-N, N7269:ZS-B, N7326:ZS-F, N7372:ZS-Y, P5117:ZS-S, P5156, T9248, T9270, T9284: ZS-J, T9313, T9317, T9365:ZS-K
Hudson Mk II	N7209, N7218:I, N7223, N7296, P5123, T9372, T9378: ZS-U, T9379, T9430:ZS-E later L, T9447, T9451:ZS-X
Hudson Mk III	AE535:ZS-F, AE591:ZS-E, AE606:ZS-M, AM536:ZS-J, AM541, AM582

Commanding Officers

2 Aug 1940 – Sep 1940	W/C HA Purvis DFC AFC
7 Dec 1940 – May 1941	W/C HA Purvis DFC AFC
May 1941 – 9 Aug 1941	W/C EC Kidd AFC AFM

No 235 Sqn
13 Mar 1941 - (Detachment)
Codes: LA

Aircraft types used	Examples
Blenheim Mk If	K7116, K7120, K7122, K7132

Commanding Officers

13 Mar 1941 – end 1941	S/L IMT Bocock

No 236 Sqn
17 Sep 1940 - 26 Oct 1940
(Detachment)
Codes: FA and ND
1 Mar 1941 –6 May 1941 (Detachment)

Aircraft types used	Examples
Blenheim Mk I	2798:G, 3600:R, K7132, K7139, K7140, K7143
Blenheim Mk IV	T1811:W, T1942:FA-J and U, T1954:V, Z5737:A, Z5739:H, Z5740:J

Commanding Officers

17 Sep 1940 – 26 Oct 1940	S/L Montague

No 245Sqn
20 Jul 1940 – 15 Jul 1941
Codes: DX

Aircraft types used	Examples
Hurricane Mk I	N2486, N2707, P2906, P3099, P3385, V7678
Magister	N3861

Commanding Officers

20 Jul 1940 – 16 Dec 1940	S/L EW Whitley DFC
16 Dec 1940 – Jun 1941	S/L JWC Simpson DFC*
Jun 1941 – 15 Jul 1941	S/L WF Blackadder DSO

No 248 Sqn
26 Aug 1941 - (Detachment)
Codes: WR

Aircraft types used	Examples
Beaufighter Mk Ic	T4628, T4657, T4660, T4661, T4664, T4668

Commanding Officers

26 Aug 1941 – end 1941	W/C HG Wise DFC

No 252 Sqn
3 Apr 1941 - 15 Jun 1941
Codes PN and BT

Aircraft types used	Examples
Beaufighter Mk Ic	T3229, T3231, T3235, T3239, T3241, T3242
Beaufighter Mk If	R2153:PN-B, R2198, R2199, R2269, T3235, T3241
Blenheim Mk IV	Z6245

Commanding Officers

26 Apr 1941 - 15 Jun 1941	W/C Kidd AFC DFC

No 254 Sqn
20 Jul 1940 -
Codes   QY
5 May 1941 - 28 May 1941
(Detachment)
28 May 1941 – 15 Dec 1941

Aircraft types used	Examples
Blenheim Mk IV	L8841, N3610, T2120, Z6025, Z6027:Q

Commanding Officers

20 Jun 1940 – end 1940	S/L Hoskins
5 May 1941 - 18 Jul 1941	F/L Illingworth DFC
18 Jul 1941 - 15 Dec 1941	F/L GCB Bernard-Smith (later W/C)

No 272 Sqn
19 Nov 1940 –1 Jun 1941
Codes: ZK

Aircraft types used	Examples
Blenheim Mk IVf	L9252, L9415, N3526, N3542, P4845, V5754:ZK-A, T1950, T1954, Z5733, Z5750, Z5752, Z5756

Commanding Officers	
19 Nov 1940 – 1 Jun 1941	S/L AW Fletcher DFC

No 280 Sqn
8 Oct 1945 - (Detachment)
Codes   MF

Aircraft types used	Examples
Warwick Mk I	HG211:MF-X
Warwick Mk VI	HF984

No 311 Sqn
26 Apr 1942 - 12 Jun 1942
Codes: KX

Aircraft types used	Examples
Wellington Mk Ic	N2752, N2772, Z1150:KX-N, DV716:KX-Z

Commanding Officers	
26 Apr 1942 - 12 Jun 1942	W/C J Snajdr

No 402 Met Flight
Oct 1936 – 15 Jan 1941
Codes: None

Aircraft types used	Examples
Bulldog	
Gladiator Mk II	N5583, N5591, N5592, N5593

No 416 Flight
25 Jun 1940 - 1 Jul 1940
Codes: None

Aircraft types used	Examples
Lysander Mk II	N1210, N1264, N1269, N1270, N1302
Oxford	

Commanding Officers

25 Jun 40 – 1 Jul 1940	S/L Humphries

No 502 Sqn
15 May 1925 - 27 Jan 1941
Codes: YG

Aircraft Types used	Examples
Anson Mk I	N5049:YG-A, N5050:YG-B, N5063:YG-N, N5104, N5105:YG-D, N5109:YG-P, N5216:YG-S, N5234, N5237: YG-V, N5374, N5237:YG-V, N5374:YG-W, N9629:YG-E, N9631:YG-Z, N9899:YG-H, N9918:YG-B, R3335:YG-N
Botha Mk I	
Whitley Mk V	P5041:YG-C, P5054:YG-C, P5090:YG-L, T4168:YG-E, T4219:YG-P, T4277:YG-J

Commanding Officers

3 Sep 1939 – 30 Nov 1940	S/L Briggs
30 Nov 1940 - 27 Jan 1941	W/C TB Cooper

No 518 Sqn
7 Sep 1945 – 18 Sep 1945 (Detachment)
Codes: Y3
18 Sep 1945 – 1 Oct 1946

Aircraft types used	Examples
Halifax Mk III	RG390:Y3-A1
Halifax Mk V	LK688:Y3-H
Halifax Mk VI	RG780:Y3-M

Hurricane Mk IIc	PG469:Y3-K
Oxford Mk I	PG969
Spitfire Mk VII	MD181

Commanding Officers

7 Sep 1945 – 1 Oct 1946	W/C EEM Angell

No 547 Sqn
Oct 1944 - Jan 1945 (Detachment)
Codes

Aircraft types used	Examples
Liberator	

No 607 Sqn
9 Feb 1941 – Feb 1941 (Detachment)
Codes: AF

Aircraft types used	Examples
Hurricane Mk I	P2617, P2874:AF-F, P2901

Commanding Officers

9 Feb 1941 – Feb 1941	S/L AW Vincent

No 774 Sqn FAA
25 Dec 1939 - 5 Jul 1940
Codes: S6

Aircraft types used	Examples
Roc Mk I	L3138
Shark Mk II TT	K8914:F
Skua Mk II	L3029
Swordfish Mk I	L2732:S6-A

Commanding Officers

5 Dec 1939 – 5 Jul 1940	Lt Cdr WGC Stokes RN

No 1402 Met Flight
15 Jan 1941 - 3 Dec 1944
Codes: DQ
8 Aug 1945 – 7 Sep 1945

Aircraft types used	Examples
Blenheim Mk IV	Z7345, Z7349
Gladiator Mk I	K7918, K7927,
Gladiator Mk II	N5575, N5576, N5590, N5591, N5592, N5620, N5637, N5703, N5717, N5900
Hampden	P1196, P1314
Hudson Mk III	V9068, V9156, V9159, FH407
Hurricane Mk IIc	PG469, PZ754, PZ756, PZ759, PZ774, PZ799, PZ805, PZ815, PZ853
Spitfire Mk Va	P8036
Spitfire Mk VI	EN176, BR298
Spitfire Mk VII	MB159, MD181

Commanding Officers

15 Jan 1941 - 7 Apr 1942	F/L Chave-Jones (later S/L)
12 May 1942 - 10 Dec 1943	F/L Heaphy (later S/L)
10 Dec 1943 - 25 Jul 1944	F/L PE Daniels
25 Jul 1944 – 8 Sep 1944	F/O Hicks
8 Sep 1944 – 6 Oct 1944	F/L RG Brown AFC
6 Oct 1944 – 3 Dec 1944	F/L EJ Woosley RAAF (later S/L)
8 Aug 1945 – 7 Sep 1945	F/L RT Saunders

No 1405 Met Flight
3 Mar 1941 – Mar 1942
Codes: None

Aircraft types used	Examples
Blenheim	L6291, V5691, V5692
Blenheim Mk IV	Z7345
Hampden Mk I	AD724
Hudson Mk III	V9156, V9161
Hudson Mk IIIa	FH407

Commanding Officers

Mar 1941 – Mar 1942	F/L Ritchie

No 1674 Heavy Conversion Unit
10 Oct 1943 - Oct 1943
Codes: Individual numbers
5 Feb 1944 – 10 Aug 1945

Aircraft types used	Examples
Fortress Mk I	AN519, AN537
Fortress Mk II	FA702
Fortress Mk IIa	FK201
Halifax	DT642, JB963
Halifax Mk II	R9434, W1060, HX176
Liberator	BZ880, EV954, KG896
Liberator Mk III	LV343:12
Liberator Mk V	BZ786
Liberator Mk VI	BZ966
Liberator Mk VIII	KK297

Commanding Officers

19 Jun 1944 - 10 Aug 1945	W/C WH Ingle

METEOROLOGICAL RECONNAISSANCE CITATION

Meteorological Reconnaissance in World War II

In early 1941, a small number of Meteorological Reconnaissance Units were established in the United Kingdom, the organization growing until, at its peak, it consisted of eighteen Squadrons and Flights with over 750 personnel involved in the task of gathering vital meteorological information to assist the Allied cause.

Meteorological reconnaissance sorties were flown predominantly by Royal Air Force and Commonwealth crews although a few airmen from the Air Forces of occupied Europe also flew these aircraft. The weather conditions encountered on many of the flights were very hostile and operations called for exceptional qualities of dedication and courage by the crews. Reconnaissance sorties were flown both deep into enemy territory and over the surrounding seas and hostile waters of the Atlantic Ocean. By the end of the War, over 16,000 sorties had been flown and 52 aircraft had failed to return. The observations were used extensively in the preparation of weather forecasts which allowed Allied Commanders to undertake military actions with increased confidence and minimum risk.

It is a pleasure and privilege to record the gratitude of both the Royal Air Force and the Meteorological Office for the endeavours of the Meteorological Reconnaissance Squadrons and Flights during the Second World War. The example and zeal of the crews set a precedent of dedicated service and excellence which remains in meteorological observing and reconnaissance flights to this day.

Air Chief Marshal Sir Peter Harding,
GCB FRAeS CBIM
Chief of the Air Staff
Royal Air Force

Sir John Houghton,
CBE FRS
Chief Executive
Meteorological Office

Appendix IV

PRESS NOTES FOR VISIT TO METOROLOGICAL SQUADRON RAF STATION ALDERGROVE ON FRIDAY 28TH SEPTEMBER 1945

Weather Flights – A Story behind the Weather Forecasts

Now guarding the highways of peace against the forces of Nature, after a notable war-time record, are the Meteorological Squadrons of RAF Coastal Command.

When hostilities ceased and thousands of aircrew had completed their task, there was no relaxation for the men of the "met" aircraft. A great organisation built up during the war years was immediately adapted to the need of peace.

Today and every day, in summer and winter, sunshine or snow, long-range aircraft from "met" squadrons based in England, Scotland, Ireland, Gibraltar and Iceland fly distances up to 1,600 miles. At regular intervals each day fighters climb almost to the stratosphere. They provide the information, which in addition to its other uses is fundamental for the forecasters who issue the Air Ministry weather bulletins, which are broadcast and published in the daily newspapers.

And, because of the growing importance of upper air observations, "met" flying, which was carried out on a small scale in pre-war days, has come to stay. With accumulating data the meteorologist has been able to extend his scientific principles to the third dimensions, and upper air observations have been found to give more faithful indications of atmospheric changes. Already plans are being formulated to extend the service with all-British Halifax aircraft, and there is a possibility that France and other Continental countries will co-operate.

The development of "met" flying during the war has been one of the less spectacular tasks of RAF Coastal Command, but one which has contributed in no small measure to the total defeat of the enemy. In September, 1939, only four "met" flights were made daily, but in May 1945, the organisation had expanded to 30 sorties each day in the European theatre alone, half of this number consisting of long-range flights with an average duration of 10 hours.

When war broke out the loss of many sources of meteorology was a severe handicap. Ships could no longer risk sending their Atlantic reports by wireless, and the once Continental section of the weather maps gradually became uncharted region. Meteorologists eagerly sought the assistance of aircraft reports in all areas.

Late in 1940 meteorological reconnaissance sorties over the Atlantic and North Sea were started. The first aircraft were Blenheims flying a total sortie of 600 nautical miles with a vertical climb at the turning point. In order to increase the range, Hudsons were later brought into these flights. In spite of the small numbers of aircraft and limited bad weather aids, these early sorties were flown with astonishing regularity and on many occasions the "met" aircraft alone were performing prodigious feats in the worst Atlantic weather to make possible the safer and more economical operation of other squadrons.

By the beginning of 1943, the widening scope of Allied operations made accurate knowledge of weather more important than ever. But the increase of "met" activities also meant that aircraft and equipment were needed everywhere in greater quantities. Only obsolescent Hampdens were available to replace the ageing Hudsons; both ground and aircrews did wonders to fulfil their commitments.

By the end of 1943 new and improved equipment arrived and, eventually, all squadrons were equipped with four-engined aircraft – Halifaxes or Fortresses. Each crew had a specially trained "met" air observer, drawn from volunteers with previous "met" experience.

Month in, month out, the "met" flights and squadrons have continued their invaluable work, providing a constant weather guard from the Arctic to the Azores. More than 20,000 "met" sorties were flown during the European War, each one adding its quota to the general meteorological picture.

In the work of balloon barrages and anti-aircraft batteries, the planning of bomber raids, the hunting and destroying of U-boats, the transport of men and material across the Atlantic, the photographic mapping of enemy territory, the invasions of North Africa, Italy and Normandy – in all these operations a vital part has been played by the meteorological reconnaissance force.

Outside Coastal Command, the United States Army Air Force made a valuable contribution to "met" reconnaissance. At first operating from this country with RAF "met" air observers, they later had their own fully trained observers and carried out scheduled sorties daily as part of the general programme. In addition, a Mosquito Met Flight of Bomber Command operated over enemy territory.

Of all the thousands of "met" sorties, three deserve particular mention. Three aircraft, one from 517 Squadron, one from 518 Squadron and one from an American Weather Squadron took off on their normal sorties on 4th June 1944. They had been briefed to meet an Atlantic "Low" which had left Newfoundland close behind the previous depression, then off north-west Scotland. The 50 nautical mile "positions" were steadily marked off, tufted wisps of frontal cirrus came into view, but with each excursion to sea level, pressure continued to rise. The evidence was unmistakable. A new ridge of high pressure was developing. Eagerly, meteorologists decoded the W/T messages, plotted the vertical soundings and prepared their high level maps. At 1800 feet the ridge became an extensive "High", covering most of the Atlantic. Some hours later the Allied meteorological crews returned to their bases, unaware of the fact that their sorties had provided the date of D-Day.

The activities of the "met" squadrons have not been entirely confined to observations of weather. Interceptions by enemy aircraft were not infrequent in the south-east and North Sea areas, and the "met" aircraft, particularly the poorly armed Hampdens, did not always get through. However, at least two enemy aircraft were destroyed and in a number of other combats the enemy received as good as he gave. U-boat sightings totalled 36 and creditable attacks were made on 11 occasions.

Here is and idea of the everyday life of an aircrew on a "met" squadron – No 518 – the first to operate long-range Halifaxes solely to take weather recordings, and still going strong.

They flew from the island of Tiree in the Western Hebrides. The airfield overlooks the turbulent waters of the Atlantic, and is subjected to the most violent storms. A strong south-westerly breeze frequently sweeps the treeless island, and in the grim winter months gales whip the rain into fury and sometimes upheave huts. So strong are these gales that they often hurl metal sheets into the air, and have been known to rip the iron doors from the hangars. Snow is sometimes heavy, and deep drifts must be cleared from the runways before aircraft can take off. Though real fog is rare there is an even greater menace than gales, rain and snow in the mist and very low cloud which at times cover the island. Whatever the weather, two aircraft take off daily. The crews are up in the early hours of the morning, breakfast and are driven to the operations room for briefing. The Halifaxes take off in darkness, beginning their 10-11 hours' journey of 700 nautical miles (805 statute) into the Atlantic. For this long journey – halfway to Newfoundland and back – the aircraft are heavily loaded with petrol carried in long-range fuel tanks. Each has a set course and a timetable, which must be rigidly followed whatever the weather conditions. Thus storms, which other aircraft would avoid, must be flown through, as well as "cold fronts" when instruments go haywire. Often snowstorms and severe icing have to be contended with.

The crew, which comprises a pilot, second pilot, navigator and three wireless operator air gunners, also includes a meteorological air observer. He is specially trained, and his work entails taking recordings from the meteorological instruments at various stages of the flight. The reports are sent direct from the aircraft by wireless telegraphy, and are picked up by the Meteorological Headquarters, and by Commands and Groups in the British Isles and Overseas.

At the terminal point of the journey, there is the stiffest task of all. The aircraft descends to sea level, and then makes a spiral climb to 18,000 feet (three and a half miles). This is a great test of endurance for the aircraft, and demands great skill on the part of the pilot. Descending to sea level is hazardous, for well out in the Atlantic the breakers sometimes reach heights of 100 feet, and violent turbulence makes aircraft control an exhausting struggle.

Only very experienced pilots are engaged on flying the long-range meteorological Halifax aircraft – those who are expert in bad weather flying. Most of them have completed operational tours with 1,000 hours flying, and some have as many as 3,000 hours to their credit. The meteorological course often involves flying for eight hours by the use of instruments, and the spiral climb is sometimes made entirely in cloud. Ground crews have been amazed at the ability of these pilots to land their aircraft after long flights when the cloud base is very low over the island aerodrome.

The navigators and wireless operators, too, are mostly experienced aircrew, carrying out their second tour of operations. During the war, crews were a mixture of nationalities, with Britons, Australians, Canadians, Americans attached to the RCAF and two of the "met" Air Observers were Poles.

A distinguished peace and war record is held by No 1402 Flight, operated from the Northern Ireland airfield of Aldergrove. Daily for nearly nine years, fighters of this Flight have made vertical ascents almost to the stratosphere. Only 12 climbs have been missed and they are still fully operational.

Four, and sometimes five, ascents are made daily by oxygen masked pilots in Spitfires and Hurricanes. Specially fitted into these fighters are pschycrometers and aneroid barometers, and a record of temperature, humidity, heights of cloudbase and top, types of cloud encountered, icing and snow levels is kept by the pilot on a pad strapped to his knee.

The pilots who fly these aircraft – the Spitfires go to a height of 40,000 feet to 42,000 feet (8 miles) and Hurricanes to 30,000 feet (6 miles) – are all stratosphere experts. A number came to the Meteorological Flight after a tour of operations in Photographic Reconnaissance Units, which at high altitude took photographs of enemy targets before and after attack. They have to be well above average in health and toughness in order to combat altitude "maladies", such as "The Bends" – air bubbles in the blood – which cause intense pain. Before they are accepted they pass through a rigorous decompression chamber test. Their 18 months in the meteorological Flight, during which they make 200-300 ascents, counts, in wartime, as a full operational tour.

The worst enemy of the stratosphere flyers is the weather they go up to record. Often they rely entirely upon instruments, taking off and landing in darkness and fog. Throughout the flight they are controlled by radio, and continually pass over the airfield within a radius of 15 miles. Storms, cloud, snow and severe icing have failed to stop them. Even the blizzards of January of this year were defied. They scraped ice and snow from the wings and took off from snow covered runways. One of the most remarkable experiences in the Flight fell to F/O J Benson, who took off in ten-tenths cloud and climbed to 38,500 feet before he came to clear weather. So expert were these pilots in bad weather flying that during the war years they were called upon to meet Flying Fortresses crossing the Atlantic in rain and low cloud and lead them to an airfield.

When No 1402 Flight began operations in November, 1936, the pilots flew in open cockpit fighters, such as Bulldogs and Gauntlets. In order to combat the intense cold at altitude, they wore three woollen jerseys and a leather jerkin and five pairs of gloves. Sometimes there was so much icing at 10,000 feet that the aircraft proceeded at only 80 miles an hour with full throttle (against the normal speed of 180 MPH). Today the Spitfires and Hurricanes have heated cockpits, and de-icing equipment, and fly 16,000 feet higher than the old-type aircraft. The latest type of Spitfire has a pressurised cockpit, which reduces the pressure on the pilot at very high altitudes.

In the earliest years of the war when there was a grave shortage of pilots, some outstanding flight records were set up. For three months there were only three pilots in the Flight, and they often flew twice daily. The record for all meteorological flying in Britain is now held by F/L PE Daniels AFC, who made 647 day and night ascents in 18 months, to beat the previous record of F/L AB Smith, with 633 ascents. A considerable number of these flights were made in unheated Gladiators.

A 6ft 5 ½ ins Australian, S/L EJ Woosley, until recently commanded the Flight. In his first six months with the Flight he made 254 ascents. Others were F/L RG Brown AFC (400 Spitfire ascents) and F/O JG Parkinson (344 Ascents).

A graphic description of bad weather flying is contained in the official report of a

Hurricane pilot. He took off in darkness in the early hours of a winter morning, and successfully carried out the meteorological reconnaissance to 24,000 feet. Descending to return to base, he found thick stratus cloud from 2,000 feet down to the ground. Failing to find a break in the cloud, he flew over the airfield at 1,000 feet and, seeing the outer perimeter lights, lost height to 200 to 300 feet in an attempt to land. But the fog thickened as the pilot felt the aircraft shudder as it hit an unknown object. The Hurricane, although unstable, was brought under control and gradually gained height.

The pilot received a call from flying control that another airfield might provide a possible diversion, and he decided that he had just sufficient petrol to make the journey. But he passed over this airfield in ten-tenths cloud, skirted a ridge of high mountains, and eventually broke cloud at 500 feet. With only six gallons of petrol remaining he made a successful belly landing in a field. This life and death drama was enacted in exactly two hours.

Appendix V

DAILY WEATHER RECONNAISSANCE FLIGHTS

The nominal tracks of the daily weather reconnaissance flights are shown below. These varied periodically for operational reasons.

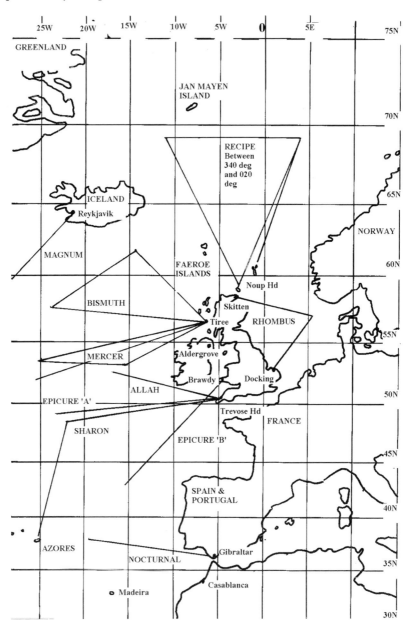

Appendix VI
No 59 SQUADRON AIRCREW PERSONNEL
15 MAY 1943

Capt & 2nd Pilot	Navigator 'B'	W/OP AG	W/OP AG
W/C GCC Bartlett	F/O FWW Cole	F/L CJ Tudor DFM	P/O S Brundell
F/S Smith E	Sgt Jones WS		
S/L PG Evans DFC	F/L JF Smith	F/O GCL Goad	Sgt Smith EG
F/S Walsh EA	Sgt Myers S	F/O JR Fox DFC	
F/L JL Heron	P/O FL Swierzynski	F/O JHG Hall	Sgt Roberts E
Sgt Schwemer WL	Sgt Curtis GC		
F/L E Knowles DFM	F/O EJA Stephenson	Sgt Honey CA	
Sgt Robinson H	Sgt Moore PC	Sgt King AE	
F/O HD Kelvin	F/O GW Green	P/O A McEwen	Sgt Yale AH
Sgt King J	P/O EJ Manuel	Sgt Williams H	
F/O EE Allen	F/O GW Laforme	P/O AW Henry	P/O HG Barton
P/O WJ Thomas	P/O LG Woods	F/O GW Flieger	
F/O AR Neilson	P/O AW Sinclair	P/O HF Tuckwood	P/O HB Clarke
Sgt Dyer JR	P/O EH Whitney	P/O LC Marriott	
F/O N Barson	F/O HR Longmuir	P/O WS Massina	Sgt Bailey AJ
F/O CE Blair	P/O JL Lees	Sgt Pilon JR	
F/O M Charlton	F/O FR Short	F/O GM Harvey	F/O MD Hutchings
F/O KRM Emmett	P/O FJ Bradley	Sgt Proudfoot LE	
F/O HAL Moran	F/O RD Stevenson	P/O L Stalker	Sgt Moorby J
P/O HR Aldcroft	Sgt Hadfield L	Sgt Regan K	
F/O FG Henson	P/O RJ Snedker	P/O AF Goodman	Sgt Richards E

P/O DSW Adams	P/O LA Ludlam	Sgt Dixon JE	
F/O TD Wright	P/O RN McCartney	P/O BA Livingston	F/S Mackenzie D
F/S Beauchamp FA	P/O HCJ Spraggs	F/S Hird W	
F/O GB Lynch	W/O Prentice WN	P/O K Wordsworth	Sgt Parker JL
Sgt Kenney A	F/S Smith T	Sgt Riley VT	
P/O SG Duplooy DFC P/O MN Black	P/O RV MacDonald	Sgt Wilson HS	
Sgt Moore LW	P/O K Coates	Sgt Knight GE	
F/O DWB Taylor	P/O MP Johnson	F/O RV Evans	Sgt Barnett P
P/O RC Penning	Sgt Hopkins LJ	Sgt Cowgill A	
F/S Hunter GO	W/O Ferris WE	F/S Diggle R	Sgt Taylor JM
Sgt Harris EW	Sgt Hodges A (AG)	Sgt Carpenter R	
F/S Loney WG	Sgt Leonard J	Sgt Field KJ	
F/S Jenkins JB	Sgt Clark JF		
F/O W Teare	F/S Goodacre JO	Sgt Barr J (WOM/ AG)	Sgt Kershaw CL
P/O GE McArthur	Sgt Hannah R	Sgt Williams (FE)	Sgt Rogers GT (AG)

SPARES

P/O DH McLean (Bombing Leaders Course)	Sgt Davies AV (replacing P/O Massina on Gunnery Leaders Course)	Sgt Haddock C

DUTIES

Adjutant	F/L S Harvey
Aircraft Dispersal	S/L PG Evans DFC
Aircraft Recognition	F/O RV Evans
Aircrew Training	F/L JL Heron
Armament	W/O Jones WM

Bombing	F/O HR Longmuir
Compass Adjuster	Sgt Chadwick B
Defence Officer	F/L JE Austin
Engineer Officer	F/O DA Winton
Electrical Engineer Officer & Salvage Officer	P/O L Holder
Gas Defence	F/O GCL Goad
Gunnery Leader	F/L CJ Tudor DFM
Intelligence Officer	P/O AC Rider
Link Trainer	F/O N Barson
Medical Officer	F/O JD Broadbent
Navigation	F/L JE Austin
Photography	F/O RD Stevenson
RDF Officer	P/O JES Fitzgerald
RDF Leader	P/O K Wordsworth
Ship Recognition	
Signals Officer	W/O Girling VJ
Signals Leader	F/O GM Harvey
Safety Equipment	F/O HAL Moran
Sports	P/O SG Duplooy DFC
Welfare	F/O HD Kelvin

Appendix VII

No 59 SQUADRON DETACHMENT
ST EVAL 5 MAY 1943

AIRCRAFT	CREW	AIRCRAFT	CREW
M	F/O Charlton	X	F/O Barson
	F/O Emmett		F/O Blair
	F/O Short		F/O Longmuir
	P/O Harvey		P/O Lees
	F/O Hutchings		Sgt Pilon
	P/O Bradley		Sgt Bailey
	Sgt Proudfoot		Sgt Davies
B	F/O Allen	K	F/O Wright
	P/O Thomas		F/S Beauchamp
	F/O Laforme		P/O McCartney
	P/O Henry		P/O Livingston
	F/O Flieger		P/O Spraggs
	P/O Woods		F/S Hird
	P/O Barton		F/S Mackenzie
J	S/L Cave DFC		P/O Adamson
	Sgt Polkinghorne		P/O Rider
	F/O Galbraith		
	Sgt Taitselis		
	P/O Summers		
	Sgt Sainthovig		
	Sgt Joanette		

GROUNDCREW

Fitter II	Fitter IIA	F Mech E	F Mech A
Sgt Cann BS	Cpl Synnock GT	LAC Rouse AE	LAC Hamilton CJ

		LAC Russell D	LAC Hopkins GT	
		LAC Ward WG	LAC Ferguson WN	
		LAC Love J	LAC Bonham K	
		LAC Davis EG	LAC Brannigan N	
			LAC Hall WA	
RDF Mech	Inst/Rep I	Elect I	Elect II
LAC Bach H	LAC Eaton HM	Cpl Cavanagh G	LAC Sykes FW
LAC Button HJ		LAC Squires C	
LAC Budzak W			
LAC McCraig RL			
WOM	W Mech	F Arm B	Arm G
Cpl Strachan JC	LAC Webber LG	Cpl Armstrong JJ	LAC Savill RHA
Arm			
AC1 Monk AJ			
AC2 Gray WC			

Appendix VIII

No 59 SQN AIRCREW PERSONNEL
25 JUNE 1943

Capt & 2nd Pilot	Navigator 'B'	WOP/AG	WOP/AG
W/C GCC Bartlett AFC	F/L CJ Tudor DFM	F/S Walker GT	
F/S Smith E	F/O FWW Cole	P/O S Brundell	Sgt Jones WS
S/L PG Evans DFC	F/L JF Smith	F/O GCL Goad	Sgt Smith EG
F/S Walsh EA		Sgt Myers S	F/O JR Fox DFC
S/L BA Sisson	W/O Whittaker W	F/O ELG Cook	F/S McLoughlin W
P/O RA Williams	P/O H Humphries Sgt Kammellard GDP		
F/L JL Heron	P/O FL Swierzynski	F/O JHG Hall	Sgt Roberts E
Sgt Schwemer WL	Sgt Curtis GC	Sgt Dickenson J	
F/L E Knowles DFM	F/O EJA Stephenson	Sgt Branagan J	Sgt Honey CA
Sgt Robinson H	Sgt Moore PC	Sgt King AE	
F/L HD Kelvin	F/O GW Green	P/O A McEwen	Sgt Yale AH
	P/O EJ Manuel	Sgt Williams H	
F/L EE Allen	F/O GW LaForme	P/O AW Henry	P/O HG Barton
Sgt Jones H		P/O LG Woods	F/O GW Flieger
F/O AR Neilson DFC P/O AW Sinclair	P/O HF Tuckwood	F/O HBClarke	
P/O WM O'Dwyer	P/O EH Whitney	P/O LC Marriott	
F/O N Barson	F/O HR Longmuir	F/O WS Massina	Sgt Bailey AJ
F/O CE Blair		P/O JLG Lees	Sgt Pilon JR
F/O M Charlton	F/O FR Short	F/O GM Harvey F/O MD Hutchings	

F/O KRM Emmett	P/O FJ Bradley	Sgt Proudfoot LE	
F/O HAL Moran	F/O RD Stevenson	P/O L Stalker	Sgt Moorby J
P/O HR Aldcroft	Sgt Hadfield L	Sgt Regan K	
F/O FG Henson	P/O RJ Snedker	P/O AF Goodman	Sgt Richards E
P/O DSW Adams	P/O DA Ludlam	Sgt Dixon JE	
F/O TD Wright	P/O RN McCartney	F/O BA Livingston	F/S Mackenzie D
F/S Beauchamp FA	P/O HCJ Spraggs	F/S Hird W	
F/O GB Lynch	W/O Prentice WN	P/O K Wordsworth	Sgt Parker JL
F/S Kenney A		F/S Smith T	Sgt Riley VT
F/O SG Duplooy DFC P/O MN Black	F/O RV MacDonald	Sgt Wilson HS	
Sgt Moore LW	P/O K Coates	Sgt Knight GE	
F/O DWB Taylor	F/O MP Johnson	Sgt Hopkins LJ	Sgt Barnett P
P/O RC Penning	Sgt Haddock G	Sgt Cowgill A	
F/S Hunter GO	W/O Ferris WE	F/S Diggle R	Sgt Taylor JM
Sgt Harris EW		Sgt Hodges A (AG)	P/O R Carpenter
F/S Loney WG	Sgt Leonard J	Sgt Field KJ	
F/S Frankis RGF/S Jenkins JB	Sgt Clark JF	Sgt Davies AV	

At Beaulieu:

F/L W Teare	F/S Goodacre JC	Sgt Barr J (WOM/AG) Sgt Kershaw CL	
	Sgt Hannah R	Sgt Rogers GT (AG)	

Spares:

F/L Catley J	F/O JA Parsons	Sgt Brooksbank H	P/O DH McLean

F/S Gamble NR	Sgt Price HJ	Sgt Coston RGV
F/O RV Evans	Sgt Oldfield L	F/O RJ Couchman DFM
F/S Drabble T DFM	Sgt Trickett HH	
Flight Engineers:		
Sgt Peacock DE	Sgt Sills WR	
	Sgt Stoneman FG	Sgt Mason AJ
	Sgt Kilby JH	

■ Appendix IX ■

ALDERGROVE LAYOUT 1945

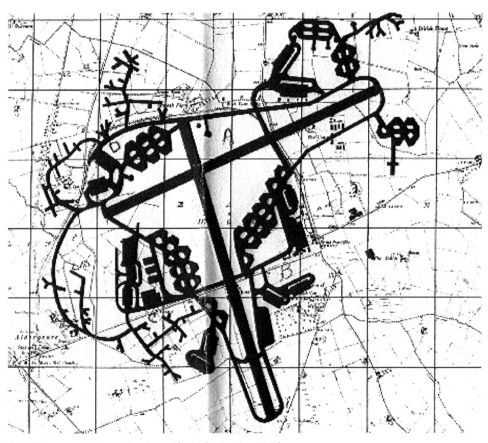

RAF Aldergrove in its wartime layout (post September 1941). *(RAF Aldergrove).*

Appendix X

ALDERGROVE SPORTS PROGRAMME 2 AUGUST 1943

R.A.F. Station, ALDERGROVE

Athletic Sports Meeting:-
ALDERGROVE – August 2nd 1943 commencing
At 14.15 hours.

COCK O' THE WALK COMPETITION between teams from
R.A.F. Station, Aldergrove,
No. 59 Squadron,
No. 86 Squadron,
No. 23 Maintenance Unit

OFFICIALS

Referee:-	Group Captain I. E. Brodie OBE
Starters:-	Major P. G. Humphrey (Events 1, 2, 4-8, 10, 11, 14-20, 22)
	S/L. E. V. Cook (Events 3, 19, 13).
Judges:-	W/C. R. D. Williams (Events 1, 2, 4-8, 10, 11)
	F/L. R.W. Leigh
	F/L. S. Harvey
	F/O. R. R. Hobbs
	S/L. N. Booth(Events 12, 14-20, 22)
	F/L. J. E. James
	F/L. W. J. P. Sloan
	F/L. P. E. Daniels
	S/L. Fraser (Events 3-9, 13)
	F/L. K. J. Cauldwell
	Clerk of the Course - S/L. F. T. Eades , DFC
	Assistant Clerk of the Course - W/O S. Storer

PROGRAMME

1.	1415	100 yards	2 entrants each team
2.	1420	100 yards – WAAF	2 entrants each team

3.	1425	High Jump	2 entrants each team
4.	1425	Sack Race	2 entrants each team
5.	1430	Sack Race – WAAF	2 entrants each team
6.	1435	220 yards	2 entrants each team
7.	1440	Bicycle Race – WAAF	Team of two
8.	1445	Old Sweats Race 100 yds - Handicap	2 entrants each team
9.	1450	High Jump – WAAF	2 entrants each team
10.	1455	440 yards	2 entrants each team
11.	1500	Three Legged Race	2 entrants each team
12.	1505	Final Tug O' War	
13.	1515	Long Jump	2 entrants each team
14.	1520	Medley Relay NCO, 1 Cpl, 1 LAC, 1 AC, 1 WAAF.	C.O., 1 Officer, 1 W.O, 1 Sen
15.	1530	880 yards	2 entrants each team
16.	1540	1 Potato, Egg & Spoon – WAAF	2 entrants each team
17.	1545	Obstacle Race	2 entrants each team
18.	1550	Obstacle race – WAAF	2 entrants each team
19.	1555	1 Mile	2 entrants each team
20.	1605	1 Mile Relay, 220, 440, 880, 220	1 Team
21.	1620	Final Six a Side Football	1 Team
22.	1640	Band Race	The Band
	1645 – Presentation of Prizes		

Appendix XI

No 120 SQUADRON AIRCREW 1943

The following list is of all aircrew serving with No 120 Sqn in 1943. This includes those stationed at Ballykelly and Iceland. It is included for completeness.

Commanding Officer:	W/C SJ Harrison DFC
	W/C PA Gilchrist
	W/C RM Longmore OBE
	W/C JK Bland
Adjutant:	F/L J Booth
	P/O J Willmott
Intelligence Officer:	F/O P Ogden
	P/O HN McGinn
Gunnery Officer:	F/L M Thompson
	F/O Howlett
Bombing Leader:	F/O Mitchell
	F/O Matthews
	F/O P Rackham
Engineer Officer:	F/O (A/F/L) FC Cooper
Navigator Leader:	F/O RM Mitchell
Signals Branch:	P/O K Revill
	A/F/L AL Furr
	P/O IB Sly (Radar Duties)
	P/O JG McNeill (Radar Duties)
	A/F/L JS Gunn
Electrical Engineer Officer:	A/P/O S Evans
Pilots:	

F/O NV Bristow	S/L PR Casement	F/L SE Esler
F/O DC Fleming-Williams	F/L AW Fraser	P/O JH Frewen
F/L R Goodfellow	F/L GL Hatherly	F/O RA Hayden
W/O AE Hayes	S/L DJ Isted	F/L FT Keill
F/L RF Kerrigan	W/C RM Longmore	F/L WJ McEwen
S/L CH Milto	F/O JK Moffat	F/L BE Peck
S/L JR Procter	F/L DJ Rose	F/O LE Ross
F/O NE Smith	P/O W Stoves	F/L L Taylor
F/L CD Thompson	W/O BW Turnbull	F/O RT Turner
F/O DC Webber	F/S M Weiner	F/L RW Wightman
P/O HJ Wilson		

Second Pilots:

F/S HJ Bennett	F/S RD Brown	F/L RL Button
F/S JD Colman	F/O JS Crank	F/S H Cruttenden
F/S WH Dunan	F/O AL Dyck	F/O AT Good
F/O H Gordon-Cropper	F/O AG Green	S/L Harnott
F/S RG Harrison	F/S EA Hughes	F/O EN Jennings
F/O RD Ker	F/S J Leach	F/S LW Lenz
F/L RD Lewis	W/O J Luker	Sgt J Milne
F/O GC Noseworthy	F/O NH Oakley	F/S NJ Oliver
F/O CG Pfeiffer	F/L DJ Rose	Sgt KG Sneller
F/O RW Tait	F/S B Threlfall	F/O SR Walker

Observers/Navigators:

W/O FJ Andrews	F/S DJ Appleton	F/O HJ Bates
P/O A Boland	F/L JN Bruce	P/O DN Bungay
F/S J Collinson	Sgt GC Crampton	Sgt JD Davies
F/S EA Day	W/O WE Ferris	Sgt W Fraser
F/O NP Gallemaerts	Sgt GA Hann	W/O DA Harborne

F/O WJ Hartrick	F/S LC Heiser	Sgt AH Jay
F/O FJ Kernaghan	F/S TJ Kempton	F/L WN Kenyon
W/O SF King	F/O HL Matthews	W/O VB McKeague
F/L RN Mitchell	F/O SJ Paine	P/O PR Rackham
F/O JW Rickard	F/O E Stanley	F/O RW Tait
F/S EF Thorpe	F/S AW Watson	F/O RM Webber
P/O RJ Wells	F/O JH Wilsher	F/S VC Wilson
W/O WG Whiteford		

Flight Engineers:

Sgt NJ Bacon	Sgt H Bailey	F/S RW Barrett
F/S CJ Bell	F/S BJ Bennett	F/S EH Britton
Sgt RL Carter	Sgt E Cole	F/S NG Cotton
P/O BM Eshleman	F/S R Fallon	Sgt AS Forward
P/O GM Goodall	F/S BH Harvey	Sgt H Healey
Sgt Hooker	F/S JG Jeans	F/S TR Jones
Sgt JK Ladkin	F/S R Meyer	F/S SJ O'Reilly
F/S AE Parsons	F/S FP Payne	Sgt JT Payne
Sgt EP Priddy	Sgt H Richardson	Sgt RN Robertson
W/O GW Robinson	F/S EA Scott	F/S Shelton
Sgt CE Stevenson	W/O AE Storey	F/S HT Wright

Wireless Operator/Air Gunners:

Sgt D Abson	Sgt AF Adams	W/O AJ Allan
F/S A Allwood	Sgt EG Arnott	Sgt DH Auld
Sgt GR Babb	F/S EB Bailey	P/O RC Baker
F/O A Barker	F/S AE Bartley	Sgt GJ Baxter
F/S R Bedford	W/O D Binns	Sgt RH Bishop
Sgt JA Blair	F/S JS Bradley	F/S MJ Brady
Sgt KJ Brickley	W/O RA Browne	Sgt DL Caldecott

Sgt TW Chapman	F/S G Clayton	F/S R Copperthwaite
F/S JP Dowling	W/O SJ Duckworth	Sgt H Dixon
F/S JA Earp	Sgt RW Elder	Sgt ME Evans
Sgt DE Farrant	Sgt FJ Fisher	P/O FH Fitzjohn
W/O JT Foy	F/L AL Furr	Sgt T Givens
Sgt JJ Grassam	F/L JS Gunn	F/S JP Hanton
F/S SC Harrison	P/O ND Hartnell	Sgt N Heseltine
Sgt JH Holland	F/S HF Hollands	F/O ET Howlett
Sgt W Hunt	Sgt JP Hunter	F/S J Jenkins
F/S K Johnson	Sgt G Kammellard	Sgt JR Kitching
Sgt RD Lauder	W/O H Lea	Sgt LW Lenz
F/S LP Lesueur	Sgt T Levinsky	F/O L Lewis
Sgt AT Liddle	F/S JH Lowry	F/S E Lund
P/O GR Lynn (attached from 1407 Flt.)	W/O GS McDonald	
F/S NR McGrath	F/O J McGregor	F/S DA McIntosh
F/S T McKie	F/S TE McManus	F/S RH Mealin
Sgt B Millward	W/O EA Mincham	Sgt W Milchreest
F/S JD Nugent	Sgt GW Oliver	W/O JJ Patterson
Sgt FB Pincott	Sgt W Poulton	Sgt RS Raynel
Sgt J Richardson	F/S RM Ritchie	F/S AW Sanders
W/O HE Scammell	F/S J Scoular	Sgt CA Sherwood
F/S PS Sinclair	Sgt R South	Sgt AE Staples
W/O W Stott	Sgt TC Stowell	F/S R Tetley
F/S JB Timoney	F/S NR Tingey	Sgt GL Turner
W/O GW Turner	F/S JF Waite	F/S FW Wallace
Sgt R Watkins	F/S AR Wood	

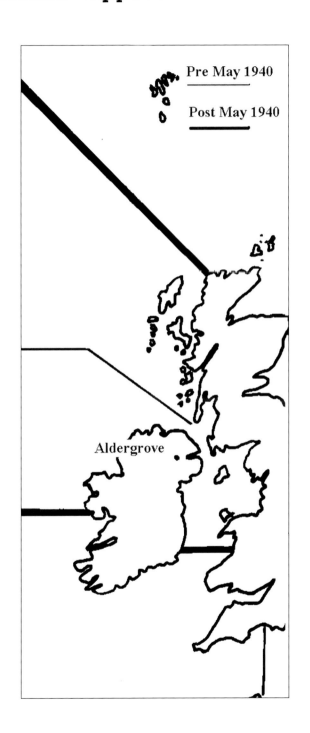

Pre May 1940

Post May 1940

Aldergrove

Appendix XIII

No 59 SQUADRON SONG

Verse:
(Tune – 'My Bonnie')

A squadron swept over the ocean,
A squadron swept over the sea,
They chased the Hun back to his harbours,
Now who could that darned squadron be.

Chorus:
(Tune – Emer's Tune)

Who makes the Hun send his convoys out only at night,
Or when the fogs and the clouds hide the blighters from sight,
And makes them scatter and shiver and tremble with fright,
Its just 59!

What makes old Hitler feel littler with each passing day,
Its just the worry and flurry of us in his way,
What makes old Goering go roaring and say he won't play
Its just 59!

Bombing shipping, everybody thinks its simply ripping,
Turning, diving, lookout for that mast or it may be your last,
So when you hear on the news that a boat has been sunk,
And Jerry's ships are reduced to a lot of old junk,
You can be sure that the aircrews whose health will be drunk,
Come from 59!

Verse:

A squadron swept over the ocean,
Their aircraft must airworthy be,
They're kept in that state by the groundcrews,
Now who could those fine fellows be.

Chorus:

Who does the work on the engines all hours of the day,
And patches the airframe when its shot away,
And tunes up the kites so they're fit for the fray,
Flight Mecs 59!

Who puts the bombs on the racks when we go on a raid,
And sees that the ammo has not been mislaid,
And checks all the guns and the turrets until they're okayed,
Armourers 59!

Tuning, testing, working all the time and never resting,
Fitters, riggers, tightening the screws that'll make the Hun lose,
And who DI and SE and are always discreet,
And makes of the wiring and circuits a feat,
Who bring the planes back to base when the raid is complete,
Signals 59!

Appendix XIV

CONVOY CODES

CU	New York – Curacao – UK
EC	Southend to Clyde, Oban or Loch Ewe (North about coastal convoys)
GU	Alexandria – North Africa – USA
HG	Gibraltar – UK
HX	Halifax – UK
KMF	UK – North Africa – Port Said (Fast)
KMS	UK – North Africa – Port Said (Slow)
KX	UK – Gibraltar (Special)
MKF	Mediterranean – North Africa – UK (Fast)
MKS	Mediterranean – North Africa – UK (Slow)
OG	UK –Gibraltar
ON	UK – North America
ONS	UK – North America
OS	UK – West Africa
SC	Halifax – UK (Slow)
SL	Sierra Leone – UK
UC	UK – Curacao – New York
UG	USA – North Africa
UGF	USA – North Africa
UGS	USA – North Africa
UT	USA – UK (Military)
WN	Clyde, Oban or Loch Ewe to Methil (North about coastal convoys)
WS	UK – Middle East and India (Military)
XK	Gibraltar – UK (Special)

Appendix XV

PROFILES OF ALDERGROVE BASED AIRCRAFT
1939-1946

The profiles produced below are by profile artist and historian Malcolm Barrass. I am deeply indebted to Malcolm for allowing me to use them in this history. The profiles are to no specific scale.

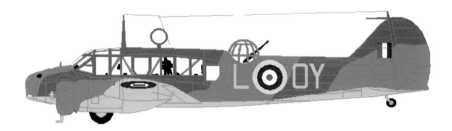

48 SQN
Avro Anson Mk I OY-L base at Aldergrove during 1940-41.

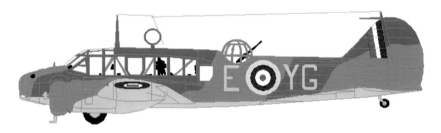

502 SQN
Avro Anson N9629:YG-E operated by the squadron in 1940.

102 SQN
Armstrong Whitworth Whitley Mk V P4995:DY-P based at Aldergrove in 1940.

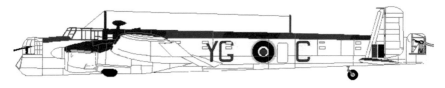

502 SQN
Armstrong Whitworth Whitley Mk V P5041:YG-C of No 502 Sqn at Aldergrove in 1941.

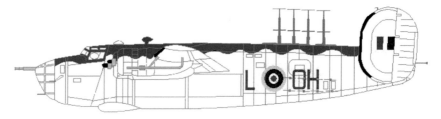

120 SQN
Consolidated Liberator Mk I AM916:OH-L in early 1943.

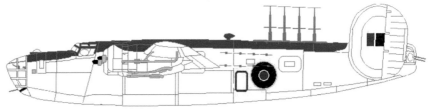

120 SQN
Consolidated Liberator Mk III coded 'O' at Aldergrove in early 1943.

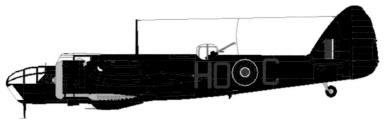

143 SQN
Bristol Blenheim Mk IVf coded HO-B of No 143 Sqn at Aldergrove in 1941-42.

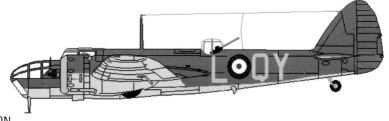

254 SQN
Bristol Blenheim Mk IV coded QY-L in 1940-41.

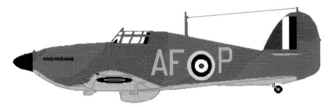

245 SQN
Hawker Hurricane Mk I P3165:DX-X at Aldergrove in 1940.

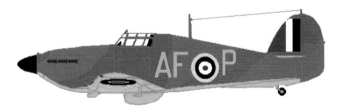

607 SQN
Hawker Hurricane Mk I AF-P of No 607 Sqn at Aldergrove in 1941

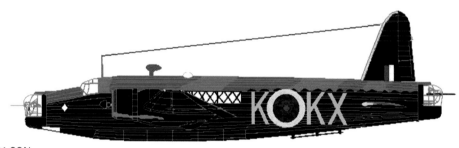

311 SQN
Vickers Wellington Mk Ic R1378:KX-K in 1942.

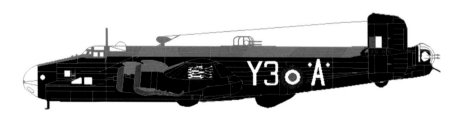

518 SQN
Handley Page Halifax Mk III coded Y3-A of 518 Sqn at Aldergrove in 1945.

518 SQN
Handley Page Halifax Mk III Y3-Q in 1946.

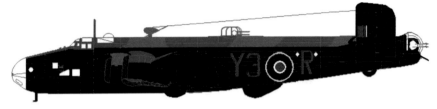

518 SQN
Handley Page Halifax Mk III Y3-R in 1945.c

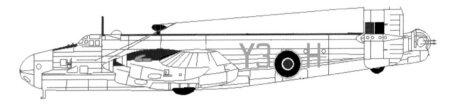

518 SQN
Handley Page Halifax Mk V LK688:Y3-H in 1945.

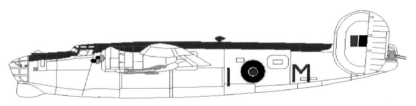

59 SQN
Consolidated Liberator Mk V coded 1-M of 59 Sqn in 1943.

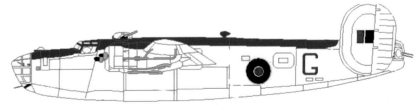

86 SQN
Consolidated Liberator Mk IIIa FK226:G in 1943.

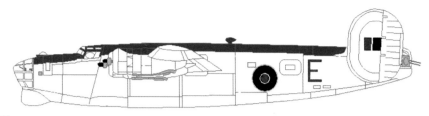

86 SQN
Consolidated Liberator Mk V BZ724:E in 1943.

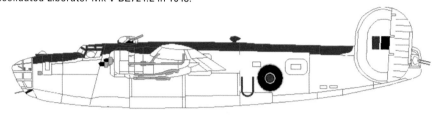

120 SQN
Consolidated Liberator Mk IIIa FK222:U at Aldergrove in early 1943.

547 SQN
Consolidated Liberator Mk VIII KK327:2V-M in 1945.

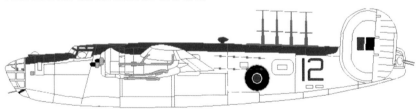

1674 HCU
Consolidated Liberator Mk III LV343:12 at Aldergrove in 1944.

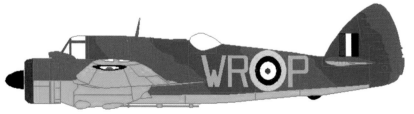

248 SQN
Bristol Beaufighter Mk Ic coded WR-P of 248 Sqn in 1941.

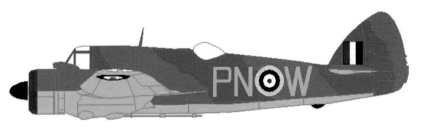

252 SQN
Bristol Beaufighter Mk Ic coded PN-W in 1941.

143 SQN
Bristol Beaufighter Mk Ic coded HO-N at Aldergrove in 1942.

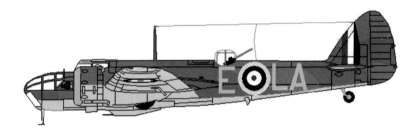

235 SQN
Bristol Blenheim Mk IV coded LA-E in 1941.

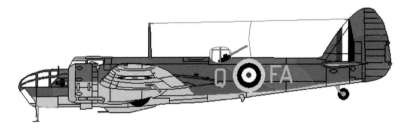

236 SQN
Bristol Blenheim Mk IV coded FA-Q of 236 Sqn in 1941.

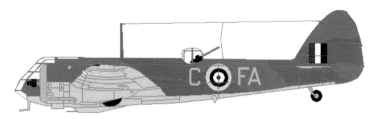

236 SQN
Bristol Blenheim Mk I coded FA-C in 1940.

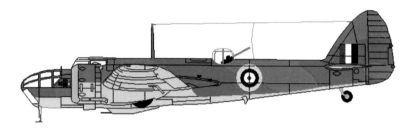

252 SQN
Bristol Blenheim Mk IV Z6245 at Aldergrove in 1941.

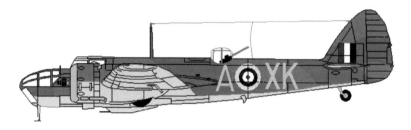

272 SQN
Bristol Blenheim Mk IV V5754:XK-A at Aldergrove in 1941.

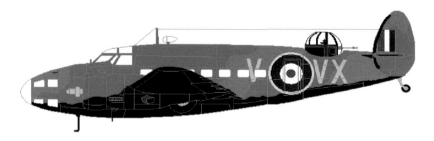

206 SQN
Lockheed Hudson Mk I coded VX-V at Aldergrove in 1941.

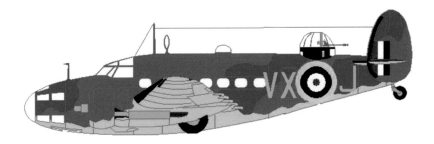

206 SQN
Lockheed Hudson Mk III T9454:VX-J in 1942.

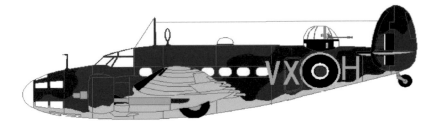

206 SQN
Lockheed Hudson Mk IV T9458:VX-H at Aldergrove in 1942.

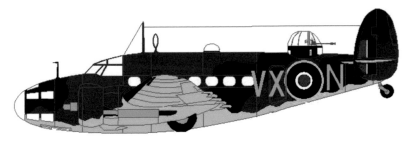

206 SQN
Lockheed Hudson Mk V AG648:VX-N in 1942.

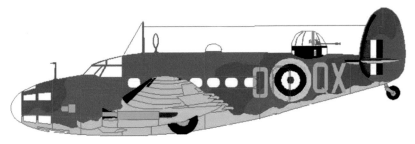

224 SQN
Lockheed Hudson Mk III coded QX-O of 224 Sqn in 1941.

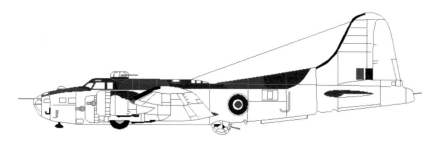

220 SQN
Boeing Fortress Mk II FI 459:.I in 1943

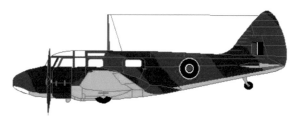

518 SQN
Airspeed Oxford P6969 at Aldergrove in 1945.

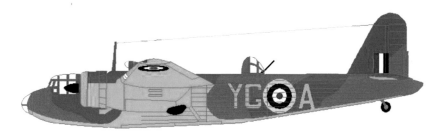

502 SQN
Blackburn Botha Mk I YG-A of 502 Sqn at Aldergrove in 1940.

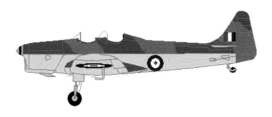

245 SQN
Miles Magister N3861 in 1941.

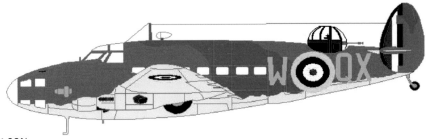

224 SQN
Lockheed Hudson Mk I QX-W of 224 Sqn in 1940.

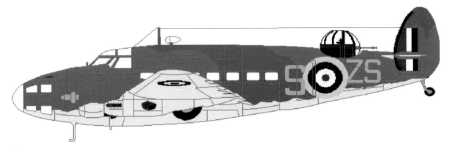

233 SQN
Lockheed Hudson Mk I ZS-S in 1940.

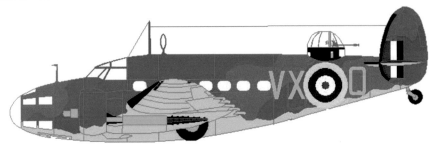

206 SQN
Lockheed Hudson Mk II T9383:VX-Q at Aldergrove in 1941.

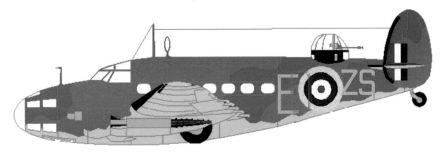

233 SQN
Lockheed Hudson Mk II T9430:ZS-E at Aldergrove in 1941.

231 SQN
Airspeed Oxford of 231 Sqn in 1940.

231 SQN
De Havilland Tiger Moth Mk II N9127 in 1940.

518 SQN
Supermarine Spitfire Mk VII MD181 at Aldergrove in 1945.

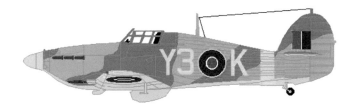

518 SQN
Hawker Hurricane Mk IIc P6469:Y3-K at Aldergrove in 1945.

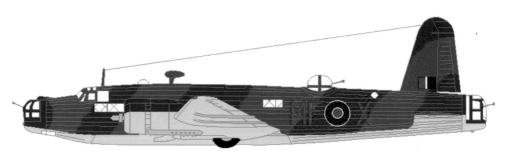

280 SQN
Vickers Warwick Mk I HG211:MF-X at Aldergrove in 1945.

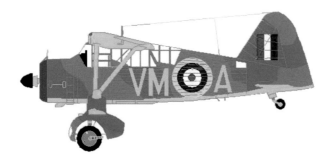

231 SQN
Westland Lysander Mk II in 1940.

BIBLIOGRAPHY AND REFERENCES ▮▮

References:

59 Sqn Diary May 1943 – Aug 1944		
120 Sqn Historical archive		
206 Sqn Historical archive		
Form 540	RAF Aldergrove	
Air 27/555	Form 540	59 Sqn
Air 27/469	Form 540	48 Sqn
Air 27/911	Form 540	120 Sqn
Air 27/978	Form 540	143 Sqn
Air 27/708	Form 540	86 Sqn
Air 27/807	Form 540	102 Sqn
Air 27/1223	Form 540	206 Sqn
Air 27/1366	Form 540	220 Sqn
Air 27/1427	Form 540	231 Sqn
Air 27/1431	Form 540	233 Sqn
Air 27/1445	Form 540	236 Sqn
Air 27/1481	Form 540	245 Sqn
Air 27/1508	Form 540	252 Sqn
Air 27/1514	Form 540	254 Sqn
Air 27/1577	Form 540	272 Sqn
Air 27/1687	Form 540	311 Sqn
Air 27/1955	Form 540	502 Sqn
Air 29/704	Form 540	1 APC
Air 29/705	Form 540	9 OTU
Air 29/863	Form 540	416 Flt
No 17 Group Operations Record Book		
RAFNI Operations Record Book		
Belfast Telegraph article 29 Sep 1945		
Inland Waterways News Vol 29 No 2		

Further reading:

SEEK AND STRIKE	Andrew Hendrie	(W Kimber)
LOCKHEED HUDSON IN WW2	Andrew Hendrie	(Airlife)
SEARCH FIND AND KILL	Norman Franks	(Grub Street)
B-24 LIBERATOR 1939-45	Martin Bowman	(PSL)
B-24 LIBERATOR AT WAR	Roger Freeman	(Ian Allan)
ACTION STATIONS 7	David J Smith	(PSL)
U333 The Story of a U-Boat Ace	Peter Cremer	(Triad Grafton)
COVERING THE APPROACHES	John Quinn & Alan Reilly	(Impact Printing)
WINGS OVER THE FOYLE	John Quinn	(Shanway Press)
THE MONTH OF THE LOST		
U-BOATS	Geoffrey Jones	(William Kimber)
BLACK MAY	Michael Gannon	(Dell)
U-BOATS DESTROYED	Paul Kemp	(Arms and Armour)

Internet Links:

www.rafcommands@currantbun.com

www.uboat.net

www.airforce.ca

www.Waafamag@beryl32.freeserve.co.uk

www.rafhaaa@aol.com

www.cz-raf.hyperlink.cz

www.rquirk.com

www.acseac.co.uk

www.dalnet.se

www.b24.mach3ww.com

www.wabakimi.carleton.ca

www.seawaymall.com

www.rafweb.org

Acknowledgements

Writing this book would have been impossible without the greatly valued assistance of a large number of ex-Aldergrove personnel, air and ground crews. In addition several fellow historians helped greatly with documents, photographs and other information during the writing of the book. My grateful thanks go out to the following:

CJ Allen
Ernest E Allen
Mike Allen
T Armstrong
Belfast Telegraph
John Bell
Andy Bird
G Briggs
Deryck Brown
Ernie Burton
Chris Charland
Peter Clare
Ian Coleman
Bert Coles
Flt Lt DJ Coombes, CXX Sqn
Neville Cooper
Ernie Cromie
Ken Davies
Flt Lt Neil Ebberson, CXX Sqn
Moira Edge
Ian Foster, 57 Rescue
Gary Fowkes
Geoff Gardiner
Betty George MBE
George Gray
PHT Green
Joe Griffith
Ken Harper
Frank Haslam
Michael Havrda
JP Hobbs
AL Holland MBE
Ken Hutson
Marylin Irvin

Ros Jefferies
Martin Kidds, Assistant Librarian, National Meteorological Library and Archive
Flt Lt S Lockyer, CXX Sqn
Ken Lunn
I Malcolmson
J Martin
R Martin
Michael McBurney
Jim McGarry (deceased)
Neil McGarry
WH McGiffin
F McLintock
Ross McNeill
Jack Meadows
Gordon Mepham
Peter Mullen
Ted Nelson
Ken Ness
R Parsons
Peter Piper
Air Cdre G Pitchfork
Ron Powers
MAEOp Eddie Pratt
Ian Priestley
RAF Aldergrove
Chris Regan
J Reynolds
R Robertson
Charles Scandrett
Ralph Schenk
Eric Schulzinger, Lockheed Martin Corporation
Mike Seymour

J Slater
Ron Smith
R Spencer
A Stamper
Flt Lt Tom Talbot, 206 Sqn
Richard Thomas
Pavel Vancata
VPI International
Stanley Warren
JF Waite
Westland Group
John Wightman
Beryl Williams

Abbreviations

AAS	Air Armament School
AC	Aircraftsman
Air Cdre	Air Commodore
AG	Air Gunner
AOC	Air Officer Commanding
AONS	Air Observer Navigation School
AOS	Air Observer School
APC	Armament Practice Camp
AS	Anti-submarine
ASV	Air to Surface Vessel (Radar)
ATS	Armament Training Station
AVM	Air Vice Marshal
BGS/B&GS	Bombing & Gunnery School
CCECDU	Coastal Command Engine Control Demonstration Unit
CCTDU	Coastal Command Trials and Development Unit
C-in-C	Commander-in-Chief
CPF	Coastal Patrol Flight
DC	Depth Charge
D/F	Direction Finding
EFTS	Elementary Flying Training School
F/L	Flight Lieutenant
Flt	Flight
F/O	Flying Officer
F/S	Flight Sergeant
FTS	Flying Training School
G/C	Group Captain
GDGS	Ground Defence Gunnery School

HCU	Heavy Conversion Unit
LAC	Leading Aircraftsman
Lt Cdr	Lieutenant Commander
Met	Meteorological
Mk	Mark
MOP	Mobile Oxygen Plant
MU	Maintenance Unit
NAAFI	Navy, Army, Air Forces Institute
OTU	Operational Training Unit
P/O	Pilot Officer
RSU	Repair and Salvage Unit
R/T	Radio Telephony
SFTS	Service Flying Training School
Sgt	Sergeant
S/L	Squadron Leader
SMO	Station Medical Officer
SNO	Senior Naval Officer
Sqn	Squadron
Sub Lt	Sub-Lieutenant
THUM	Temperature and Humidity
VLR	Very Long Range
VR	Volunteer Reserve
W/C	Wing Commander
W/O	Warrant Officer
WOM	Wireless Operator Mechanic
WOp/AG	Wireless Operator/Air Gunner
W/T	Wireless Telegraphy

A

X, Y, Z